BODY QUESTIONS IN PRACTICE

Body Questions in Practice is a comprehensive multimedia guide to exploring life transitions and decision-making, supporting readers during these processes by engaging with body movement and dance. Blending original music composition, illustrations, accessible movement exercises and reflective journalling, this book helps readers understand the important messages our bodies communicate, leading to deeper self-awareness and providing insight into interpersonal relationships.

Through practical case studies in creative and therapeutic settings, each chapter illustrates the application of key stages of embodied decision-making. Readers will discover methods to enhance communication, bolster confidence and articulate potential courses of action both in their own practice and in working with others. Underpinned by the principles of dance movement therapy, this framework facilitates embodied exploration, unveiling significant insights into individual movement preferences and cultural influences, while informing effective strategies for managing life's challenges and opportunities.

This dynamic integration of practice and theory provides a space for readers to reconnect with their bodies and deepen their understanding of movement, ultimately enriching their creative or professional endeavours. With activities tailored to all abilities and experience levels, it will resonate particularly well with mental health practitioners, arts therapists, artists, students, academics and advocates for wellbeing.

Thania Acarón (she/her) is a dance movement therapist, researcher and performer. She leads the postgraduate degree in Arts, Health and Wellbeing at the University of South Wales. Thania is also founder of The Body Hotel CIC, which focuses on movement-for-wellbeing training for healthcare professionals, burnout prevention and dance movement psychotherapy services for marginalised communities. Social media: @thebodyhotel

BODY QUESTIONS IN PRACTICE

DECISION-MAKING THROUGH MOVEMENT AND THE ARTS

Thania Acarón

Music: Ross Whyte

Illustrations: Eve Pyra

Routledge
Taylor & Francis Group

LONDON AND NEW YORK

Designed cover image: Getty Images

First published 2025
by Routledge
4 Park Square, Milton Park, Abingdon, Oxon OX14 4RN

and by Routledge
605 Third Avenue, New York, NY 10158

Routledge is an imprint of the Taylor & Francis Group, an informa business

© 2025 Thania Acarón

British Library Cataloguing-in-Publication Data
A catalogue record for this book is available from the British Library

ISBN: 978-1-032-42045-5 (hbk)
ISBN: 978-1-032-42044-8 (pbk)
ISBN: 978-1-003-36095-7 (ebk)

DOI: 10.4324/9781003360957

Typeset in DIN Pro
by Apex CoVantage, LLC

Access the Support Material: https://resourcecentre.routledge.com/books/9781032420448

This book is dedicated to my mom Ellen, who continually has shown me the value in connecting wholeheartedly and seeing the strengths in others, and to my participants and mentors, who demonstrate the importance of community, curiosity and belonging.

CONTENTS

Contents

Contents

Contents

PREFACE

When I tell people how I became a dance movement therapist, I can mark my journey as a spiral across the world. Every career change, every shift, every country entailed many (what seemed to most people as impulsive) decisions. Reflecting on this, however, there was always a catalyst prompted by my body. If I listened closely, I felt a sense of seeking change, new experiences, and knowledge deep in my core. These Body Questions led to moving countries, dancing, throwing tantrums, and ultimately doing what I love.

I refer to a Body Question as a piece of information offered to and by our body. Body Questions emerge when we connect to the arts and creativity both to experience joy and pleasure and also to tackle life's challenges. Many decisions in life are based on early Body Questions we negotiated through movement since infancy and have practised throughout our lives. Most of us did this without being consciously aware of how we were interacting with the world nonverbally. Here is your chance to learn or revisit a different approach to making decisions, practicing new approaches, and taking some well-deserved time to get to know yourself.

Why Decision-Making Through Movement and the Arts?

Many articles, practices, theories, and models suggest 'thinking' our way through this process. There are many positive skills and research that use a mind-based approach to making decisions. The problem with this is that not only can we get stuck in thinking loops (rumination), but also we are neglecting a powerful source of information we already have: our body. Movement cuts across language, culture, age, ability, and all facets of our identity. Often words may fail to describe how we feel and how we want to engage with the world. In *Body Questions in Practice*, we have both mind and body represented, and we will work constructively on this connection. You will practise these skills through activities and reflective exercises and apply them to real-life and work transitions.

Body Questions in Practice aims to explore the connection between decision-making and self-reflexivity in personal and professional development. To be self-reflexive means to continually examine, challenge, and question interactions between ourselves, others, and our environment. How these elements coexist and, many times, clash between each other is examined through the body and artistic media to instigate growth and change.

What Are the Multimedia Elements of This Book?

I collaborated with renowned Scottish composer Ross Whyte and Lithuanian illustrator and yoga teacher Eve Pyra to create a multisensory experience for you to engage, enjoy, and discover at your own pace. The book is dynamic, meaning you can start anywhere in the book to tailor it to your own decision-making process! If you are working with others as part of your job, you can get ideas for activities to try and create spaces for reflection and support others' decisions/transitions. The activities are meant for people of all abilities, with many variations and adaptations to suit your needs. I will explain the symbols, icons, music, and unique format of the book in the introductory chapter.

This book is practical but also includes the theoretical elements from which the role of movement in decision-making was initially developed. You will learn about the research that underpins these concepts and better understand human development and the connection between movement, behaviour[1], and daily life. I include activities I have applied throughout my international professional career in dance movement therapy, arts, health and wellbeing, and higher education, which I fine-tuned during my experiences as an international trainer and facilitator since 2006, developed during my doctoral research at the University of Aberdeen in Scotland, and applied during my experiences as a researcher and educator at the University of South Wales.

My wish is to share with you all the different ways I have encountered decision-making in my own 'Jane of Many Trades' professional life and how we can inform our decisions by using the body as the central source of information and as a guide for change and transformation.

One of my greatest dance movement therapy inspirations and my first mentor, Dr Diane Duggan, positively impacted me while I was contemplating a huge life/work change to travel to a new country in search of my purpose. She said to me: "You are a seeker. The path of a seeker is always challenging and never-ending. You will always want to seek your own truth. Sometimes it will never be enough, but you will not stop seeking". This is why I decided to write this book. For the ones who are seeking (or have stopped seeking) and those who are supporting and guiding others to see.

ACKNOWLEDGEMENTS

Firstly, I send appreciation to all my colleagues, teachers, and friends who have engaged in this process. Special thanks to Diana Acarón Katz, Michael Katz, Aisha Robinson, and Eider Valle Encinas for their support in the editing process and providing a much needed outside eye in this labour of love. Thanks to Gareth Pahl for his creative insight and to the Queens of House of Deviant for helping me reconnect with the value of reflexivity and non-judgement. To Peggy Hackney for her rich and influential movement practice and to Rena Kornblum for her valuable activities which I still apply today. Much appreciation to the students and participants of the workshops and organisations who offered their time and life experiences to trial out these interventions, with particular thanks to those who participated in the case studies.

I am also especially grateful to the University of South Wales for believing in this project, funding its inception, and providing spaces to record, move, and create, and to Startup Stiwdio for being The Body Hotel's 'home base'. Thankful for my clinical supervisor Melanie Beer for being a steady rock in tough times. Finally, a massive thanks to Eve Pyra and Ross Whyte, whose incredible talents helped transform letters and movements into images and sound. Thank you all for making me feel heard and seen, for your creative laughter, immense dedication, and your belief in this work. ¡Gracias! Diolch!

Note

1 I debated between US (United States) English or British English options for this book, and I have chosen to apply British English, as it is the place where most of my recent practice has taken place.

How to Use This Book

Body Questions in Practice is a multimedia guide to making decisions and exploring transitions using dynamic activities for all abilities, with an exciting feature of bespoke music and engaging illustrations to guide your way, as well as downloadable worksheets (available at https://resourcecentre.routledge.com/books/9781032420448). Whether you are considering a career change, debating a crucial personal issue, or going through a life transition, engaging with movement can help you cope with life events through insightful discoveries. This book is meant for everyone. If you are completely new to movement or are interested in deepening your movement practice – welcome! If you are a dance/movement student and/or advocate, a dance movement therapist or a professional in mental health, allied health, or the caring professions, you can gain new ideas to work with your clients, as well as apply these to your personal development. In this book, you will get a chance to

- Creatively map out your decisions and their possibilities
- Develop new skills to reflect and get fresh perspectives
- Understand how movement and body awareness help us to know ourselves better
- Reconnect with your body in the process!

ABOUT THE AUTHOR

Dr Thania Acarón (she/her) PhD, BC-DMT, R-DMP, FHEA, is a lecturer, performer, researcher, and dance movement psychotherapist from Puerto Rico, currently based in Wales. Acarón obtained her PhD on the role of dance in violence prevention at the University of Aberdeen. She is certified as a clinical supervisor and dance movement therapist in the United Kingdom and the United States, specialising in generating safe spaces for LGBTQ+ and marginalised communities. Thania currently works as a course leader, lecturer, and researcher in creative arts therapies and arts, health, and wellbeing at the University of South Wales. She founded her own company, The Body Hotel CIC, which offers international workshops on movement for employee wellbeing, burnout prevention, and embodied decision making in healthcare and corporate settings. Social media handle: @thebodyhotel

ACTIVITIES INDEX

MOVEMENT BREAKS AND REFLEXIVE EXERCISES

Some of the activities have an audio description recording available. You can listen to the audio description while playing the music files on a separate device, use separate tabs on your browser, or engage with each element separately. In addition, visit https://resourcecentre.routledge.com/books/9781032420448 for downloadable worksheets for your use.

The full audio description playlist can be found on YouTube via this link: www.youtube.com/playlist?list=PLtGm4qYm5yBQZqgY5_PFpJHa4jgs2R6Cw, or via the following QR code:

Body Questions
Book Audio Description Playlist

Narrated by: Dr Thania Acarón

Symbol 🎧 indicates that an audio description recording is available.

Chapter 1: Introduction: Decision-Making Through Movement

- 🎧 Spirals
- 🎧 Body Check-In Exercise
- 🎧 Kinesphere

Chapter 2: Attention Stage: Environment and Alternatives

- 🎧 Safety Backpack/Rucksack
- 🎧 Directness
- 🎧 Indirectness
- Reflexive Exercise: Space Effort Continuum
- Spreading and Enclosing
- Role Play on the Communication Stage

Chapter 3: Intention Stage: Needs and Priorities

- 🎧 Vertical Plane.
- Rising and Sinking

PART 1
DECISION-MAKING FRAMEWORK

1

INTRODUCTION

Decision-Making Through Movement and the Arts

DOI: 10.4324/9781003360957-2

The decision-making through movement stages encompass five categories: Flow/Tension, Attention, Intention, and Action/Non-Action[1] with embodied reflection/evaluation embedded in each stage (Figure 1.1). The model is dynamic, interactive, and non-linear. It can also be used in proactive, reactive, and retrospective ways of exploring decisions/transitions. This means that you can reflect before, during, or after a decision has taken place or when you are considering a life transition. Developmentally (in 'typical' progression), the decision-making stages resemble tasks, challenges, and opportunities you learned to tackle throughout your early childhood and have practised billions of times into your adulthood.

While we might have been unaware of how we have been approaching these negotiations when we were younger, the reflexive exercises in this book will support you in making those connections. In *Body Questions in Practice*, we get to reflect on movement patterns, preferences and embodied sensations, thoughts, images, and emotions[2] related to the decision-making stages of Flow/Tension, Attention, Intention, and Action/Non-Action, which I will explain in more detail next.

In 'typical' human development, the negotiation of tasks in terms of decisions and transitions supports the process of learning how to crawl and walk. Table 1.1 describes the parallels between decision-making and some of the key developmental issues we typically grapple with in infancy. The second row of Table 1.1 offers themes emerging out of the Movement Pattern Analysis (MPA) profiles which is one of the movement analysis systems we use in the book. We will return to MPA in the next sections. This is a brief intro into the system to help you get familiar with each stage. Each chapter will explain these developmental negotiations in more depth.

Cultural caveat here: I acknowledge that everybody has a different developmental journey and that 'typical' is not always universal. I acknowledge that discussing development usually involves an ableist view which sometimes ignores how many people have progressed through development differently. I use the word 'typical' to be mindful of differences in how humans develop. I want to draw attention to the fact that there is no such thing as 'normal' development and to demonstrate developmental progression in some bodies to help explain the movement concepts.

FIGURE 1.1 Decision-Making With Flow/Tension at Its Core

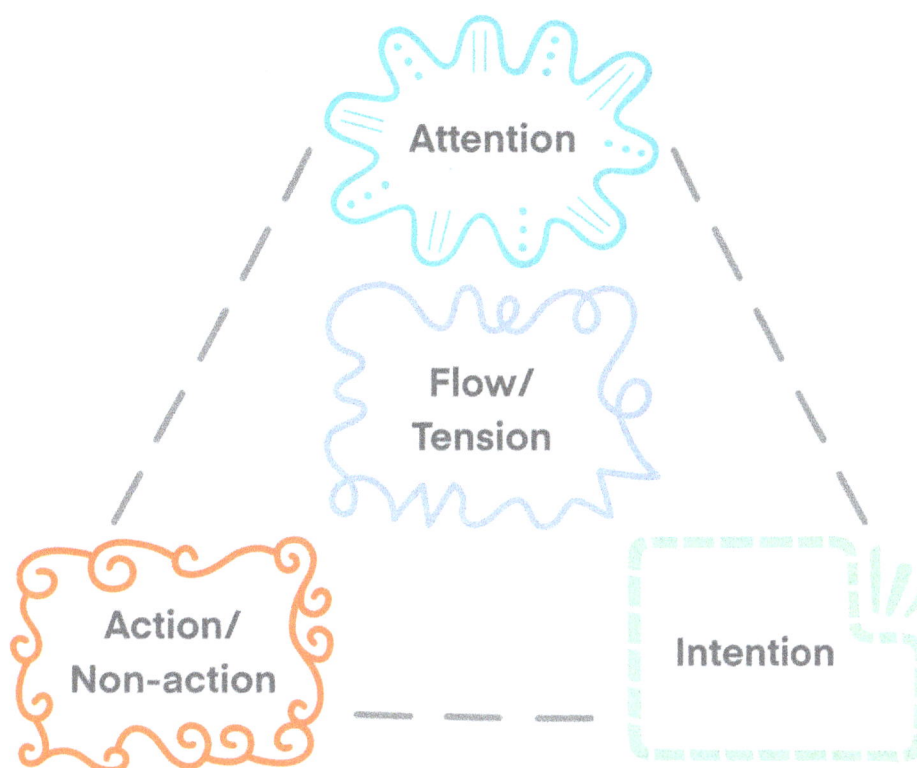

These are the underlying Body Questions manifested through the five stages:

Flow/Tension – How? – current bodily state
Attention – Where? – environment and alternatives
Intention – What (we need)? – priorities
Action – When? – timing and commitment
Reflection/Evaluation – So what? Micro- and Macro-Processes (Chapter 7 and 8)

The **Flow/Tension stage** is usually the stage where you know something needs to change – but don't quite know how to go about it yet. Or you had a wonderful experience that felt so incredible and want to make some changes to feel that way more often. This stage is fundamental, as it relates to the embryonic stage in human development. We were once surrounded by amniotic fluid, listening to the sounds of heartbeats, fluid, and organs. Most people are born through fierce muscle contractions – high levels of tension, which give in to a release into the world. I locate Flow/Tension at the centre of the decision-making through movement system (Figure 1.1), as I argue that this stage symbolises the ongoing communication with our body that gives us clues which underlie the precursors for change. (Consult Table 1.2 on page 41 for a visual representation of the developmental stages.)

The **Attention stage** engages our awareness of the environment, considering options and researching alternatives. In 'typical' development, these movement negotiations occur in early infanthood before babies can crawl. As babies gain strength in their neck to be able to look around fully, and work on core strength to turn themselves over, one of the main tasks is regulating focus. Infants then learn to distinguish different factors in their surroundings through their senses. In this book we reflect on how we experience our immediate environment and communicate information to others.

The **Intention stage** involves asserting oneself and identifying one's priorities and needs, which is negotiated in the toddler's stages when they start exploring their own verticality and work their way to standing up. This is the time when you start to 'find your feet' literally and figuratively, negotiating your centre of weight. In later life, this negotiation helps you determine what is important and essential.

The fourth stage either involves a plan of **Action** or a time frame which we can commit to or retreat from. **Non-Action** is also considered here, as the pressure of decision-making should not be always on 'doing' or 'acting' on things, but to consider timing, pacing, and how sustainable our decisions might be. In 'typical' development, we observe this as toddlers take their first steps and start negotiating acceleration and deceleration, sometimes much to the dismay of their parents! In adulthood, this is when we start to stumble forward, procrastinate, and/or pull back. This might be the stage when we decide it is not time to act but to revisit another stage. This is what makes this system so dynamic and non-linear; this process could take milliseconds, and we can get stuck in these stages. We will explore this system as a micro-process (going through all the stages) and a macro-process (looking at common themes) in Chapters 7 and 8.

These are just some of the highlights of human development, and we will get into more nuance later in the book. The important aspect to remember is that the body continues to be a source of query, challenge, and information throughout the decision-making stages. At each stage and throughout our lives, we tackle Body Questions that help us problem-solve, cope, heal, or repair.

Table 1.1 Human Development and MPA Equivalents to Decision-Making Stage

STAGE	ATTENTION	INTENTION	ACTION/NON-ACTION
Developmental Negotiations	Focus	Force	Timing
Movement Pattern Analysis	Communication	Presentation	Operation

We will also be discovering our own movement preferences (Chapter 6) to help us understand how we navigate the preferences inherent in our own cultures and subcultures. Movement preferences are our 'default' way of interacting with people/ situations, which represent a lens through which we perceive and interact with a particular issue. Chapter 6 (Movement Styles) will introduce an interactive way to understand our own preferences. All these Body Questions help you assess the role you play within a decision and what factors are involved in change.

The decision-making through movement framework, in practice, is learned sequentially and then explored in non-linear and dynamic ways. During the professional development workshops I held, participants were invited to explore each stage individually, with ample time for creative interventions and reflection (drawing/writing/journalling). As a culminating activity in the workshops, the participants chose an important decision that related to their professional identity and moved through all the stages in whichever order they felt was relevant to their situation. You will be engaging with a version of these exercises in the latter chapters of the book (Chapters 7 and 8).

This introductory section outlined some of the key points of the decision-making through movement system and its Body Questions. In developmental terms, we discussed how 'typical' human development progresses from the embryonic/birth stage (Flow/Tension), to crawling (Attention), standing (Intention), and walking/ locomoting (Action/Commitment). Of course, it is important to acknowledge that not everyone's developmental process has been the same. Crawling, standing, and walking is not always possible for everyone, and it is not a requirement for you to engage with this book. As we will discuss, movement qualities are present in all kinds of behaviour, and we will be able to understand our bodies through this movement language and find our own way within this system.

Main Concepts and Format of This Book: Non-Linear and Dynamic!

This section will offer an overview of the innovative dynamic format of the book. It will also offer some context into how I came into the work and present some of the fundamental theories that shaped the research and underpin our activities and concepts.

Life Transitions

Life transitions are times of change that provoke both welcome and unwelcome situations. This book will help you engage with the body as a protagonist (sometimes antagonist) and guide for transitions and life changes. Life transitions can be[3]

- Career-related (e.g. relocation, returning to work from leave, retirement, graduation, and career change/unemployment)
- Relationship-based (e.g. loss/bereavement, gaining/losing a romantic relationship, changes in familial constituency, changes in significant friendships or support networks)
- Age/developmental stage (e.g. entering/leaving college or family home, children leaving home, menopause, having/not having children, retirement
- Health-related (e.g. ill health of self/loved one, mental health, accident, medical diagnosis, disability)
- Identity (e.g. gender identity, sexual orientation, cultural identities)
- Other life-altering circumstances (e.g. seeking asylum).

You might be considering some options regarding any of these transitions and/or just want to gain some more skills in reflecting on personal decisions or supporting others.

Dance/Movement

Moving 'for movement's sake' is when you just dance, rock to your favourite song, or move because you want to, and it feels good. Dance brings vitality, neurological connections, activation of the body, relaxation, and so much more. It is impossible to list the innumerable sources that cite how powerful dance has been since the beginning of time. One example is the dance research from the World Health Organisation, which highlighted its benefits for people with Parkinson's, young people, trauma, and across the entire spectrum of community groups[4].

Many people have been curious as to why body movement-focused professions often include and differentiate between the terms *dance* and *movement*. I consider dance/movement to include both dance as an art form with cultural significance and a focus on body movement. I offer some context into why I have chosen to include them both and refer to them separately. Movement is a release of energy at a muscular level[5]. It is inherent in all life, essential not only for bodily functioning but also for communicating internal worlds to external worlds. Dance draws on movement and on cultural forms, which express the deep-rooted aspects of lived experience dynamically and physically[6]. Gestures, fine motor and gross motor actions, and nonverbal language exist as part of quotidian living without necessarily being considered as dance[7]. Dance represents a conglomeration of movements which function to express the interrelation between body, space, place, culture, and history[8]. Dance draws upon social meaning and has its own movement vocabulary, which each socio-cultural context decodes in a multiplicity of ways. Dance movement therapist Sabine Koch states that, "Dance movement therapy/psychotherapy includes movement but focuses on its expressive communication in order to access and engage parts of the self that no exercise, words, or repetitive action can contact"[9]. Therefore, it remains important to distinguish between these terms as many practitioners use one or both depending on their background, experience, and how they want to position themselves in the sector. As I come from a dance background, I felt it was important to highlight both aspects in this book.

Dance Movement Therapy

This book is influenced by dance movement therapy (DMT) training and research. After many years of practice, I define DMT[10] as

> A postgraduate level profession that incorporates training in psychotherapy, movement analysis with dance/movement practice. DMT offers a system of

embodied skills to help make, maintain, and repair the relationship to body, self and other(s). DMT training involves helping clients ask body questions through dance/movement, drawing connections between movement behaviour and life stress, and transforming relationships through the vehicle of psychotherapeutic creative expression.

In dance movement therapy, we work on integrating verbal and nonverbal information and apply the powerful aspect of symbolism to help people cope and process their lived experience. Using the principles of dance movement therapy can therefore have many constructive implications for health, science, and business.

Dance movement therapy is part of the umbrella category of the creative arts therapies (art psychotherapy, music therapy, and drama therapy). I focus on two main processes we share with the other arts therapies: **Representation** and **Activation**, which I will explain in the following "Variables of Insight" section.

There is also the field of arts, health, and wellbeing that uses some of the therapeutic aspects of the arts but does not engage at a psychotherapeutic level. DMT often gets confused as a profession with other fields, and although there are some crossovers in terms of practice, it is important to make professional distinctions to help clarify the varying responsibilities and approaches. Therefore, it is important to make a distinction here that while DMT is the baseline of all my research, the activities here would be considered under the category of movement-for-wellbeing, therapeutic dance, or embodied approaches to decision-making.

Movement Analysis: Underlying Framework

Movement analysis is a system to help us understand movement by experiencing the concepts through our body by observing, writing it down, and trying to understand how human beings interact nonverbally. Movement analysis feeds the vocabulary of most of this book. Movement specialists can train in movement analysis observation and notation (writing movement down via symbols) and become certified movement analysts. In general, movement analysis is offered at undergraduate and postgraduate levels, which take years to master. However, there are many concepts from the movement analysis systems which are useful for anyone. What I am trying to do in this book is to reconfigure this system to think about ourselves, how we move, and how to use this information to help us make decisions, rather than interpret how others behave.

The foundations of the decision-making through movement come from movement analysis and contributions made initially by movement specialists Rudolph Laban (Hungarian dancer and architect), Irmgard Bartenieff (German dancer, choreographer, and physical therapist), and Warren Lamb (British dancer and management consultant) and many collaborators who have continued and developed this work worldwide. Many movement analysis systems have had a substantial impact on the fields of arts practice, arts therapies, and arts education (dance, music, orchestral conduction, theatre)[11]. Movement analysis systems[12] date back to the early 1900s and became more developed during the Industrial Revolution. The Laban Bartenieff Movement Analysis (LBMA) system specifically has been applied to physical and mental health, physiotherapy, psychotherapy, and occupational therapy. Most recently, it has even been used in analysing motion and design in robotics[13]. As movement analysis is often used in many professions, it offers a common language that ties into my background as a dance movement therapist but I will also explore some cultural caveats of these systems in future chapters.

In this book, we will focus on two systems, one of which is widely known as LBMA and Movement Pattern Analysis (MPA), which evolved from collaborations between the founders of both systems. In this book, I call the LBMA system the Body Effort Shape Space (BESS) system to acknowledge its many collaborators and evolutions of the system since its inception. In the spirit of my eclectic practice, I also bring in some influences from other movement analysis systems such as Kestenberg Movement Analysis[14], and Bartenieff Fundamentals, which I explain more about throughout the chapters of this book.

If movement analysis systems are unfamiliar to you, don't worry! We will break down each concept into its most essential forms, with examples and activities to guide you. The book is meant for everyone – you can delve more into the theory if that's of interest, or you can skip over to the movement. Decisions and life transitions are unique to each person, and as such you should make the activities and processes here your own.

My Background and Experience

During my doctoral research[15], I examined how dance/movement could contribute to violence prevention and peacebuilding. Dr Martha Eddy's (US-based certified movement analyst and somatic movement educator) work on violence prevention through physical activity in schools served as a strong base for my research. Eddy studied the connections between decision-making and movement analysis and suggested this could be a way to evaluate school curricula and build awareness to prevent bullying. Rena Kornblum's curriculum for violence prevention through movement in schools was also seminal[16], as I had come from working in the New York City public school system. The aim of my thesis was to widen the decision-making framework scope to understand how dance/movement practitioners work across the world and suggest contributions movement can make to understanding, preventing, and healing from violence[17]. I wrote an article building on these principles, arguing that decision-making systems are fundamental to conflict resolution[18].

In the beginning stages of my doctoral process, I was asked to facilitate interactive creative workshops on these principles by dance movement therapy associations in Greece and Norway, and it was this application of theory which illustrated the practical aspects of this model for practitioner and artist training. I spent a month of my thesis write-up period with the DMT Programme at SRH University in Heidelberg, where I presented this work to dance movement therapy students for the first time. Transforming the theory into practical workshops started to lay out the foundations for what this book is today. I have held this workshop on decision-making for the Norwegian Dance Movement Therapy Association (NODAK) and the University of Southeastern Norway every year since then.

Years later, I decided to apply this framework with postgraduate students during a module called Professional Practice and Employability at my university. By doing this work with higher education contexts, I noticed that this system could be useful for different types of transitions: from students contemplating their thesis topics to building confidence in our own unique value proposition (formerly known as USP – Unique Selling Point). From these workshops I also wondered – what if I focused on business students and professionals from fields that had not engaged with the arts before? This is when the process started to really take a new perspective.

In Wales, I engaged with the Entrepreneurial Women's Programme and the freelancer incubator Startup Stiwdio, which gave me a chance to pilot some of the interventions you will encounter here. I trialled the activities with freelancers and graduate entrepreneurs and at University of South Wales (USW) with business students, trainee nurses, sports, music, health, cybersecurity, drama and arts health, and wellbeing postgraduate students, who offered incredible insight into potential applications. Then the process started to take even more shape as I opened workshops to a wider community. I quickly sensed that even when people spoke about their transitions and decisions, we could gauge if they were in the Attention, Intension, Action, or Flow/Tension stages by the types of words they used to describe their situation! I saw, experienced, and felt these decision-making stages wherever I went and witnessed its wide applicability.

Structure of the Book

In this book, you will use movement, drawing, writing, and explorative play to gain new ways of understanding ourselves and others to make decisions about your career, relationships, life paths, and key transitions you are going through. It is a multimedia book with music, visual language, and creative activities to help you reflect on transitions and change.

Part 1 of the book dedicates one chapter to each of the stages (Chapter 2–6). Ideally, you will consider a query about a decision/transition to practise throughout the book. You will explore your decisions/transitions through movement activities related to the four stages in the system. Each chapter breaks down each stage into its movement components, connections to human development, with *Case Examples* and practical activities (called *Movement Breaks*). The system is non-linear and dynamic– so here is a twist: you may start at any chapter in Part 1 and read them in any order! Figure 1.4 has some suggestions of different orders you can read the chapters and the reasoning behind them.

The icons we use throughout the book are shown in Figure 1.2.

All the activities in this book can also help you reflect on your wellbeing. Wellbeing involves the ability to cultivate resilience by

- Self-regulating under stress
- Expanding coping skills
- Identify and develop inner resources[19]
- Investing in external support systems.

If you find that the activities here activate issues that need further support, I highly encourage you to seek out your local mental health organisation and recommend contacting a creative arts therapist/mental health practitioner to provide you with the care you might need. The more protective factors we have, the better!

FIGURE 1.2 Icons Legend

ICONS LEGEND

Body
Questions

Body
Reflexivity

Culture
and
Caveats

Case
Example

Movement
Break

Review

Skip or
Bookmark

The elements in this book are meant to prompt reflection without self-judgement. You are welcome to just enjoy the movement and come back to the exercises as often as you need to, or delve deeper into the theory behind the concepts. Here are the types of sections and corresponding icons you will encounter throughout this book:

The *Body Questions* sections explore some of the emerging explorations related to decision-making by proposing questions that connect body and mind. These are the questions you should consider surrounding your decisions/transitions. You will continually return to these throughout the book as they serve as a guide for the whole process. You will find *Body Questions* at the beginning of each chapter to get you ready for each stage. Worksheet 1.1 has all the questions in one place for you to get a sense of the whole system before delving into each component.

The *Body Reflexivity* sections offer ideas to reflect deeper on the concepts covered. These reflection sheets are there for you to come back to as you progress through the book. Search for this symbol if you want to take a break and do some reflecting.

The *Culture and Caveats* sections critically analyse some challenges and opportunities from a multicultural lens. This is one of the core values considered in the writing of this book. Search for this symbol if you want to understand more about some counterindications to the concepts and some reflections on culture, power, and difference.

Case Examples are short vignettes in which I show you how I have applied the system in my practice. There are examples of real-life applications which might help you understand how decision-making through movement can be used in business, education, therapies, and other professions.

Review: At the end of decision-making chapter, we will have time to review what we have done so far and make some recommendations for further exploration. You can jump to these to get a sneak peek at the concepts in case you are not reading the book in linear form or come back to them when you need a recap.

Skip or Bookmark: This is a section which you can come back to later or bookmark for when you want to reflect more. This icon will signal you to the next chapters and give you more information in case you are not following the sequential order. See Figure 1.4 for examples of different reading orders for Part 1 of this book.

Movement Breaks: This symbol is used throughout the book whenever we need to practise a concept. I use plain language in each of these exercises, with modifications and alternatives for all abilities. You can always browse across sections if you need to move. There are choices of music for you and an audio version where I talk you through the exercises, so you can enjoy the activities using different senses. You can play these using separate tabs on your computer browser, if you want to engage with these at the same time, or you can use separate devices for audio description and music.

Format Option for Movers and Shakers: If you are more interested in the practical bits of this book, and just want to move and experience the system, search for the Movement Breaks symbol.

The chart in Figure 1.3 provides a short summary of the decision-making stages to give you a sense of how each chapter will progress with their corresponding symbols in keeping with the visual language used in this book.

Some examples of the order in which you could read Chapters 2–5 (there are 24 possible combinations) are listed in Figure 1.3.

Chapter 6, "Movement Styles" (your movement preferences – called Action Drives in BESS) – I must confess this section is the one I usually start with in workshops, particularly the ones I did with business students. It is a very down-to-earth model for understanding our body and how the whole world operates based on movement preferences. Movement styles help you identify and reflect on your 'default settings' in movement, and you will get a lot of information about how you engage with others and behave nonverbally in situations. I have used this to train people in negotiation skills, nonverbal communication, and leadership. I decided to put this section after the decision-making stages in Part 2 since it is a distinct application complementary to decision-making and serves as a standalone component. You could start there if you want to know more about your own movement behaviour and how this can influence your relationships before embarking on the decision-making theory and practice.

Additional Media Used in the Book

Our illustrator Eve has designed some symbols as a visual guide that will prompt the type of sections you will encounter. All the stages also have icons assigned to them, with each stage having a specific colour and shape (see Figures 1.3 and 1.4) so you can identify them throughout.

Many of the *Movement Breaks* also comes with a QR code so you can have the accompanying music if you need it. There are also additional music tracks to support reflection (drawing/moving/writing) time (see Music Index on page 267). Make use of all of Ross Whyte's amazing tracks or use your own music if you prefer.

FIGURE 1.3 Introduction to Icons of the Decision-Making Stages

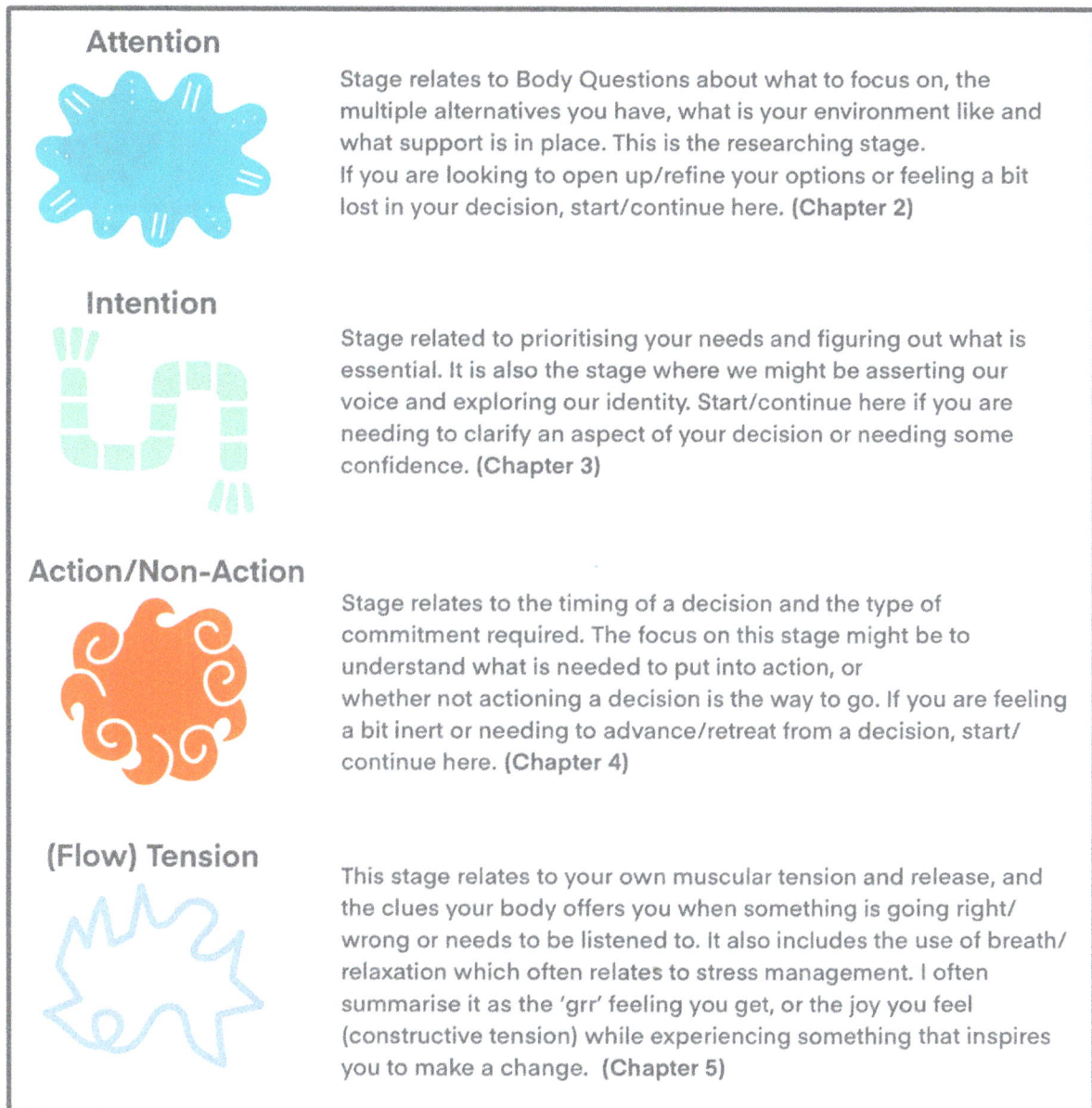

Attention

Stage relates to Body Questions about what to focus on, the multiple alternatives you have, what is your environment like and what support is in place. This is the researching stage.
If you are looking to open up/refine your options or feeling a bit lost in your decision, start/continue here. **(Chapter 2)**

Intention

Stage related to prioritising your needs and figuring out what is essential. It is also the stage where we might be asserting our voice and exploring our identity. Start/continue here if you are needing to clarify an aspect of your decision or needing some confidence. **(Chapter 3)**

Action/Non-Action

Stage relates to the timing of a decision and the type of commitment required. The focus on this stage might be to understand what is needed to put into action, or whether not actioning a decision is the way to go. If you are feeling a bit inert or needing to advance/retreat from a decision, start/continue here. **(Chapter 4)**

(Flow) Tension

This stage relates to your own muscular tension and release, and the clues your body offers you when something is going right/wrong or needs to be listened to. It also includes the use of breath/relaxation which often relates to stress management. I often summarise it as the 'grr' feeling you get, or the joy you feel (constructive tension) while experiencing something that inspires you to make a change. **(Chapter 5)**

FIGURE 1.4 Decision-Making Stage Order Examples

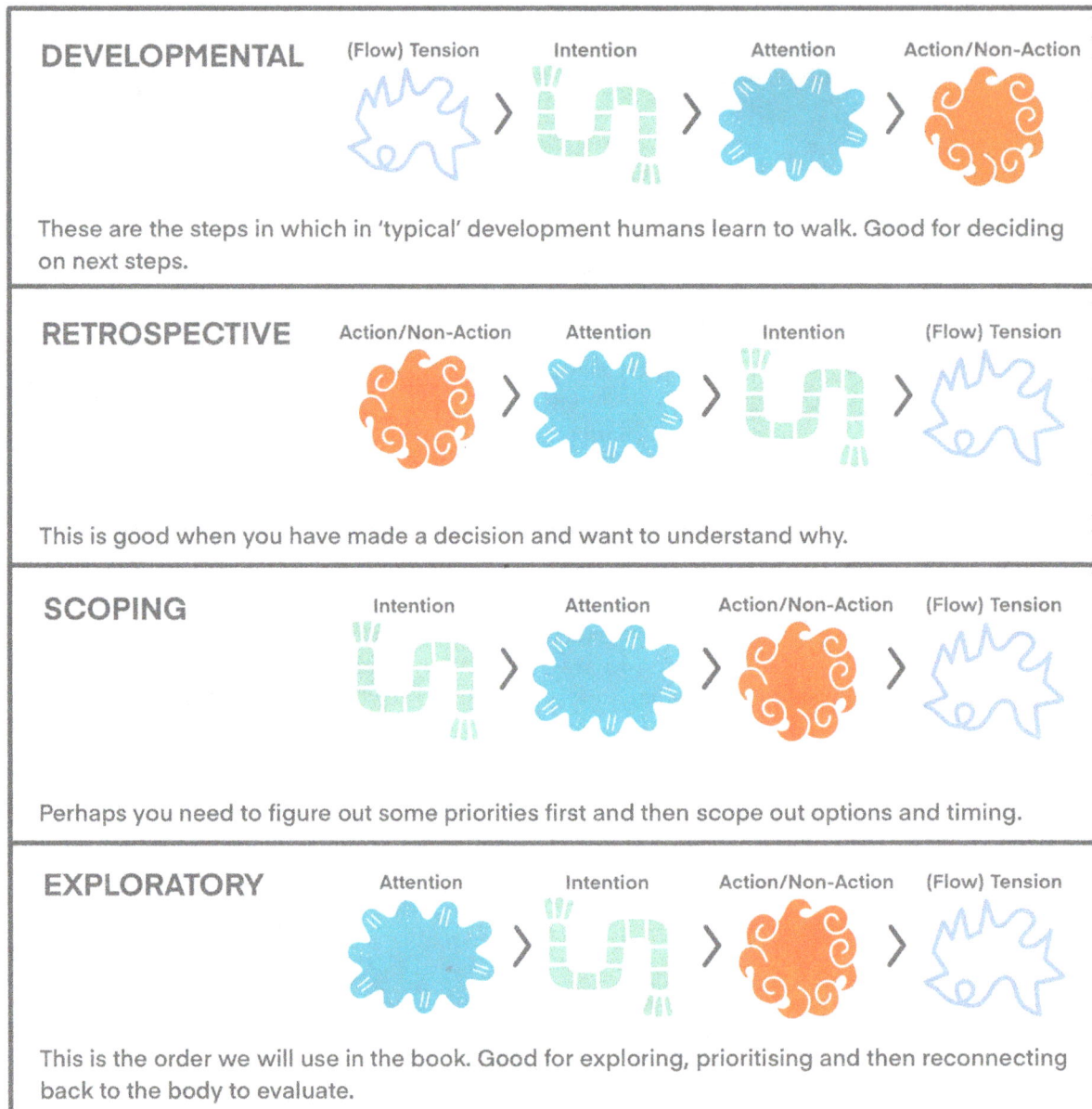

DEVELOPMENTAL — (Flow) Tension > Intention > Attention > Action/Non-Action

These are the steps in which in 'typical' development humans learn to walk. Good for deciding on next steps.

RETROSPECTIVE — Action/Non-Action > Attention > Intention > (Flow) Tension

This is good when you have made a decision and want to understand why.

SCOPING — Intention > Attention > Action/Non-Action > (Flow) Tension

Perhaps you need to figure out some priorities first and then scope out options and timing.

EXPLORATORY — Attention > Intention > Action/Non-Action > (Flow) Tension

This is the order we will use in the book. Good for exploring, prioritising and then reconnecting back to the body to evaluate.

The book includes workbook-style sheets to assist your reflection along with review points and illustrations. A full index of all worksheets can be found in the Appendices section towards the end of the book. These are also available to download at https://resourcecentre.routledge.com/books/9781032420448.

Part 2 combines all the concepts together, and you practice the four stages together. We will look at common themes across your life and reflect more if you are 'stuck' in a stage, or which ones you might prefer! I recommend you cover these sections after you have read all the decision-making stages in Part 1.

I have attempted to include adjustments to the activities in this book for all considerations: neurodiversity, physical differences, levels of fatigue, and options for working in pairs, groups, or individually. The great thing about movement practice is that it can always be modified and evolve. Make sure you make these your own and keep yourself and your body safe. Not all the activities are suitable for everyone – if you are engaging with this book to get ideas for working with others, please make sure you know your client group well, as some of these activities might require more familiarity with participants. However, I have tried to select the activities that would suit most groups and individuals and offered caveats for others that might need more training.

Towards the end of the book, we pull together all the decision-making stages to explore how the Body Questions system integrates, and how reflexivity will yield themes and patterns to frame our decisions. The goal here is that you feel more connected and listen more to your body and can apply the information your body provides in your daily life. The movement exercises will help you expand your repertoire of skills to cope with challenging decisions/transitions.

In the epilogue, Ross, Eve, and I talk about the process 'behind the scenes' of creating a multimedia book and the important discussions about representation and interdisciplinary collaboration.

Author Positionality: My Own Culture and Caveats

I want to be fully congruent with the fact that I write this book with a Western bias, and that as a Latinx queer cis woman who has lived in many countries, I will inherently come with some assumptions. I also am an able-bodied person without any (known) disabilities to date and want to introduce this as a bias in the way I frame the exercises in this book. I want us to remain mindful that not everyone can walk or locomote without assistive equipment, and I invite alternatives and offer modifications to all exercises. Ultimately, you know your body and its possibilities.

I must also disclose that none of this book has been created using artificial intelligence (AI) tools. It is all about the connection between home-grown research and practice.

Variables of Insight Through Movement: Processes You Will Be Undertaking

This section describes the main processes underlying movement, which make it an incredible way to understand why and how you engage with the world the way you do. In *Body Questions*, we use movement to reflect, represent, and discover parallels to our lived experience. I call these aspects Variables of Insight because they are the mechanisms through which we can reflect on decisions and transitions by using dance/movement. This section will tell you more about fundamental processes that make movement an important tool for reflection and change.

Variables of insight are categories that explain the relationship between dance/ movement and decision-making. I integrate the knowledge from dance movement therapy research and the movement analysis frameworks with Body Questions to look at the 'bigger picture' of movement in the context of health, wellbeing, and quality of life.

Processes of Change

It is a challenging task to question our ways of being, which are so entangled with our core values and identity. There are many times when I have controversially said, "people modify – they won't change at their core, unless something transcendental happens". I say this to provoke discussion about how hard it is to change and perhaps how change often is intertwined with anxiety and resistance. It takes a lot of effort to change some of the fundamental patterns and behaviours we have engaged with for long periods of time. There is a reason why these patterns and behaviours arise and how they serve us in navigating relationships with ourselves, family, loved ones, co-workers, and people in general.

According to anthropologist George Herbert Mead[20], reflecting on our actions and creatively engaging with reflexivity allows for an "imaginative rehearsal" of alternatives, performing scenarios before choosing which path to take[21]. By engaging with creative play and embodied reflexivity we can then rehearse, understand, and discover ways of engaging, with the aim to implement these techniques in our daily life.

> **Variables of Insight** is an umbrella term that incorporates the underlying practices that support arts therapies, arts, health and wellbeing, and decision-making.

In Figure 1.5 I delineate the two fundamental processes that guide the activities in this book: Representation (Life-Through-Movement) and Activation (Movement-Evokes-Life).

Representation: Life-Through-Movement

Representation usually involves a task that asks us to 'translate' a situation, experience, memory, or interaction and express it through movement (Figure 1.5). The underlying theory behind this process is that mind and body are connected, and there are movement concepts (as we have evidenced through this book) that are intrinsically connected to human behaviour. There is a world of possibility in using the symbolic power of movement to express what we think and feel. Other arts therapies also make use of representation through visual art, music, drama, and poetry; here we emphasise dance/movement but have also included some elements of other arts genres as well.

FIGURE 1.5 Representing Life Through Movement

DMTs Koch and Fischman state that dance/movement provides an enactive and reflexive embodied 'rehearsal'[22], which can be very healing. Enactive approaches are defined by DMTs as activating movement patterns that emerge from a person's repertoire of movement and through their relationship with others[23]. You can therefore practise new ways of moving and being, thus expanding your embodied possibilities[24]. Symbolism allows such a rehearsal to take place in an immediate time and space and for body action to 'rehearse', replay, or re-enact experiences without explicit consequences[25]. Many of the activities here will ask you to represent something in movement. The goal is to work instinctively, without overthinking it, and to witness the many surprises and insights these movements offer.

Activation: Movement-Evokes-Life

This process describes when dance and movement prompt us to reflect or gain perspective. Often, this emerges out of listening closely to our body or engaging with movement for movement's sake, which generates a feeling of connection to a past or present experience. This often consists of 'AHA!' moments when we are moving that may come up as sensations, thoughts, images, feelings, or memories, as your body helps you work through things. Movement-evokes-life also involves the feeling of vitalisation that happens when you dance to your favourite tune.

The crucial element here is to understand that both processes allow movement to provide meaning and context to situations, which set the backdrop not only for decision-making, but also for understanding how movement can support wellbeing and reflexivity in general. The following case example shows instances of both representation and activation.

Case Example: Why Movement Is Important: AHA! Moments

My 'AHA!' moment about one of the processes that makes dance movement therapy distinct from other practices and linked to decision-making came during a one-off individual movement-for-wellbeing session with a participant interested in getting an online 'taster' of the practice during the pandemic. I did a brief assessment of what she needed from the session in the beginning, and she wanted to understand more about DMT as a practice and get more connected to her body as she was living with a chronic pain condition. As I went through the initial warm-up exercises, she kept drawing parallels between what I was suggesting and other practices such as mindfulness, yoga, somatic therapies, Tai Chi, etc. For example, I suggested some visualisation and paying attention to the breath – and she associated this with mindfulness. The participant was in quite some pain, and I offered a body check-in and some light movement, but she likened this to Feldenkrais.

Internally, I was feeling some pressure (it happens) as I wanted her to get the most out of the session – *How do I distinguish this practice? How do I communicate what we do in the short time we have together?*

I was also aware that we were doing this session online, and it was meant as a one-off, which also added pressure to the situation. I nevertheless repeated in my head the mantra I learned as a student and often use with my own students (much to their dismay): *Trust the process.*

I stayed attuned to what she needed in movement and started observing her patterns of movement to get a sense of how she moved and how it resonated in my own body. As she moved, she clarified she was struggling to ground and anchor. Paying attention to her body brought back some connection to her chronic pain, which was a concern. Here is when I decided to shift from doing something more introspective, which brought more attention to her body, to something more activating and an activity that used symbolism, which wouldn't bring too much attention back to the body pain and would get us moving together and flowing more (Representation). Symbolic distance[26] is a way in which we use metaphors or symbols to get some perspective.

> Decision-Making through movement is a system that explores movement to activate body-based change.

I decided to suggest the Safety Backpack activity from page 56 where we collected real or imaginary objects/people/places that make us feel safe. I thought potentially some metaphoric content would help her clarify her Intention for the session. This is when the dynamic completely shifted between us and in her body. She began to engage her whole body as she picked up objects both literally and symbolically. She started making connections to her life and what functions these objects could serve in her safety backpack. She started creating more awareness of the space. She said, "I have never done this quite like this!", which I took as a signal we could then shift into a space of exploration. She allowed the movement to surprise her and offer meaning. She reported feeling less pain and sensing her body activated and awake (Activation). Something settled in my chest, and I felt that symbolic content, enacted through or by movement, was the factor that made a difference for most of my participants. The connections we make between movement and lived experience is what we aim for, as they can help us generate, repair, and reflect on our relationships to others and to ourselves. Here, by suggesting an activity which focused the work on a symbolic representation activity, the participant was able to connect to her experience through objects. By engaging deeply with the images of safety, she was then able to activate positive bodily sensations and connect to endearing memories of the protective factors in her life.

Our First Movement Break: Spirals 🎧

Here is a movement exploration where we will embody some spirals, which will involve both activation and representation. (Yes, both can occur at the same time!) I will write small notes about the process as we go along.

Suggested Music

Track Title: Earthy

Duration: 03:00

Music Composer: Ross Whyte

Link for QR Code: https://youtu.be/2DdF7PG8d2Y?si=RgB_PFtGs8idSkMF>

🎧 Link for Audio Description playlist:
www.youtube.com/playlist?list=PLtGm4qYm5yBQZqgY5_PFpJHa4jgs2R6Cw

Draw spirals with your whole body. You can draw spirals in the air or on the body itself. Experiment with specific body parts – hands, elbows, knees, top of the head, and any other ones you can explore with. **Try bigger, larger spirals or smaller ones.** Do this without any expectations but with curiosity. If exploring these spirals in movement feels too challenging at the moment, you can start by drawing spirals on a piece of paper.

Notice the flow patterns that are emerging with the spiral. Do they follow a rhythm? How are the movements accompanied and supported by your breath? **Play with increasing or decreasing the tension while you move.** You can also try spirals becoming lighter or heavier.

Notes on Process: This would be the aspect of the exercise in which we engage with a movement concept through a task. While executing the exercise, it might evoke some aspects in your life, but the main goal even if it doesn't is to engage the body in a full range of movement.

Once you have explored this as long as needed, **visualise how you are feeling today:**

- What type of spiral represents it best? (If it's not a spiral, you can come up with any geometrical figure in the space that symbolises it more accurately.)
- What is the shape of the spiral pattern? How does is flow?
- Is there an ideal Flow pattern which is different, or would it need to change?
- What new possibilities are there?

After exploring, take some time to do some drawing reflection.

Notes on Process: This is the aspect which I term as representation – drawing the parallel between the movement concepts and constructing/connecting meaning from our own life experiences.

How did your first movement break go? Smoothly? Was it fun? Or was it a challenge? It is okay either way, as movement practice is an ongoing process. Before I move on to discuss other elements of the work, I want to take a brief pause to recognise the crucial element of non-judgement. It is an important principle that

I aim for when I lead groups, but it is also important to be non-judgemental about ourselves first.

The connection to the Variables of Insight of movement and the application of creative methods allows symbolic content to help us investigate our context further. I encourage you to continue to investigate the two processes – moving and seeing if meaning emerges (**Activation**) and/or having an intention/image and representing this through movement (**Representation**). This interplay between listening to the body for new information and representing our daily life through movement is part of the richness of embodied practice. How they interweave continues to be a source of new discovery.

Movement Break: Body Check-In Exercise 🎧

Before we start introducing the concepts that we will be using for the book, we will begin by checking in with our bodies. This is sometimes the way I start groups, or prepare myself before starting to move, so that I feel present, put any unwanted thoughts or mental tasks on pause, and prepare for my movement practice.

Suggested Music

Track Title: Goofy

Duration: 03:12

Music Composer: Ross Whyte

Link for QR Code: https://youtu.be/18H-vcxs2Io?si=e7D95H-WTl_apONF

🎧 Link for audio description playlist:
www.youtube.com/playlist?list=PLtGm4qYm5yBQZqgY5_PFpJHa4jgs2R6Cw

---

Find a comfortable position either sitting or standing. If you are sitting, place your feet flat on the ground or with the bottoms of your feet on a steady surface. If you are standing, place your feet a bit wider than your hips and make sure you are not holding any unnecessary tension in your knees. I often say to participants to imagine their knees are like memory foam – bouncy and resilient.

We will start by taking an 'inventory' of our body parts. This helps us feel more connected if we are too much in our head. I will take you through a guided suggestion, but feel free to spend more time on this on your own. **Close your eyes and tune in to your body.** I often use the imagery of the light of a photocopier machine – scanning from feet to head. Start by wiggling your toes and bringing awareness to the heels and imagine making footprints by treading through the feet. Sitting – or standing – you can shift the weight from one foot to the other. Then, shift the attention upwards to the major joints: ankles, knees, sit bones, belly button, lower back – travelling up the spine up to the top of the skull. Take some time in each, noticing the body parts. **Pat, wiggle, massage, or shake to bring any parts into consciousness.** Try not to judge where the body is at, but just notice and acknowledge. Take your time as needed. Scan the front of the face to the jaw, then travel down the neck into the shoulders, elbows, wrists, and hands. **Move as your body needs in this moment to warm up and feel activated.** Stretch, yawn, shake, and then bat open your eyes. Notice your environment with a softened gaze. We are ready to begin.

We also have a body check-in chart available to you (Worksheet 1.2) in case you want to also incorporate drawing into this exercise.

WORKSHEET 1.1 Decision-Making Stages and Their Body Questions

ATTENTION (SPACE)
What is my environment like?
What options/alternatives can I explore?
What do I need to research/know more about?
What information do I already have?
What is my support system like?

INTENTION (WEIGHT)
What do I need?
What does my body need?
What are my priorities right now?
What is at the core of the issue?
What kind of internal/external pressure am I facing?
Is it an internal/external pressure or both?
What is essential?

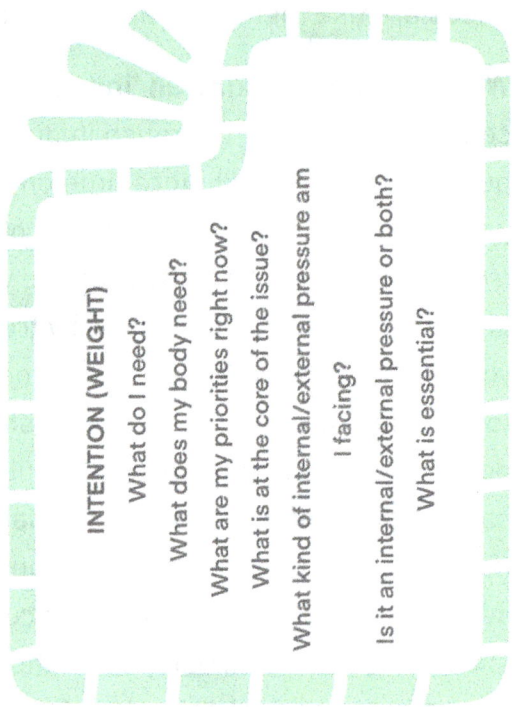

(FLOW) TENSION
What tension exists?
What sparks joy/pleasure? (Constructive Tension)
What produces annoyance/discomfort and/or curiosity?
Where do I feel this is my body?

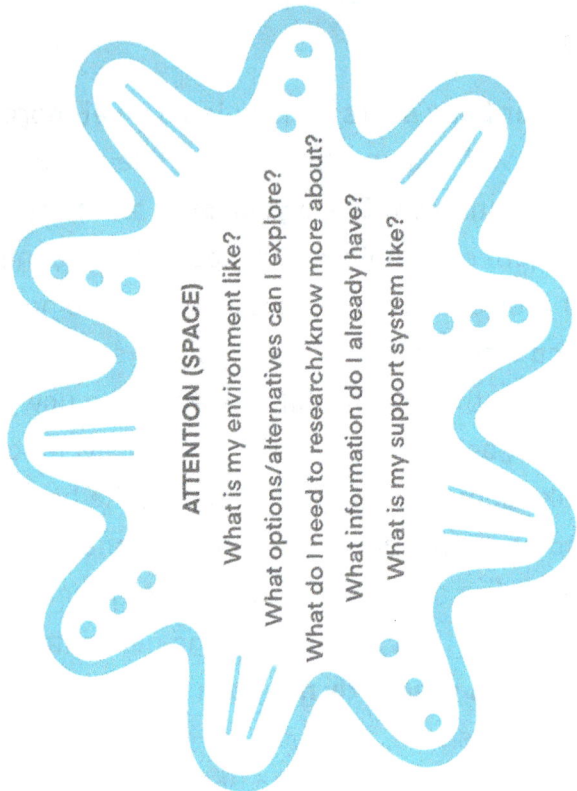

ACTION / NON-ACTION (TIME)
What can I commit to?
What timing does this need?
What actions or next steps can I take/not take?
Is non-action an option?
Do I need to move to a different stage?

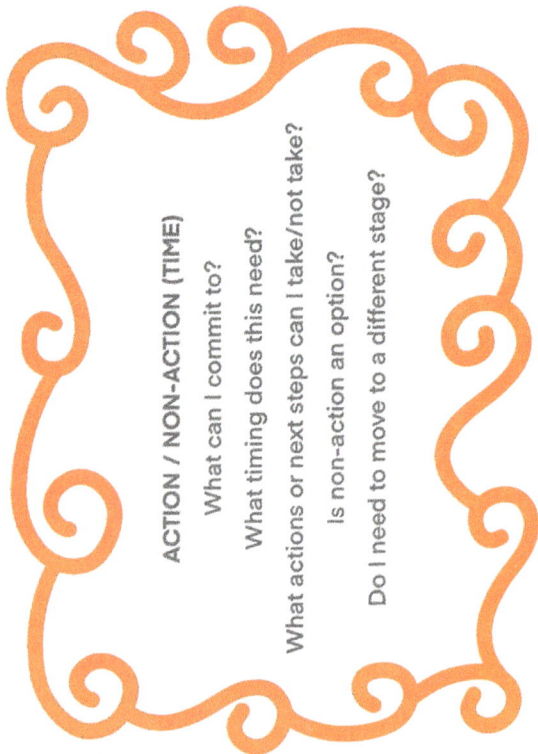

WORKSHEET 1.2 Body Check-In Chart

Body Check-in Chart

Exercise

Connect to your body by drawing, colouring or writing anywhere on this page

My body feels...
OR
I am aware of ... in my body

How are you feeling before the exercise?

Low	Meh	Ok	Good	Great!
☐	☐	☐	☐	☐

How are you feeling after the exercise?

Low	Meh	Ok	Good	Great!
☐	☐	☐	☐	☐

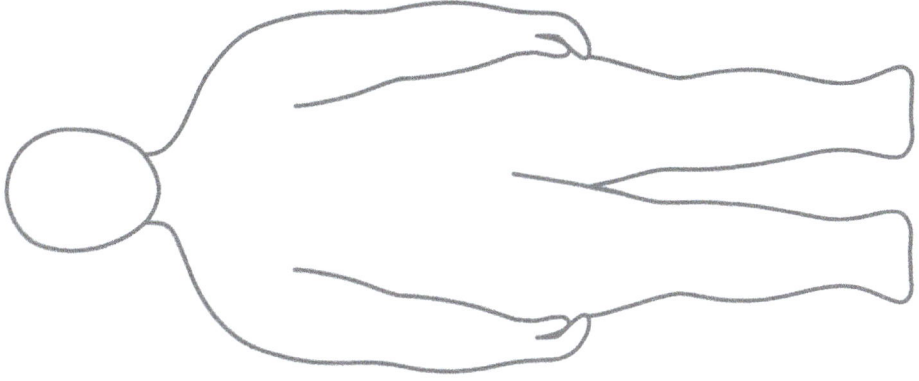

REVIEW: WHAT WE HAVE COVERED SO FAR

- You went through the format of the book and its visual language consisting of icons, colours, and shapes.
- Representation is one of the processes underpinning our movement breaks where we translate real life into movement or artistic media.
- Activation occurs when we move, and through this embodied experience make connections to our life
- You also received an overview of the four stages of decision-making and started to understand their connection to development:
  - Flow/Tension – embryonic stage
  - Attention – before crawling when infants regulate focus
  - Intention – when toddlers explore their relationship to gravity and 'typically' work their way to standing
  - Action/Non-Action – toddlers negotiate timing while advancing/retreating attempting to walk

Before we continue to the Attention stage in decision-making (Chapter 2), I will introduce the frameworks I use as a theoretical anchor for this book. I will also introduce some movement concepts to get us started working with the body.

The next section goes more into detail about movement analysis concepts.

The Whole Movement Analysis System at a Glance

Before we get to each of the stages, I will introduce some of the common categories within the BESS (Body Effort Shape Space). This chapter will also offer a comprehensive overview of the categories we will explore in each of the decision-making stages. If you'd like to take a sneak peak at the themes we will be covering in each stage, you can take a look at Worksheet 7.2 on page 202. The movement qualities that we will cover for each stage are detailed on Worksheet 1.3 at the end of this chapter on page 47.

If you have had enough of terminology and want to come back to these categories later, please skip to the chapter pertaining to the decision-making stage you'd like to start with. Figure 1.4 on page 18 offers you the different order formats in which you can read Part 1 of this book.

Each stage, within the BESS movement analysis system, includes a combination of concepts related to these wide categories:

Body: This is the most fundamental aspect of the system since it usually looks at our body shape, posture, and the gestures we make. We can take notice of how we negotiated developmental tasks as young children and how our body 'works' in movement[27].

Effort Qualities: This relates to the effort required to move. Effort Qualities are ways to describe the dynamics of movement which relate to exertion[28]. Efforts are key to understand how we move, relate to the world, and in what way we are investing our energy. Efforts are the main components of our movement styles covered in Chapter 6.

Shape elements: This category connects body to space and relates to how we mould and adapt to the space around us[29]. We often perform many movements to accommodate our body within our environment, include/exclude other people/ objects, and negotiate boundaries, among many other functions!

Space/spatial elements: We might not have considered that we move in three-dimensional space. These elements help us understand how we map out the space we use. Space does not refer to outer space, but how we measure and negotiate interpersonal space in relationship to other people, or how we move in different directions[30].

Effort and Shape combined together are the main elements we will focus on in this book. They each will form part of each of the decision-making stages we will cover.

Starting With the Body: Our Kinesphere

The *kinesphere*[31] refers to a bubble around our body in which all our movements take place. This was a concept attributed to the works of Rudolph Laban, and many body theorists down the line describe it as the space which we can palpate around us, which culturally is additionally interpreted as 'personal space'[32]. The kinesphere has several layers (see Figure 1.6), and it expands/contracts depending on mood, stress, and sense of safety[33].

Although this concept is more abstract, you can probably picture someone in your life who takes up a lot of space around them and someone who wishes to be as small and unnoticeable as possible. Understanding how you use your kinesphere is the first step towards increasing your body awareness.

The third Movement Break of our book will help you practise this concept more.

FIGURE 1.6 The Kinesphere

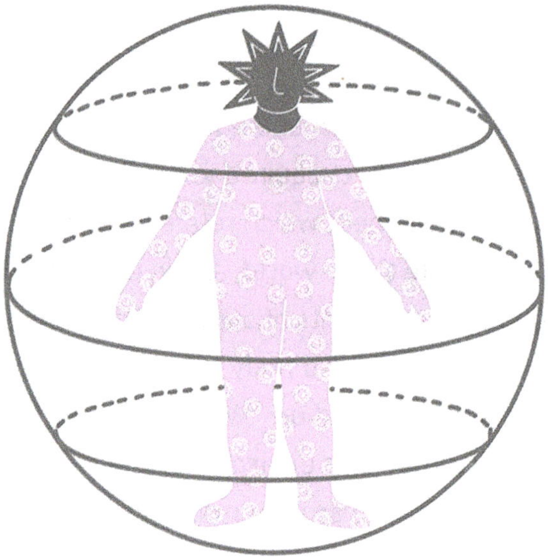

Movement Break: Kinesphere 🎧

Suggested Music

Track Title: Dreamy / Wintery

Duration: 1:30

Music Composer: Ross Whyte

Link for QR code: https://youtu.be/7Quy4s4x4jQ?si=ZZTXf0T1SawwZQz0>

🎧 Link for audio description playlist: www.youtube.com/playlist?list=PLtGm4q
Ym5yBQZqgY5_PFpJHa4jgs2R6Cw

Rub your hands together, and imagine you are putting paint on your hands with your favourite colour or texture. **Use your hands to invisibly paint a big bubble around you which extends 360 degrees in all directions** as far as you can reach. This is called the kinesphere. We will experiment with three layers of the bubble, called *kinesphere reach* (Figure 1.7).

Take some time to move within the kinesphere (while standing or sitting still). Then **try out doing any free movements, getting closer and closer to your body** until you are moving almost 5 cm (≈ 2 inches) from your skin. This is your **'small space bubble'**, as dance movement therapist Rena Kornblum termed it[34]. Play with the idea of moving super close to the body without making contact with your skin.

Once you have finished, **put your hands on your hips and explore *mid reach*,** which is at elbow distance, or around 24 cm (≈ 9 inches) around your body[35]. Explore movement at this distance. You can try moving forward or back – just try not to extend your elbows. This is your medium space bubble.

FIGURE 1.7 Kinesphere Reach and Kinesphere Levels

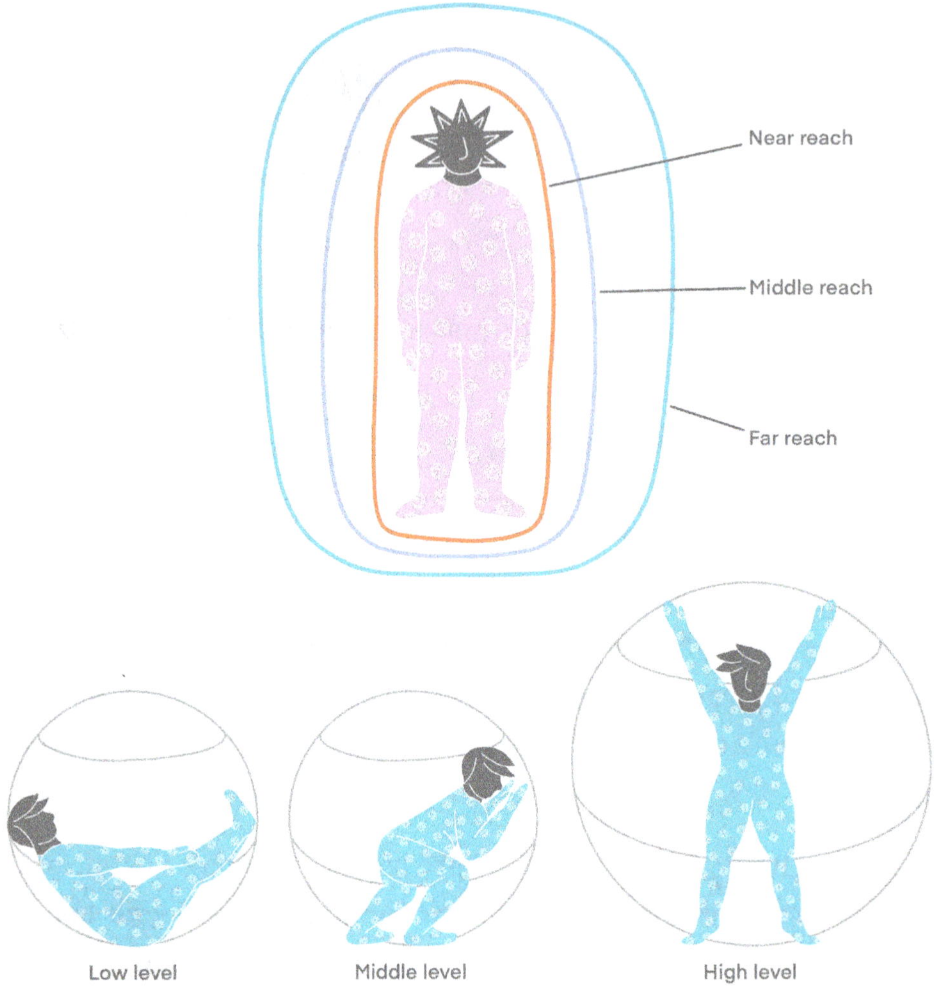

Near reach

Middle reach

Far reach

Low level　　　　Middle level　　　　High level

Then try *far reach*, your largest expansion of space (large space bubble). This is as far as you can extend without bending your elbows or moving from your spot. **Trace all the edges of your bubble.** Move around the space to see what spatial negotiations you encounter. **Try different combinations of bubbles:** small, middle, or large. How do they feel?

You carry this bubble and engage with the world at different levels, which highly depend on your context, culture, upbringing, and how comfortable or uncomfortable you are. These bubbles will also interact with other people's bubbles very dynamically, which makes for a lot of spatial negotiations (which may involve intimacy, friendship, and conflict, amongst many other states). Notice for yourself how much space you have at this moment in time. How much space do you want? How much space do you need?

In each of the activities, I will encourage you to move differently perhaps from what you might be used to. I suggest you move in different types of space 'slices' as you will see shortly.

Slicing the Kinesphere (Challenges for Each Movement Activity)

One way we can slice the kinesphere is by exploring movement in levels – low level (close to the floor), middle level at level of our torso, and high level upwards towards our head and as far as our arms can reach (Figure 1.7 bottom – left to right). This is great for when you want to stretch up to your maximum reach or use the floor to get new insight in movement.

Reach: Near to Far (Figure 1.7 top image)

We explored this on page 32 as part of our kinesphere movement exploration. This expands from near reach to mid reach to far reach. This is great for when you want to experiment with how much space you take up while moving.

IMPORTANT NOTE: We will be getting even more technical about movement analysis concepts in the following section. You can come back to this section later if you are getting too saturated with the terms. At this point, you know the main categories we will cover, so that should be enough to jump to the decision-making chapters (Chapters 2–5). Each decision-making chapter will include each of these movement concepts as default sections.

Introduction to Terminology

Planes of Movement

Each decision-making stage (except Flow/Tension [see Figure 1.8*]) will have a plane assigned to it. We will be practising these planes as part of each stage. Planes are 2-D, like a piece of paper. For each plane, we will conceptually separate the body into 'halves' so that we can understand its movement components.

FIGURE 1.8 Stages Diagram

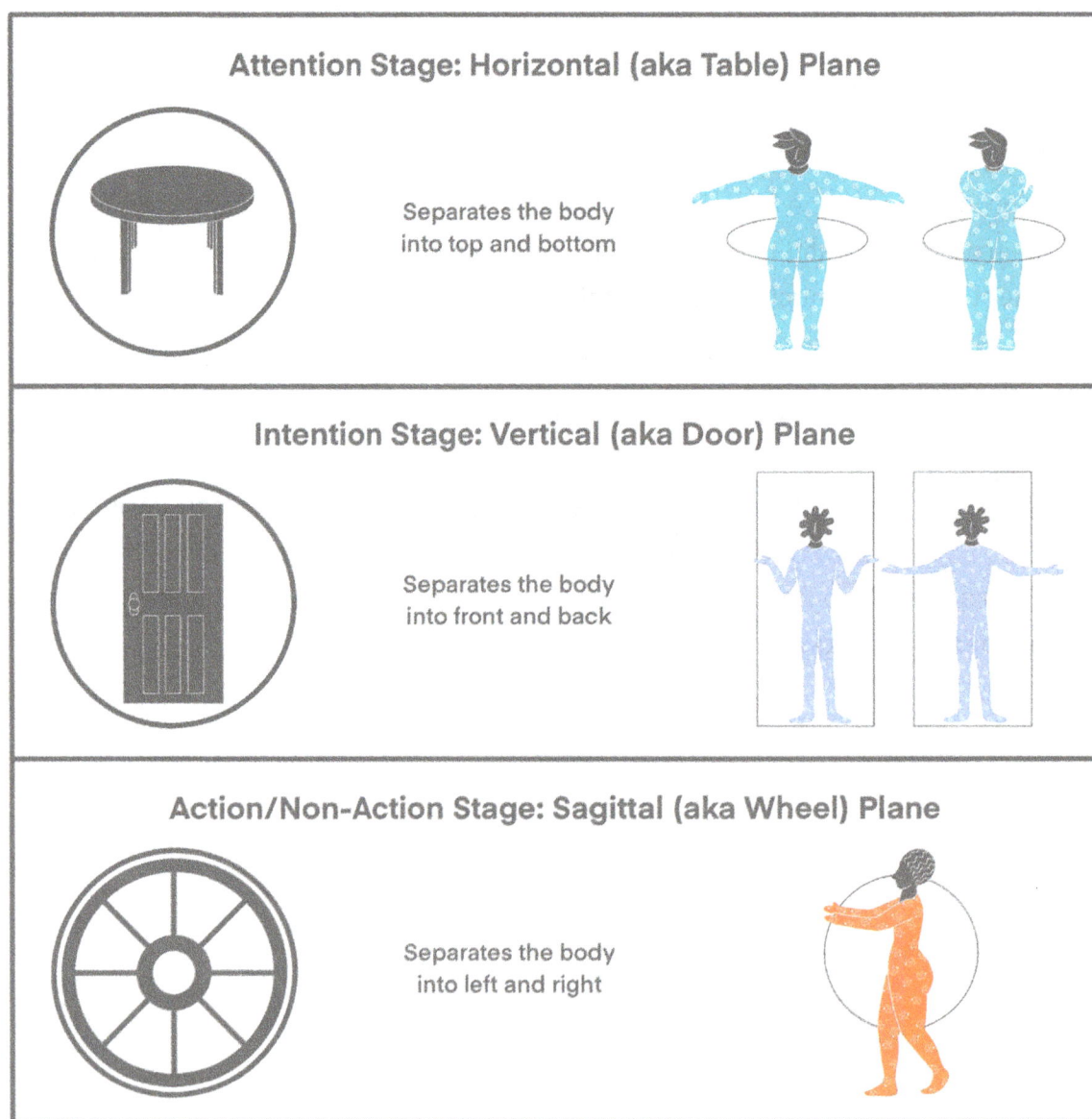

Attention Stage: Horizontal (aka Table) Plane

Separates the body into top and bottom

Intention Stage: Vertical (aka Door) Plane

Separates the body into front and back

Action/Non-Action Stage: Sagittal (aka Wheel) Plane

Separates the body into left and right

*Flow/Tension doesn't have a plane because that stage relates to your own muscle tension and connecting back to your body to reflect/evaluate.

Figure 1.9 shows the directions involved in each plane.

FIGURE 1.9 Dimensions Diagram

1. Combination of Two Directions called a Dimension[37] (2-D)

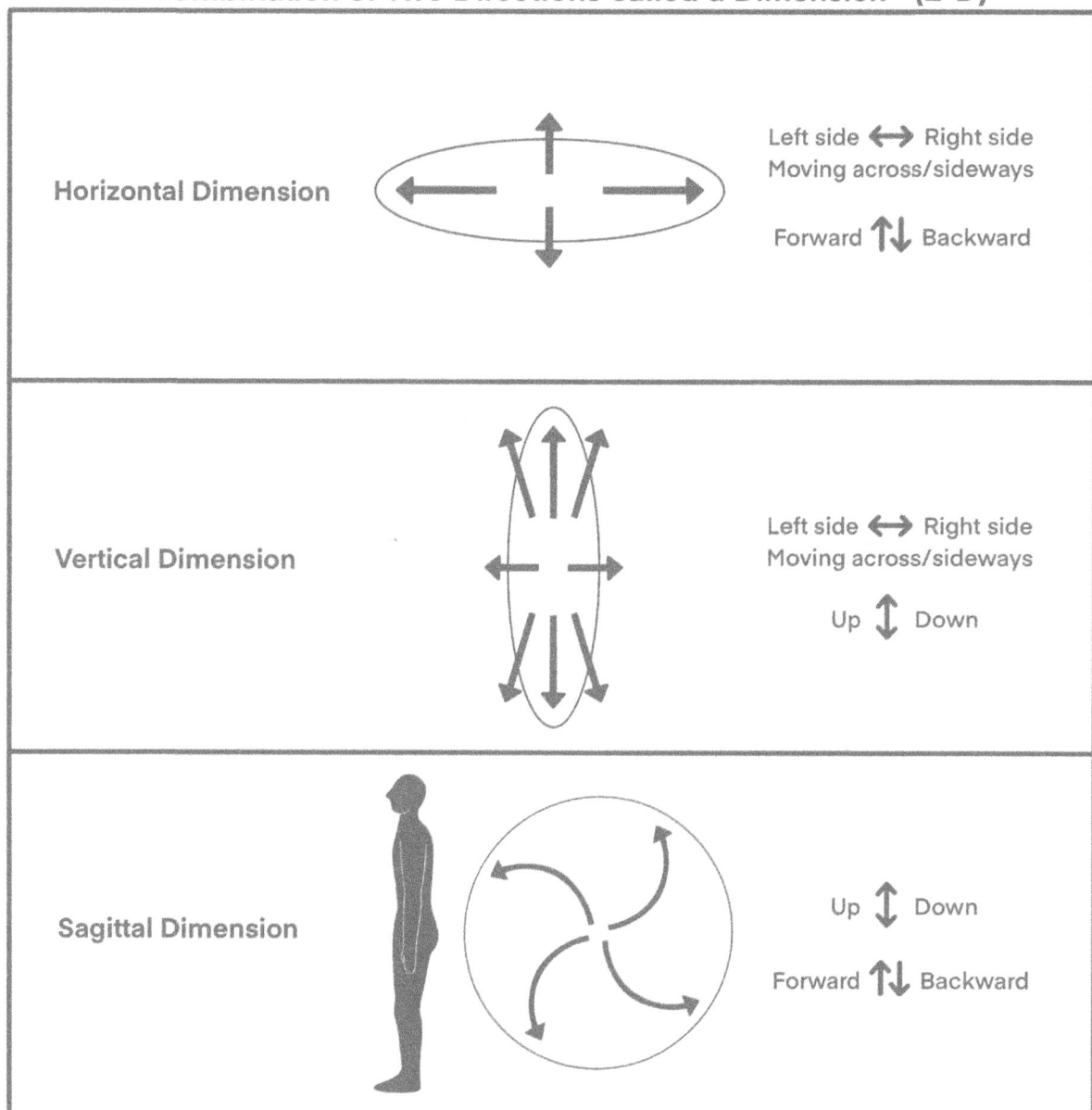

Horizontal Dimension — Left side ⟷ Right side Moving across/sideways; Forward ↑↓ Backward

Vertical Dimension — Left side ⟷ Right side Moving across/sideways; Up ↕ Down

Sagittal Dimension — Up ↕ Down; Forward ↑↓ Backward

In BESS, there are four Effort categories: Space, Weight, Time, and Flow (Figure 1.10).

1. Combinations of Effort Qualities. Effort is what movement theorists define as the dynamics of movement. "Effort gives the feel, texture, tone or colour of the movement or energy"[36].

FIGURE 1.10 Effort Categories Icons

Space: Regulation of focus – from direct (specific attention) to indirect (expansive focus). Where are we focusing? Too many options? Too narrow focus?

Weight: Regulation of Force – from light uses of pressure to strong exertion. How much pressure are we giving a situation? Are we having a light touch? Or applying too much strength?

Time: Regulation of time acceleration or deceleration – pacing and rhythm – negotiating the timing of any decision. When is the right time for a decision? Are we pacing ourselves? Moving too quickly or taking too much time?

Flow: Regulation of tension/release in our muscular system and bodily organs (e.g. lungs, stomach). Are we tense? Are you releasing tension? What is happening to your breath?

2. Shaping Qualities these are movements that happen when we mould or shape the space around us (e.g. like a hug) (Figure 1.11). We open or close our body to engage with objects, people, and places. The different types of shaping qualities indicate 'towards where' we are opening or closing.

FIGURE 1.11 Shaping Qualities

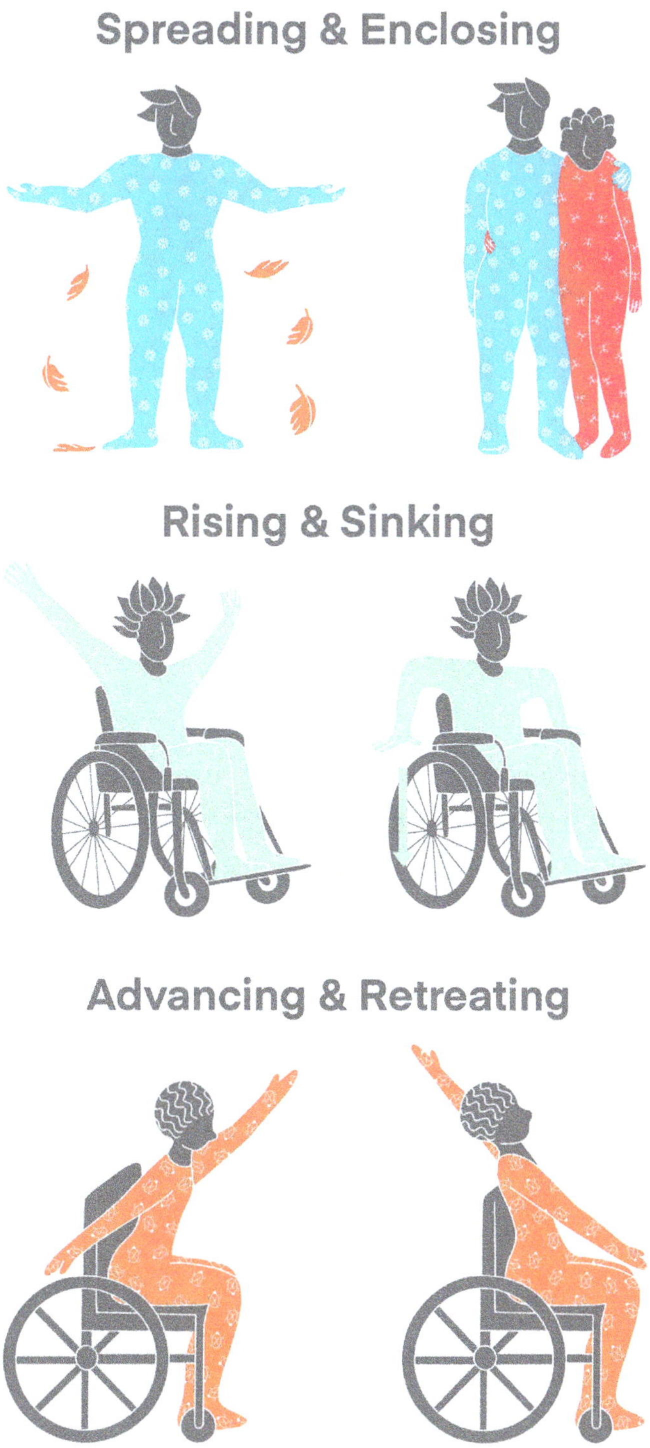

Spreading & Enclosing

Rising & Sinking

Advancing & Retreating

The next three chapters will cover the decision-making stages – Attention, Intention, and Action/Non-Action. Each decision-making stage will all include the following 'recipe': PLANES + EFFORTS + SHAPING QUALITIES (See Figure 1.12).

However, Chapter 5, which focuses on the Flow/Tension stage will only focus on efforts, since Flow/Tension has no spatial components.

FIGURE 1.12 Components of Each Decision-Making Stage

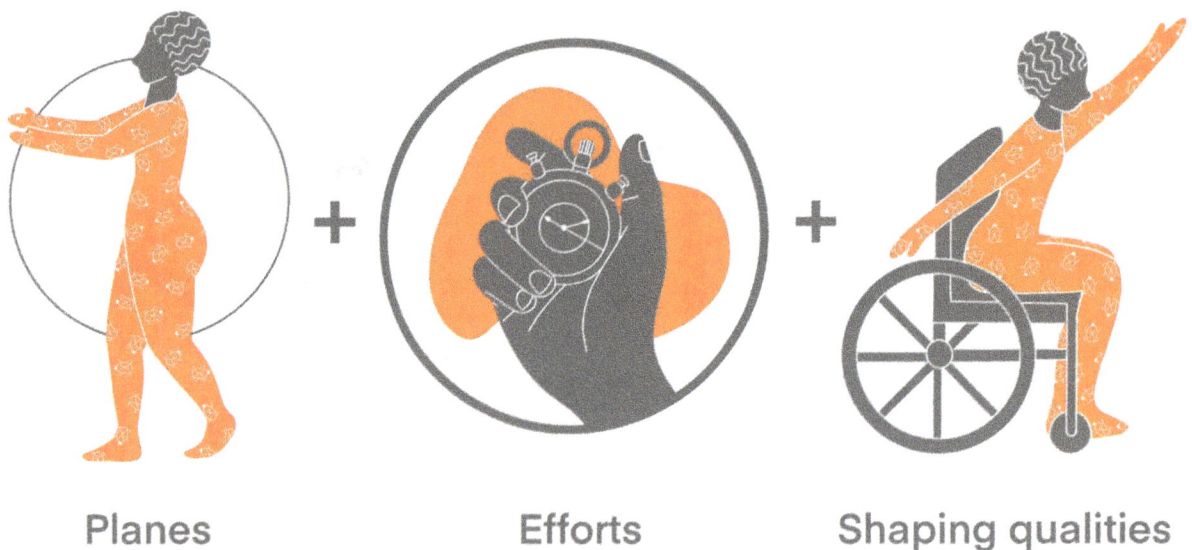

Planes   +   Efforts   +   Shaping qualities

An interesting development is that recent dance movement psychotherapy research has connected the planes to cultural competences[37] to keep developing awareness when engaging with different cultures. We will draw some connections in more detail in each Chapter 7 and 8. Table 1.1 on page 7 offers themes emerging out of the Movement Pattern Analysis profiles and emerging research, which were initially developed by movement analyst Warren Lamb and many of his associates[38].

Table 1.2 pulls the whole system together for those of you who want an overview of the system before we get into its detail in future chapters. The aim is that as we navigate through the book, these alignments will make more sense, and you will be able to come back to it to review and clarify.

Things will start to make more sense when we move them! For each stage we will connect all these movement qualities, issues, themes, and developmental tasks together as different layers.

TABLE 1.2 Overview of Decision-Making Through Movement Categories

STAGE	MOVEMENT QUALITIES	ISSUE	THEME	DEVELOPMENTAL STAGE
(Flow) Tension	EFFORTS: Bound / Free Flow SHAPE FLOW QUALITITES: Growing / Shrinking	How?	Current Bodily State	
Attention	PLANE: Horizontal EFFORT CATEGORY: Space EFFORTS: Direct / Indirect SHAPING QUALITIES: Spreading / Enclosing	Where?	Environment & Alternatives	
Intention	PLANE: Vertical EFFORT CATEGORY: Weight EFFORTS: Light / Strong SHAPING QUALITIES: Rising / Shrinking	What?	Priorities & Needs	
Action / Non-Action	PLANE: Sagittal EFFORT CATEGORY: Time EFFORTS: Quick / Sustained SHAPING QUALITIES: Advancing / Retreating	When?	Timing & Commitment	

How I Struggled With, Overcame, and Applied Movement Analysis

If you have gotten to this point in the book thinking: *This is too technical! I'll never get this!* Please bear with me as I tell you my own story and how I came around to apply movement analysis in my practice.

My first encounter with movement analysis was not a peaceful one. In fact, my first LBMA teacher often labelled me as 'resistant'. I didn't get what the fuss was about and why I needed to qualify movement that was inherent in me, as I had been dancing since I was three years old. I rebelled against this structure in my own way as a questioning and challenging postgraduate student should do (much to my teacher's constant dismay). For example, we started to learn about notation, where we needed to learn symbols pertaining to all the movement concepts in LBMA (don't worry – we won't do that here). I was so confused by this; I decided to substitute the formal symbols with little animals and shapes that I found familiar to me. This apparently was a *faux pas* in movement analysis which still makes me giggle a bit. I remember the frowns and exasperation from my teacher when I drew rabbits for Quick Time and turtles for Sustained Time instead of using 'proper' notation. I found it hard and inaccessible, and my body and mind struggled in understanding these concepts. Given that I was coming from an undergraduate degree in business, I needed a more pragmatic approach to this world of analysing movement[39]. However, when I delved deeper into my internships and embodied practice, this started to change. I found a way in while I was a DMT intern in a residential school setting in New York, which made a huge U-turn in my relationship to movement analysis. My DMT supervisor at the time, Anne Perrin (total rockstar) informed me I was to lead my own class of neurodivergent middle school young people for the first time. She cautioned me by saying, "Please don't mention the word 'dance' or the whole class will protest. You will have to use other methods to get them moving".

I was clueless as to how to breach this barrier, and the anxiety of leading this group was high for weeks on end. Then I had an idea. I approached the class and, as a DMT often does, started with their interests and needs. I asked them what TV, movies, or video game characters they loved. We had to start with what they brought to the group. They named their favourite characters, and back in the early 2000s, my group members loved *Sonic the Hedgehog* (90s video game), *Police Academy* (80s movie) and *Monty Python* (British comedy sketch show which started in the 60s). These were just some of the eclectic and amazing examples the young people offered.

I told the group that there was this 'code' that very few people knew (BESS), which could classify different movement concepts. The uniqueness of this code sparked interest, so I took that as encouragement. I then laid out some big, white, laminated cardboard signs with graphic representations of movement concepts, which is a simplified version of notation used in school curricula at the time, called Language of Dance™ (LOD). Luckily this was taught at my MA, and I loved how simple and accessible it made the whole system and how it opened up creativity in dancemaking. The cardboard signs represented movement actions, such as jumps, rotation/turns, stillness, gestures, movements of different body parts, and others. One of the boys, (around 11–12 years old) was instantly curious. He asked if there was a keyboard to represent this code. I smiled internally at this and replied that there weren't any yet, and he replied, "Hmm – I can probably create one", which I took as a definite sign of interest (even though he did not end up making one). It was all very cognitive at this point, and I wondered how I could get them to embody these concepts, which was the therapeutic objective of working with this group. The group organised these signs and laid them out on the floor, but getting the group to move was still a challenge. They could conceptualise all the movement concepts and memorised the 'code' (in one session!) but embodying was a no-no. I had to go slow. I set them up with tasks in each session:

1. Draw their favourite characters on large pieces of paper.
2. Look through the Language of Dance™ cards and select the appropriate ones for their character.
3. Create their own movement profile for how their character would move.

For example, the lumberjack from *Monty Python* would use strong effort movements to wield his axe; Sonic the Hedgehog used rotation on the low level to roll across the floor on the video game; Mahoney from Police Academy would use arm gestures on the high level (gesture in a high diagonal) to stop criminals in the movie.

One day I took a big risk and said, "I wonder how these characters would move their symbols in real life? Could someone show the class how their character would move?" I gulped. I thought this was the day the protest would begin. To my surprise, they really got excited about showing each other how the characters moved! We had a common language, a structure to work with, and in the end we were moving like different characters, demonstrating the diversity of options we had using all our bodies. This is when I came round to the idea of movement analysis, by engaging with representation and activation. I understood that having a way to make movement accessible, particularly in working with neurodiversity, could help us reach common ground.

During the six years I worked across the New York educational system, I used movement analysis concepts for many purposes. When I taught fifth grade (12–13 year olds) choreography class in an inner-city school, they got to create and direct their own dances. We also used movement analysis concepts to offer feedback to other students on how the dances were communicating choreographic intention. By focusing on movement qualities, we could offer constructive ways to discuss how choreographers could support their dancers in learning the dances and communicate messages through their dances. It also helped tone down some of the potentially critical feedback the kids were using with each other beforehand.

Across different schools, the young people and I co-created dances about specific movement concepts, had BESS-themed dance offs, and generated movement improvisational tasks to come up with new choreographic material. This meant breaking down the concepts into its simplest form, which set up the roots for working in higher education and professional development today. Like me, my students also experienced resistance, rebellion, questions, and challenges to the system, which I still enjoy when experimenting with this system today. I haven't used the symbols/notation themselves at university level and haven't had any rabbits or turtles drawn in protest; yet I am still finding new ways I can reflect on my own movement preferences and choices across my career.

I do not intend for movement analysis in this book to be used to decode others or prescribe what others can do. I wish to stay away from creating recipes for how to move since as I will describe and will repeat across many chapters, there is no 'right' way to move, and all movement qualities are adaptive, dynamic, and respond to the many social structures we contend with on a daily basis. My intention is for this book to be about reflecting on our movement decisions, either zooming in or zooming out of specific life situations, and offering ideas as to how to apply movement concepts to understand how we engage with others. This system is not new, it is even contended and debated in many circles as I will also discuss. I am conscious that I am not creating any new type of method nor do I desire to do so – my goal is to contribute activities and new applications of the work to make these concepts available to anyone who wants to integrate/develop their movement practice in everyday life.

What I provide here is a 'user-friendly' approach to movement which can be accessed by a range of experiences with movement – for people who have never moved in an expressive manner and want to try moving more, DMT students, or experienced professionals who want to engage in discussions about embodied reflexivity.

Some Early Caveats About Movement Analysis

I note that no movement analysis system is a blanket solution to all problems, and there are many cultural challenges to the systems since most of them were developed with a Western and European lens. For example, Laban underwent some of the initial work on this system in Germany during World War II, which also has brought up some historical challenges and numerous debates in DMT[40]. I acknowledge this and have consciously considered cultural contexts in this book. You will notice there will be some sections titled "Culture and Caveats" throughout to help address this and embed this model into the current social, political, economic, and cultural contexts at the time when this book is published. Intersectionality is the consideration that we are made up of many different identities. I aim to propose intersectional Body Questions, challenges, and opportunities along the way.

REVIEW POINTS ON CHAPTER 1

- The section "Introduction: Decision-Making Through Movement: Human Development" introduced key concepts, my background, and the structure of the book.
- The section "Variables of Insight Through Movement: Processes You Will Be Undertaking" synthesised the two main processes involved in using dance/movement to reflect: Representation and Activation.
- The section "The Whole Movement Analysis System at a Glance" offered an introduction to what constitutes a decision-making stage. It broke down each stage into its bare movement components (Worksheet 1.3 offers a preview of the qualities that you will learn as part of each chapter):
  - Planes (which include two dimensions)
  - Shaping Qualities (how we form/shape the space around us)
  - Efforts – the dynamics of movement
  - Developmental stages linked to each decision-making stage
  - Themes associated with decision-making according to the framework of Movement Pattern Analysis (MPA) and BESS.
- Table 1.2 has a summary of themes and overview of the system.
- I offered some case examples of my own experience and my work with individuals and groups to get us thinking about the applications of decision-making.
- Chapters 2–5 will detail each decision-making stage individually. You may start at any chapter and choose your own order within Part 1 of the book.

WORKSHEET 1.3 Decision-Making Stages and Their Movement Qualities

ATTENTION

PLANE: Horizontal

EFFORT CATEGORY: Space

EFFORTS: Direct / Indirect

SHAPING QUALITIES:
Spreading / Enclosing

INTENTION

PLANE: Vertical

EFFORT CATEGORY: Weight

EFFORTS: Light / Strong

SHAPING QUALITIES:
Rising / Shrinking

(FLOW) TENSION

EFFORTS: Bound / Free Flow

SHAPE FLOW QUALITITES:
Growing / Shrinking

ACTION / NON-ACTION

PLANE: Sagittal

EFFORT CATEGORY: Time

EFFORTS: Quick / Sustained

SHAPING QUALITIES:
Advancing / Retreating

Notes

1 Lamb, Warren. *Posture and Gesture: An Introduction to the Study of Physical Behaviour* (G. Duckworth, 1965); Lamb, Warren, and Elizabeth M. Watson. *Body Code: The Meaning in Movement* (London and Boston: Routledge & Kegan Paul, 1979); Lamb, Warren, and David Turner. *Management Behaviour* (New York: International Universities Press, 1969); Moore, Carol-Lynne. *Movement and Making Decisions: The Body-Mind Connection in the Workplace* (New York: Dance & Movement Press, 2005); Moore, Carol-Lynne. 'A Primer on Movement Pattern Analysis' (1977); Eddy, Martha. 'Body Cues and Conflict: LMA-Derived Approaches to Educational Violence Prevention' (2002). www.wellnesscke.net/downloadables/Body-Cues-Conflict.pdf; Acarón, Thania. 'Movement Decision-Making in Violence Prevention and Peace Practices'. *Journal of Peace Education* 15, no. 2 (May 2018): 191–215. https://doi.org/10.1080/17400201.2018.1463913.

2 These four concepts are derived from Authentic Movement, a method in dance movement therapy. I have found them useful in my practice to stimulate different types of reflection and to structure feedback. Adler, Janet. *Offering from the Conscious Body: The Discipline of Authentic Movement* (Simon and Schuster, 2002).

3 Evans, Elizabeth, Martin Hyde, Jason Davies, Suzanne Moffatt, Nicola O'Brien, and Gill Windle. *Navigating Later Life Transitions: An Evaluation of Emotional and Psychological Interventions* (Calouste Gulbenkian Foundation UK; Centre for Ageing Better; Swansea University, 2019). https://europepmc.org/backend/ptpmcrender.fcgi?accid=PMC4318792&blobtype=pdf; Goodman, Jane, Nancy K. Schlossberg, and Mary L. Anderson. *Counseling Adults in Transition: Linking Practices with Theory* (New York: Springer Publishing Company, 2006). http://ebookcentral.proquest.com/lib/usw/detail.action?docID=291321; Sullivan, Sherry E., and Akram Al Ariss. 'Making Sense of Different Perspectives on Career Transitions: A Review and Agenda for Future Research'. *Human Resource Management Review* 31, no. 1 (March 2021): 100727. https://doi.org/10.1016/j.hrmr.2019.100727.

4 World Health Organization (WHO), Daisy Fancourt, and Saoirse Finn. 'Health Evidence Network Synthesis Report 67: What Is the Evidence on the Role of the Arts in Improving Health and Well-Being? A Scoping Review (2019)' (World Health Organization, November 2019). www.euro.who.int/en/publications/abstracts/what-is-the-evidence-on-the-role-of-the-arts-in-improving-health-and-well-being-a-scoping-review-2019.

5 Hanna, Judith Lynne. *To Dance Is Human: A Theory of Nonverbal Communication* (Austin: University of Texas Press, 1979).

6 Sheets-Johnstone, Maxine. *The Phenomenology of Dance*, 2nd ed. (London: Dance Books Ltd., 1979).

7 Hanna, 1979; Thomas, Helen. *Dance, Modernity, and Culture: Explorations in the Sociology of Dance* (London: Routledge, 1995). http://site.ebrary.com/id/10099778?ppg=180.

8 Sheets-Johnstone, 1979.

9 Sabine C. Koch, 'Arts and Health: Active Factors and a Theory Framework of Embodied Aesthetics', *The Arts in Psychotherapy* 54 (July 2017): 85–91. https://doi.org/10.1016/j.aip.2017.02.002; Lauffenburger, Sandra Kay. '"Something More": The Unique Features of Dance Movement Therapy/Psychotherapy'. *American Journal of Dance Therapy* 42, no. 1 (June 2020): 16–32. https://doi.org/10.1007/s10465-020-09321-y.

10 I use dance movement therapy (DMT) and dance movement psychotherapy (DMP) interchangeably as terms for the profession and research. The term dance movement therapy is used across most countries, while the term dance movement psychotherapy is used primarily in the United Kingdom.

11 A comprehensive list of recent LBMA resources and applications can be found in https://labaninstitute.org/what-we-do/research-development/.

12 Other movement analysis systems not covered in this book are: (list is not exhaustive)

   Benesh Notation: Benesh, Rudolf, and Joan Benesh. *An Introduction to Benesh Movement-Notation: Dance*, vol. 16 (Dance Horizons, 1969);

   Embodied Cultural Competence Framework: Robinson, Aisha Bell, kyla marie Gilmore, and Charla Weatherby. 'Embodied Cultural Competence Framework: A Body-Based Method to Examine Cultural Identity Development and Bias'. *American Journal of Dance Therapy* (March 2024). https://doi.org/10.1007/s10465-024-09399-8.

   Kinesics: Birdwhistell, Ray L. *Kinesics and Context: Essays on Body Motion Communication* (University of Pennsylvania Press, 2010).

   Paul Ekman's Facial Affect Scoring Test: Ekman, Paul, Wallace V. Freisen, and Sonia Ancoli. 'Facial Signs of Emotional Experience'. *Journal of Personality and Social Psychology* 39, no. 6 (1980): 1125–1134. https://doi.org/10.1037/h0077722.

   Movement Psychodiagnostic Inventory: Davis, Martha. 'Movement Characteristics of Hospitalized Psychiatric Patients'. *American Journal of Dance Therapy* 4, no. 1 (1981): 52–71; Cruz, Robyn Flaum. 'Validity of the Movement Psychodiagnostic Inventory'. *American Journal of Dance Therapy* 31 (2009): 122–135. https://doi.org/10.1007/s10465-009-9072-4.

13 Laumond, Jean-Paul, and Naoko Abe. *Dance Notations and Robot Motion* (Springer, 2016). https://doi.org/10.1007/978-3-319-25739-6.

14 Kestenberg Amighi, Janet, Susan Loman, Penny Lewis, and K. Mark Sossin. *The Meaning of Movement: Developmental and Clinical Perspectives of the Kestenberg Movement Profile* (Amsterdam, The Netherlands: Gordon and Breach, 1999).

15 Acarón, Thania. 'The Practitioner's Body of Knowledge: Dance/Movement in Training Programmes That Address Violence, Conflict and Peace' (University of Aberdeen, 2015). http://ethos.bl.uk/OrderDetails.do?did=1&uin=uk.bl.ethos.683450; Acarón, 2018.

16 Kornblum, Rena. *Disarming the Playground: Violence Prevention Through Movement and Pro-Social Skills, Activity Book* (Oklahoma City: Wood 'N' Barnes Publishing, 2002).

17 Eddy, Martha. 'The Role of Physical Activity in Educational Violence Prevention Programs for Youth' (PhD Thesis, Columbia University, 1998); Eddy, Martha. 'The Role of Dance in Violence Prevention Programs for Youth'. *Dance: Current Selected Research* 7 (2009): 93–143; Acarón, 'The Practitioner's Body of Knowledge', 2015.

18 Acarón, 2018.

19 Ogden, Pat, and Kekuni Minton. 'Sensorimotor Psychotherapy: One Method for Processing Traumatic Memory'. *Traumatology* 6, no. 3 (2000): 149–173.

20 Mead, George Herbert. *George Herbert Mead; Essays on His Social Philosophy* (New York: Teachers College Press, 1968).

21 Hamilton, Peter. *George Herbert Mead: Critical Assessments* (Taylor & Francis, 1992).

22 Koch, Sabine C., and Diana Fischman. 'Embodied Enactive Dance/Movement Therapy'. *American Journal of Dance Therapy* 33, no. 1 (June 2011): 57–72. https://doi.org/10.1007/s10465-011-9108-4.

23 Koch and Fischman, 2011.

24 Koch and Fischman, 2011.

25 Acarón, 'The Practitioner's Body of Knowledge', 2015.

26 As early as 1912, Bullough talked about "psychical" distance, which later dramatherapist Robert Landy developed into the concepted of aesthetic distance. Aesthetic distance is where we can use the arts as a way to get some separation from the issue being explored (Landy, 1983). I later used these concepts applied to movement in an article in which I combined psychodrama techniques with movement for clinical supervision.
   References: Bullough, Edward. '"Psychical Distance" as a Factor in Art and an Aesthetic Principle'. *British Journal of Psychology* 5, no. 2 (1912): 87–118; Landy, Robert J. 'The Use of Distancing in Drama Therapy'. *The Arts in Psychotherapy* 10, no. 3 (September 1983): 175–185. https://doi.org/10.1016/0197-4556(83)90006-0; Acarón, Thania. 'Traversing Distance and Proximity: The Integration of Psychodrama and Dance Movement Therapy Techniques in Supervision'. *Body, Movement and Dance in Psychotherapy* 11, no. 1 (November 2015): 1–15. https://doi.org/10.1080/17432979.2015.1109550.

27 Hackney, Peggy. *Making Connections: Total Body Integration Through Bartenieff Fundamentals* (New York: Routledge, 2002).

28 Dell, Cecily. *A Primer for Movement Description Using Effort-Shape and Supplementary Concepts* (New York: Dance Notation Bureau Press, 1977); Hackney, 2002, 219–222.

29 Studd, Karen A., and Laura L. Cox. *Everybody Is a Body* (Indianapolis, IN: Dog Ear Publishing, LLC, 2013), 97–100.

30 Studd and Cox, 2013, 87–96.

31 Longstaff, Jeffrey Scott. 'Kinesphere'. Laban Analysis Reviews, Research, Documentation (1996). www.laban-analyses.org/laban_analysis_reviews/index2.htm; Laban, Rudolf. *The Language of Movement: A Guidebook to Choreutics*. Edited by Lisa Ullman (Boston: Plays, Inc., 1966).

32 Sommer, Robert. 'Studies in Personal Space'. *Sociometry* 22, no. 3 (September 1959): 247. https://doi.org/10.2307/2785668.

33 Many theorists work with this concept. I wrote an article summarising key works and categorisations in interpersonal space via the following article: Acarón, Thania. 'Shape-in(g) Space: Body, Boundaries, and Violence'. *Space and Culture* 19, no. 2 (2016): 139–149.

34 Kornblum, *Disarming the Playground*, 2002.

35 Hackney, 2002, 223.

36 Studd and Cox, 2013, 159.

37 Robinson, Bell, and Gilmore, 2024.

38 Lamb, 1965; Lamb and Watson, 1979; Lamb and Turner, 1969; Moore, 2005.

39 I ended up travelling to Drexel University to take Kestenberg Movement Profile courses, which helped consolidate a lot of the movement analysis knowledge and make connections to applications to my work with children at the time.

40 Imus, Susan D., Aisha Bell Robinson, Valerie Blanc, and Jessica Young. 'More Than One Story, More Than One Man: Laban Movement Analysis Re-Examined'. *American Journal of Dance Therapy* 44, no. 2 (December 2022): 168–185. https://doi.org/10.1007/s10465-022-09370-5; Beardall, Nancy, Valerie Blanc, Ebony Nichols, Yaya Cofield, Fernanda Greco Quentel, Sofia Lee, Marea Newroz, Sahita Pierre-Antoine, and Stephanie Sinclair. 'Creating Spaces for Discoveries in Movement Observation and Beyond'. *American Journal of Dance Therapy* (January 2024). https://doi.org/10.1007/s10465-023-09395-4; Robinson, Gilmore, and Weatherby, 2024; Preda, Rachele. 'Power Dynamics in Dance Movement Therapy'. *Body, Movement and Dance in Psychotherapy* 17, no. 1 (January 2022): 71–80. https://doi.org/10.1080/17432979.2021.1994010.

2

ATTENTION STAGE

Environment and Alternatives

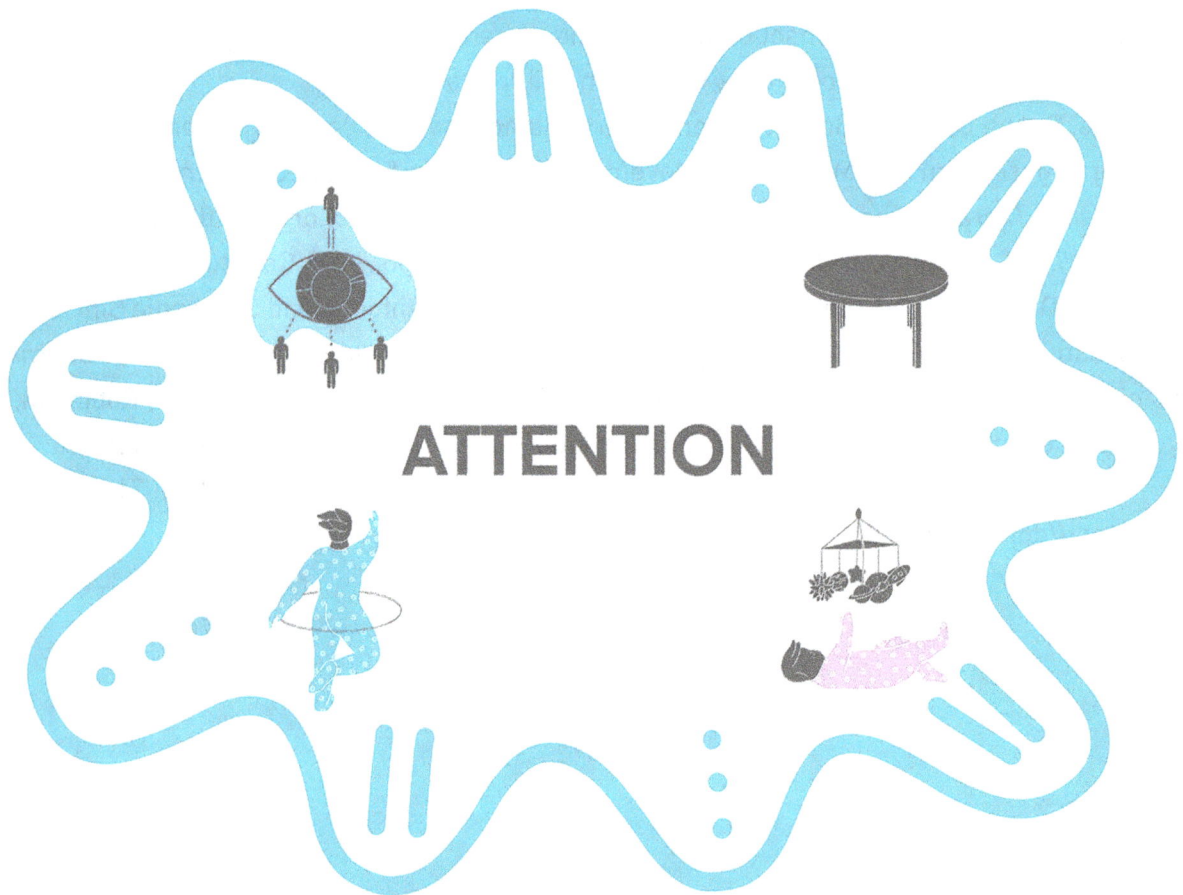

ATTENTION

DOI: 10.4324/9781003360957-3

Body Questions to Consider in This Chapter

- What is my environment like?
- What options/alternatives can I explore?
- What do I need to research/know more about?
- What information do I already have?
- What is my support system like?

In Development

The Attention stage is where we explore different alternatives, understand our environment, and engage in communication with others. We often play peek-a-boo with babies, and as they start to smile and connect, they also trial out ways of communicating their needs. Regulating attention comes in handy across our lifespan, as it helps us consider both fine details and consider the big picture.

Cognitive psychologists concur that infants develop the ability to scan the environment and locate objects in space[1]. Babies are often placed in prone (belly down) or supine (belly up) positions (Figure 2.1), which alter their perspective on what they can see and have access to. Ever wondered why mobiles are so popular on top of cribs? Mobiles, with their colours, movements, and shapes help stimulate a relationship beyond the baby's kinesphere and help motivate their engagement with the outside world. This task sets the precedent for our focus and attention.

Practising focus is a key developmental task we develop around early infancy, which serves as the building block for how we assess, evaluate, research, and explore. 'Typical' developmental tasks involved are the precursors for visual attention and motivation[2], and have been linked to the speed at which we process things, recognise cues from others or the environment, and self-regulate later in life[3]. Attention is engaged through all our senses – auditory, perceptual, olfactory – dependent upon our physical capabilities. You can perceive through your skin, muscles, and joints via proprioception, which has been added to the original five senses. The proprioceptive system is the reason we can sense our body without having a look at the body parts we need to move. Proprioception allows us to engage with action and location[4]. This

FIGURE 2.1 Infant Development

Prone (face down)
position in infants

Supine (face up)
position in infants

is very important to understand as it is essential in our exploration of transitions and decisions, as we begin to reflect on our own positioning.

In the Attention stage within the decision-making through movement framework, we can make important assessments of our environment that can help support or deter us from a decision. In human evolution, this regulation of attention helped preserve our existence against predators and hostile environmental conditions. Therefore, our spatial awareness also connects to our feelings of safety/unsafety in a space. Represented in the body, attention to alternatives allows possibilities to be activated for situations in which you may feel entrapped or hopeless. By mapping out what your environment and plausible options are, you can begin to understand which directions might feel more feasible.

Decision-Making has traditionally associated attention (and all other stages) as a mind-based process. We often connect decision-making to thoughts, preoccupations, or procedures. However, there is recent development into 'embodied cognition', with claims that "the body intrinsically constrains, regulates, and shapes the nature of mental activity"[5]. Understanding both your body and your environment shapes and informs mental processes[6]. A stronger claim from embodied cognition research is that the way you think is also shaped by your previous embodied experiences[7]. Therefore, embodied cognition research concludes that experiences you have felt in your body influence the way you think[8].

A fundamental principle of dance movement therapy is that the body and mind are interconnected, and the wider your movement repertoire available to you, the more coping mechanisms you can access to deal with challenges[9]. By intervening with the body, you can thus expand movement patterns to understand behaviours, emotions, situations, and relationships. We can practice our own adaptability to remain flexible and available to what comes our way[10].

However, what is missing from this description is the body, which is where the Body Questions come in. I won't be able to dedicate too much time to the emerging research of embodied cognition, or dwell too much on the debate of embodied versus cognitive processes, I bring it into this discussion to root us in a body-mind approach when contemplating decisions and transitions.

The Body Question involved here is also linked to spatial awareness skills – understanding where our body is located and taking in information about what surrounds us. For example, people who are active leaders in their communities often generate open spaces, looking to connect and understand their community needs, and widen access by developing strong networks. Notice what happens in your body when you visualise welcoming spaces (actual or ideal) where there is a shared connection and warmth. However, challenges may arise when we are unable to negotiate space[11], become territorial, are intrusive of other people's spaces or other people invade our space. We will keep exploring the pros and cons of each stage to introduce the many possibilities we need to negotiate. After all, the system needs to accommodate a multitude of realities and stories.

Some positives usually associated with the Attention stage are the ability to connect with others and communicate constructively and be open to exploring new alternatives. Listening to others, building community, holding both specificity and multiplicity, and being curious are all facets that emerge out of this stage.

Movement Break: Safety Backpack/Rucksack 🎧

Suggested Music

Track Title: Contemplative

Duration: 05:52

Music Composer: Ross Whyte

Link for QR code: https://youtu.be/hlfecLU5T30?si=Xb_FA-rMV737FzHc

🎧 Link for audio description playlist: www.youtube.com/playlist?list=PLtGm4q Ym5yBQZqgY5_PFpJHa4jgs2R6Cw

The Safety Backpack exercise is the activity I mentioned doing with a participant in the "AHA! Moment" Case Example on page 22. The activity can support group members to explore what makes them feel safe as individuals and communicate this back to the group, thus contributing to group safety. The exercise activates the imagination and is usually one of my warm-up activities to help us feel grounded and ready to do creative, meaningful work. This activity incorporates all the movement elements of Attention we will be discussing later in this chapter.

We will be visualising a safety backpack/rucksack/container which contains elements which help us feel safe. Before we start, I would like to acknowledge that feeling safe is often a privilege, and it is never fair to assume safety; therefore we will aim to feel "as safe as can be" for this exercise[12].

Find a place to sit, either on a chair or on the floor, and close your eyes. **We will do a quick senses inventory, a checklist of our senses to help us feel more present.** We will cover proprioception (which is the sense of where your body is positioned), smell, taste, touch, sound, and sight. If any of these are not available to you, please feel free to adapt this activity.

Feel the ground underneath you and the parts of your body making contact with the floor or the chair. Shift from side to side very subtly, and then find your centre. **Notice the temperature of the room**, and any effect it has on your skin: whether there is any breeze, air currents, or heat. Bring the awareness to your mouth and your sense of taste. What do you notice? You might want to **move your tongue inside your mouth to become more aware of your taste buds**.

Shift to your sense of smell when you are ready. Food, flowers, perfume, sweat: Are there any smells that come into awareness? **After some exploration, switch attention to the sounds.** Some senses may be more heightened than others. Feel free to go back to any senses that you might need more time with. Open your eyes and notice the difference in your body.

Try and capture the whole environment of your room via sight, sound or touch if that is available to you. Remember to also engage your tactile sense and proprioception. Concentrate on the details (using any of the senses) which you might not have noticed before: a crack in the wall, some paint chipping, the curvature of an object, what else do you notice? **Pay attention to textures, colours, vibrations and patterns around you.**

Now **imagine a backpack/rucksack/container/bag in front of you where you can reach it**. Your imagination can help design the rucksack you think would be fitting. Imagine the texture, material, and colour of this bag – whether it has straps or handles, pockets, wheels, etc. (see Figure 2.2 for examples). I encourage you to be as detailed and creative as possible. I like to use the image of a rucksack (backpack) but perhaps pick a handbag or piece of luggage you can carry with you. Another fun feature of this imaginary bag: It expands as big or as small as it needs to, and there is no budget involved in what it can contain!

If visualising/imagining the container is challenging, not to worry, you can pick a bag you currently own and a couple of objects to practice. Feel free to play some nice music while you collect the items or access any of our reflexive music tracks created by Ross Whyte (links in the Musical Index on page 267). **Place the imaginary bag in front of you and then mime the movements of lifting it in a way in which you can 'carry it'.** It can be on your back, across your shoulder, or you can hold it in front of you and imagine the feeling of being safe and content. **Notice the imaginary weight of the rucksack** on your body – how heave/light is it? Does it feel comfortable to carry? Then move around the room or reach from your chair towards objects, people, and/or aspects (real or imagined) that help you create your own sense of safety. Who/what makes you feel safe?

Spend some time collecting these objects/people/experiences and 'placing' them inside your bag by miming the actions like in the game of charades. It helps to do the actual movements of gathering and placing them inside the container, even

FIGURE 2.2 Safety Backpack Examples

when these are imaginary. When we do the movement while envisioning something, you can get some somatic information of the weight, shape, and lots of body-based feedback. In these situations where we represent something through movement, you will be surprised at the intuitive choices your body makes while you move, which can offer you some insight. Once you have gathered all the key aspects in your bag (take your time with this) – place the bag in front of you and have a look through all the items you have collected. You may also do some drawing or journalling here to capture the essence of the objects you gathered, so that you can come back to it later. Then carve some time to do some movement reflections and visualise all those objects and how safety feels in your body.

How would this sense of safety transfer to your actual life? Are there some objects in your bag that you can draw from in your day-to-day? What are the embodied sensations of safety in your body? Where do you feel safe in your body?

This exercise is useful for yourself as a grounding exercise, and you can imagine these objects and those sensations before difficult meetings, encounters, or situations. This backpack helps you maintain access to strong anchors to keep you centred and feel protected. It is also an exercise I have often done with participants to set up a safe space in sessions and understand how they can feel safe while engaging with movement therapeutically. We usually do this exploration together and then pick out one 'object' representing something they want to bring/ contribute to group safety. I have found this exercise in groups quite powerful in contributing to group cohesion and group relationship-building. Worksheet 3.1 uses the guiding words: Sensations, Images, Thoughts, and Emotions to explore or you can journal any other way you'd prefer.

In Professional Practice

Some professions really rely on the Attention stage. This stage might be very appealing to philosophers, listeners, explorers, evaluators, assessors, detectives, and people who really enjoy the search for knowledge. For example, in the corporate world, according to Lamb, strategists and market researchers usually spend a good proportion of time 'taking in' and considering factors that will later lay the groundwork for an implementation[13]. In research, this stage might be prevalent when we are engaging with research day-to-day, taking a survey of a group of people, analysing patterns amongst massive amounts of data, scoping relevant literature, or figuring out the research questions. In the caring professions, therapists thrive in this stage, as it relies on communication and holding people's multiple perspectives. Assessing the environment (workspace, landscape, maps, systems, etc.) will come quite easy to people (and professions) that thrive in this stage. What other professions do you think may thrive in or predominantly use the Attention stage?

In terms of your decision, the Attention stage would then help you map out the options you might have. You might be at a crossroads in terms of your issue or be quite stuck in one way of doing things, and the Attention stage can therefore help you expand your focus to consider what else is out there. Conversely, if you have too many options, you could also use this stage to narrow them down to a manageable number. (Then the Intention stage might come in handy to figure out what is truly needed.) Before we get too much in our head, let's have a break to embody the qualities of the Attention stage. After your body has this in its repertoire, you might make more connections to the application of this stage to your decision.

Movement Components of the Attention Stage

As we detailed in Chapter 1, each stage has movement qualities that are prevalent when embodying this stage. The images within each Chapter marker image, such as the one on page 52, offer you a visual map of the concepts we will be illustrating.

Review of Attention Stage:

Plane:	Horizontal (Table)
Two Dimensions:	Front Back + Left side Right side
Effort Category:	Space
Effort Qualities:	Direct/Indirect
Shaping Qualities:	Spreading/Enclosing

We will discuss each of these elements in the next sections. First, let's embody the Horizontal (Table) Plane (Figure 2.3).

Using your full arm (or leg), extend it in front of you, and move it from front to side while still extended, and then across to the other side, as if tracing the horizon.

FIGURE 2.3 The Horizontal or Table Plane

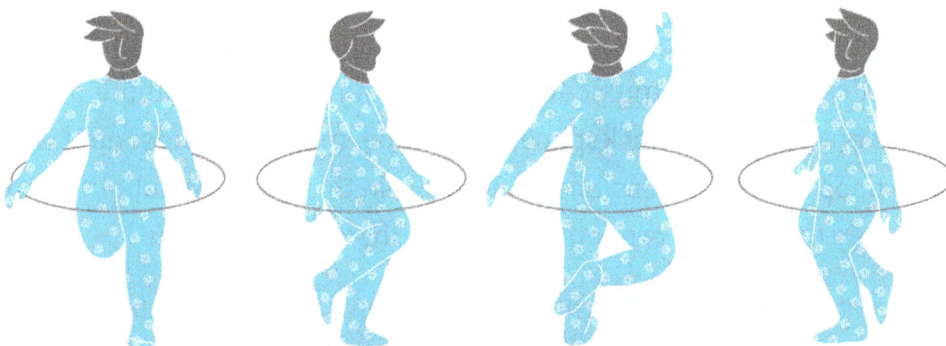

Continue sweeping your arm across by twisting your torso, almost with an aim to point towards the back as much as you can. If you prefer to do this with your lower half, you can trace a half circle with the tip of your shoe. Follow this arc with front/back and side-to-side motions.

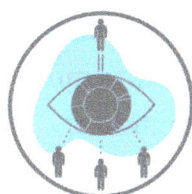

Effort Qualities (Indirect and Direct Space)

Within BESS, the Effort Qualities considered here are Direct and Indirect Space. If you are already familiar with these terms, feel free to do some of the *Movement Break* exercises or skip along to further sections. If you aren't familiar, or need a review, I offer some initial descriptions of both.

Effort Qualities: Direct Space

Direct Effort speaks to the ability for us to focus on a specific aspect and move with a succinct intent. An Indirect Effort quality refers to the ability to scan and take in the whole environment and/or encompass multiple perspectives. We often think of scanning only ascribed to sight, but our whole body's sensory system receives information constantly[14] to contribute towards what we decide to give attention to. Together with our nervous system, our senses help us filter through those inputs to help us understand where we are, how safe it is, and what factors we need to mediate/contend with.

Movement Break: Directness 🎧

Suggested Music

Track Title: Efforts: Directness

Duration: 7:58

Music Composer: Ross Whyte

Link to the QR code: https://youtu.be/-4MKcLih_QU?si=6ci6bgJyPkZI8FZq>

Link for audio description playlist: www.youtube.com/playlist?list=PLtGm4qYm5yBQZqgY5_PFpJHa4jgs2R6Cw

---

Let's take a movement break and explore the Directness Effort with some music.

Have a brief scan of the room either visually or through touch to take an inventory of the room around you: What is in the room? (furniture, objects, walls, etc.) Focus on a specific object or direction. Make a gesture towards that object/direction. You may point, reach with any of your limbs, or visualise that reach. If you are able to move around, try out movements towards that object/direction, and have an intention of establishing a connection. Walk or use your wheelchair to locomote forward in a straight line to touch the object or arrive at a particular destination. Then travel backwards (if it's safe to do so) while still maintaining a connection to the object.

Direct movements have a certain specificity. Think of a bullseye target or a salute – your whole body wants to achieve this one gesture. A playful image is John Travolta's traditional disco dance pointing up and down in a diagonal, or a cheerleading pose.

Now let's practice some actions that require directness. Start with punching movements in the air in front of you. Try that for some time and then slow it down. Open your hands with palms facing outwards, pushing the air in front of you towards that object/direction. Now try using more pressure and strength. Notice the tension building in your body, as if you were pushing away a very heavy wall.

If your arms get tired, lighten the pressure more and start to reach towards the object again but with a gentle touch, as if you were trying to poke the air lightly. Consciously pick a new direction and repeat the movements. Migrate the movement to other body parts – can you still embrace their clarity and precision? Try any other movements that involve accuracy or a narrow focus. Think of different scenarios here and have a go at other Direct movements. All these actions are part of the movement analysis system which is one part of the Space Effort.

We use all kinds of body metaphors to address Directness in daily life. We often say, "let's get straight to the point", "keeping me on the straight and narrow", "(in business) so-and-so is a sharpshooter". Being able to focus, go deeper into a subject, pinpoint a particular area, or communicate something without deviating from the subject are all examples of how Directness comes into play. In our bodies, Directness also allows you to grab groceries at the store, observe your favourite plant in detail, examine a scrape on your elbow, and switch a light on or off, amongst so many of your daily actions. In decision-making, Directness helps you zoom in to a specific direction, set a goal, clarify an alternative, and visualise a path forward.

Body Question

- What kinds of images, feelings, and sensations did this exercise evoke?

Some images and examples of movements that have come up in my workshops about Direct Efforts are "karate chops", "military marching", "cheerleading poses", "YMCA song's infamous movements", and the "Macarena" movements, among many other popular responses.

Effort Qualities: Indirect Space

Let's explore the movement qualities of Indirectness and have another movement break.

Movement Break: Indirectness 🎧

Suggested Music

Track Title: Efforts: Indirectness

Duration: 8:01

Music Composer: Ross Whyte

Link for QR code: https://youtu.be/l2hLxDxpK9g?si=A9G-jxQ6f0Ma0WP-

Link for audio description playlist: www.youtube.com/playlist?list=PLtGm4q Ym5yBQZqgY5_PFpJHa4jgs2R6Cw

Pick a spot in the middle of an open space where you can sit/stand/rest in. **Begin by scanning the room or close your eyes and try to (safely) explore your surroundings** through touch without a particular aim. Move towards the centre of the space and with eyes open or closed, **use your arms to trace your kinesphere**. Make sure you don't hold any direction or final ending point. You are exploring and taking it all in.

Come back to a neutral stance and notice if your awareness of your environment has shifted. We can then try different movement qualities in combination which highlight the effort quality of Indirectness. First, **explore any movements related to the feeling of Floating**[15] **in water or the air** by slowing down and becoming lighter, while keeping this aimless quality in your movement. Notice what sensations, images, or memories come up while engaging with this movement. Once you have explored this for some time, **try quickening the pace, engaging with Flicking movements with**

your hand as if swatting away a fly or brushing something off your shoulder. You can try Flicking with different body parts or doing Flicking movements in the air. Try to maintain an Indirect Effort with all these elements, without getting too direct. **If it feels right, start gaining more momentum and force.** As those Flicks become stronger and bigger in space, they become Slashing movements downward as if you were waving a whip in the air like in the circus. Play with accelerating and decelerating rhythms while you Slash. **Notice your breath as you try on Slashing movements** – exhale as you start to let go into the momentum. Remember to pause if it gets too tiring! After exploring, **slow the timing down, but keep the strong Force**. Explore some Wringing movements as if you were trying to get water out of some dense, thick towels. See how you can engage with increasing the tension in those movements.

After you have explored enough, **shake everything off, and connect to any of actions that resonated with you**. In this exercise you have been doing the following actions: Float, Flick, Wring, and Slash (which are Action Drives we will explore in Chapter 6). Remember to not get stuck if an image or movement doesn't appeal to you – try your own exploration and notice which feels the most comfortable or uncomfortable. You might want to try combining Indirect and Direct movements in another exploration and notice the difference between the two Efforts. Which one do you prefer?

Indirectness involves an expanded awareness of the space which surrounds you, absorbing the multitude of variables within a situation and exploring different alternatives available. Indirectness can also be used as a defence mechanism, to deflect from situations, shrugging off something stressful or avoiding conflict. It can also aid us in relaxing at a beach, researching several articles and communicating to a group, amongst many other practical actions. After this movement break, it might be good to reflect more on this experience. Take an inventory of the images/

sensations/words associated with this movement exercise through journalling or drawing. We will come back to this list at a later point.

Space Effort Qualities in Daily Life

While we fluctuate constantly between Direct and Indirect Effort qualities, at times of conflict or difficulty, we can become stuck at one end of the continuum (Figure 2.4). We can either get lost or overwhelmed with so many options or get too overly focused on one thing and hold on tightly to one perspective. Being fixated in directness is sometimes called hyper-focus. Hyper-focus is often defined as the feeling of being completely immersed in an activity to the point where other external sources of information are shut off. Hyper-focus has been often associated with "autism, schizophrenia, and attention deficit hyperactivity disorder"[16], especially if it becomes detrimental to our daily life and relationships if we are unable to regulate attention flexibly. In decision-making scenarios, it could present itself as a harmful persistence related to a stressful task (both to us and to others). While often associated with high productivity, hyper-focusing can often alienate others, disregard the environment, and often provoke a disconnection to our bodies, sensations, and feelings. However, hyper-focusing for short periods of time can sometimes help get a task done. It is always important, in the context of mental health, to reflect on behaviours that serve us, whether they help us cope, and whether they are sustainable in terms of our wellbeing, relationships, and environments we navigate.

Engaging solely with Indirectness may provoke a feeling of relaxation and openness, but if we get stuck too long, we can find ourselves procrastinating, delaying, or daydreaming, and we will struggle with immediate action or setting concrete tasks. A persistence in Indirectness can often feel like and/or communicate a lack of commitment or conviction to others. Other participants in my workshops have

FIGURE 2.4 Space Effort Continuum

Indirect SPACE Direct

reported they felt a sense of being lost or ungrounded. Some connected it to always seeking the better option and struggling to commit to a decision.

An Effort Quality maybe also be incongruent with what we need to do or what others expect from us, which will require us to transition and change. For example, if we need to transition from being at the beach to going to take a train home, a shift will often be needed from one state of attention to the other (and many other Effort Qualities will also come into play as we will explore further). Take a pause and contemplate other uses for Directness and Indirectness in your life – how do they currently serve you?

Space Effort Qualities in Professional Practice

Work cultures express their preferences for Efforts; these might be explicit, or hidden. By analysing work culture, we can reflect on the dynamics at organisational level, or in your direct team, and you will start to notice some patterns emerging. While we have stressed that in this book we are not going to be observing and analysing other people, let's shift the focus into how external demands affect us and our movement preferences. Here we will only focus on Spatial Effort Qualities (Direct/Indirect). I will delve into the other Effort categories in Chapters 3 (Weight/ Force) and Chapter 4 (Time).

Some work cultures really prioritise directness. You will often be encouraged to "tell it like it is", there would be low tolerance for what is considered small talk, and "beating around the bush" will be discouraged. Email communication will dive straight in without a preamble, this would be deemed as a more 'efficient' style of communication. In other work cultures this type of directness would be considered rude. Emails would include some preamble and a check in on how the person is doing with some personal detail. Direct statements might be considered abrupt, and a more 'roundabout' way of speaking will happen in meetings. Some people might notice the body metaphor phrases: "talking around", or the saying "circling back to something" (which is quite common in recent United States vernacular) and many actions would require numerous stages of consultation, as the systems might be set up to engage with indirect ways of approaching action.

There are many factors that influence an organisation's cultural value system, such as: where the company is based geographically and culturally, sociocultural makeup and diversity of employees, historical trajectory and previous experiences at organisational/micro-level, and company values. Reflecting on the ways in which our bodies need to compromise, invite, completely forgo our movement preferences, or go out of our comfort zone can generate interesting Body Questions about the power dynamics in the cultures/subcultures that surround us.

Sometimes the movement priorities of a group might clash with your own cultural and/or moral values or create some discomfort. If systems (and people) do not recognise differences, they might perpetuate oppressive practices. People may feel that they do not belong or receive explicit/implicit messaging that they must always modify their own movement, identity, and behaviours to "assimilate" with the dominant culture. The Embodied Cultural Competence Framework recently emerged to understand our own cultural bias by using the planes, which adds new exciting dimensions to movement work and further understanding cultural nuance[17]. The Embodied Cultural Competence Framework argues that exploring each plane through movement can aid us in understanding our embodied responses to difference, our biases and perceptions of others[18]. It is a wonderful way to reflect on more connections between movement and behaviour.

Space Effort Qualities Reflection and Review

Often, this stage features processes of differentiation in our Attention: we may need to adjust our focus, much like we can adapt a zoom lens to broaden our attention to evaluate, explore, or reconsider options. We may focus on a particular issue to examine it with precision or expand our variables to see the whole picture. Do you have any other examples for when you would move with Directness or Indirectness? Does your decision require an expansion of options or precision? Or a combination of both? Let's pause and reflect.

Reflexive Exercise: Space Effort Continuum

Suggested Music

Track Title: Attention

Duration: 04:50

Music Composer: Ross Whyte

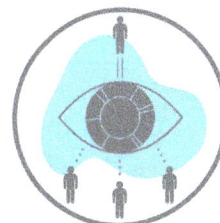

Link for QR code: https://youtu.be/pZJhAoMas3Q?si=v8dEUoe_FWGwAqqp>

In movement workshops, I draw from our heavily tech oriented climate to refer to movement preferences as our "default settings". If left to our own devices, how would we like to move? What feels like a 'me' kind of movement? There are many factors that influence our movement preferences: age, disability, gender identity, personality, upbringing, culture, development, and prior experiences, among many other factors. In the Kestenberg Movement Profile movement analysis system, they theorise that there are movement determinants of personality as early as infancy[19], which serve as precursors or early indicators of what our movement styles will develop later in life (which we will explore in Chapter 6). However, the way we are brought up and life-altering experiences will influence how these movement styles evolve. Nature and nurture doing their inevitable dance to shape how we are.

I often get asked by participants – "I can do both – how can I pick one?" My position on this is to encourage you to understand what you tend to do and where your comfort zone lies. Our jobs or training we've had before (e.g. martial arts, dance, sport) will also have stamped their own movement language and might have had some influence on the ways in which we have grown accustomed to moving. We can map our preference and range (at this point in time) and map it out for the rest of our lives as constant points of reflection. Ongoing reflections about our movement practice can also aid you in cultivating more flexible/responsive approaches to Attention/Focus.

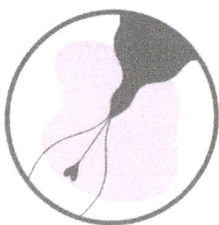

Reflexive Body Questions

We are all able to access both Space Effort Qualities, but when we are at 'baseline' or "default":

- What is your preference – Directness or Indirectness?
- Which exploration and descriptions felt more comfortable? Why?

I invite you to fill in the spectrum in Figure 2.6 by doing a shading of the breadth/ range of Space Efforts and where your preference is. Figure 2.5 has an example of my spectrum (at this point in time). There is space for you in Figure 2.6 to fill out your own.

We will use the following questions as a guide:

- How comfortable are you accessing full Indirectness or full Directness on this spectrum?
- How much of each quality can you access without feeling uneasy?

As you can see, the diagram in Figure 2.5 reflects my preference (Direct vs. Indirect) and my range (how much range of Space Effort Qualities I feel I have now). I have a clear preference for Directness. I love getting straight to the point, even tracing routes in maps to find which is the most efficient road somewhere. I feel most comfortable when I have a set goal in mind or themes to work under, and usually I do not like taking the long way around subjects. When I was training as a dance movement therapist, I struggled with Indirect explorations – I often felt lost or ungrounded. One of my DMT students had a similar preference of Directness but a short Indirect Effort range, and they said they got nauseous when exploring Indirectness!

FIGURE 2.5 Space Effort Qualities Spectrum (Thania's Example)

Indirect SPACE Direct

FIGURE 2.6 Space Effort Qualities Spectrum Reflection; Please Fill in Your Preferences

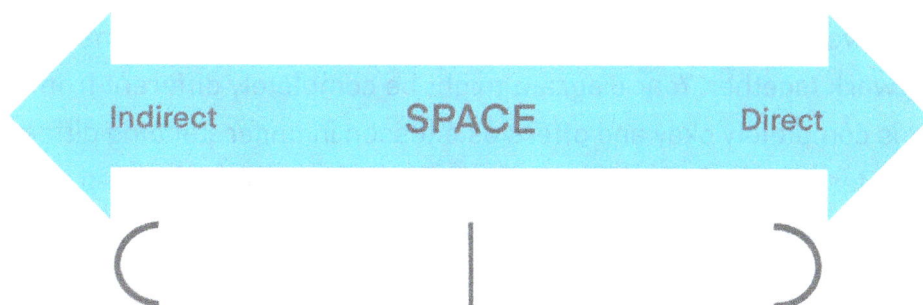

Indirect SPACE Direct

Through my psychotherapy training, I discovered I could access Indirectness a lot easier by slowing down (Time Effort). It was a challenge, but I noticed it was of benefit to my clients/participants. Allowing things to process, scanning the room, and opening questions to explore felt really open and a wonderful way to connect to clients. My experience as a facilitator also improved as I learned to hold spaces for large groups, and I became more exploratory in terms of movement practice – the more access I had to the continuum, the better equipped I felt. This also helped me as part of my professional network experience, which involved gathering input from international practitioners with very different socio-cultural backgrounds. In higher education, this became key when investigating my PhD and allowing this long process to ebb and flow and take shape. I must admit I always have to work on the Space Effort category, as I am so naturally direct. It has changed over time, but I believe it was much narrower when I first started my teaching practice. This is the lovely aspect of embodied principles – they are a lifelong investment in change and adapting to new realities.

Take time to fill out your own range – of course this might change over time, and we will return and collect these for all our decision-making stages.

It is okay to keep reflecting on this aspect throughout the book with as little judgement as possible and honouring that there are other approaches to making decisions different from our own. There will be Effort Qualities where we will have lots of range or be limited in others. These will also vary throughout the day – particularly in the days when you feel more tired or more excited. You might draw your preferences completely on one spectrum or the other. These might have changed, or you might want them to change, but that is a different story altogether. Let's focus on how these preferences show up for you in the present.

I often give out handouts of these spectrum worksheets (Worksheet 6.1 provides an example of one with all Effort Qualities on page 170) to my groups so that we can analyse the movement styles present in our group and get more information about how we can work together. Your diagram might be completely different from someone else's. That is completely okay and offers us a lesson in understanding differences. Movement preferences give us insight into the variables we need to keep working on to expand our life repertoire. There is no right or wrong. It is just a measure of where you are. All movement is valuable information that your body is providing you.

This next section adds a new BESS layer: Shape.

Shaping Qualities (Spreading and Enclosing)

Shaping involves your body engaging with moulding, adapting to the world around you. We might not have become aware of the space around us, but we are exerting relationships every day through our uses of shaping. Shaping Qualities look at the 'Where' in movement and our attitude towards the space around us – "how our body forms itself in space"[20]. Here, sign language comes to mind as an example. If you have ever had the amazing experience of watching a sign language interpreter work, their gestures have a specific attitude towards the space. I learned from a sign language consultant who came to help us with one of our performances that slight variations in space and intensity will mean different things to someone else. I accidentally did a gesture with too much intensity, and they told me the sign meant I was shouting, which was accidentally perceived as rude. I truly hope I can learn sign language someday, as the possibilities of communication get expanded and enhanced.

The Shaping qualities pertaining to the Attention stage are Spreading/Enclosing. For example, we often spread our arms wide for a hug or enclose a pillow in our arms at night.

In 'typical' development "spreading and enclosing form the basis for giving/taking and accepting/refusing in the Horizontal Plane. These early patterns form the basis

FIGURE 2.7 Shaping Qualities – Spreading and Enclosing

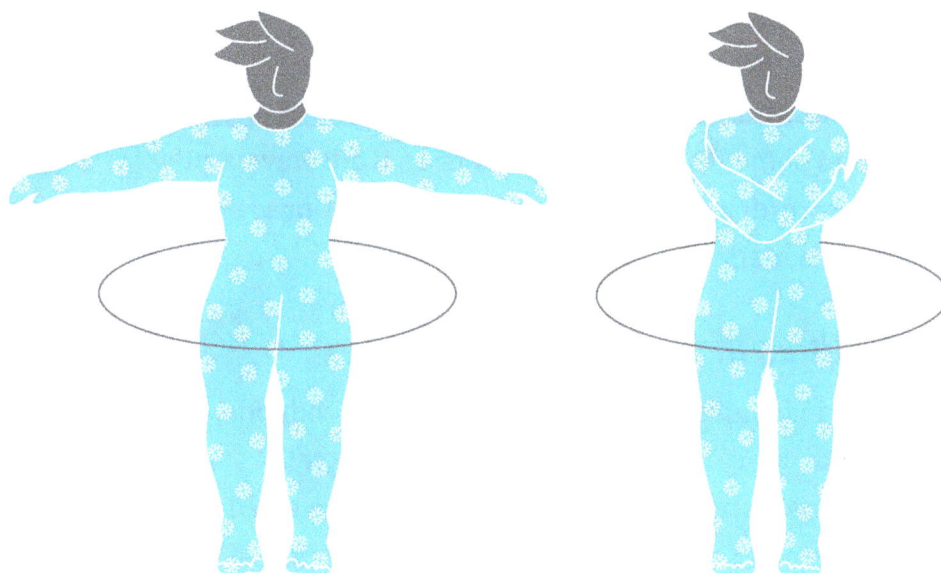

of reciprocal types of communication"[21]. In essence, this means that we begin to differentiate between personal and interpersonal space. We use the space around us to negotiate how to communicate/engage with others. Think about times when you felt uncomfortable with someone's proximity or wanted to get closer to someone to show affection. As we go through life, communication patterns gain complexity when we start socialising in groups and needing to cope with multiple viewpoints/experiences.

Movement Break: Spreading and Enclosing

Suggested Music

Track Title: Spreading/Enclosing

Duration: 04:50

Music Composer: Ross Whyte

Link for QR code: https://youtu.be/pZJhAoMas3Q?si=iCe4Paf6jM92xXod

Here is a chance to spend a few minutes exploring Spreading and Enclosing as an open movement exploration. Play the following piece of music in the QR code or pick your own and **engage with your whole body in these two movement tasks of moving shaping qualities in the Horizontal Plane: Spreading and Enclosing**. Practice engaging different body parts and use the different levels (low/middle/high) from page 34. Use the floor, walls, chairs, and/or any surface to help you investigate. Remember to also **explore different directions** – both sides, all your front, and as much as you can towards the back (minimise the up/down movements). You can add some twisting and some diagonal movements as well! **Have a play for 2–5 minutes and then write down/draw some words, images, feelings, and/or sensations** associated with this plane.

Shaping Qualities in Daily Life

The Attention stage features the negotiation of focus with one or multiple relationships. If you think about political figures, storytellers, performers, some celebrities, or charismatic leaders, you might have perceived their full engagement across all the movement planes, but primarily the Horizontal Plane. Charismatic speakers usually have movement qualities in both voice and body which are dynamic, using Directness/Indirectness, while also using their arms to spread or enclose – often in sync with their arguments. Shaping qualities underlie the dynamics of communication and are the foundation of managing relationships. Flexibility and breadth in the movement qualities of Horizontal Plane, Space Effort, and Spreading/Enclosing Shaping Qualities make the Attention Plane an excellent one for transmitting and receiving information.

The combination of Shaping and Effort Qualities – within BESS, Kestenberg Movement Profile (KMP), and MPA systems – are often associated with communication styles, patterns, and behaviours.

Great leaders involve the whole audience, connect with them, and make them feel like a community, while also reaching out to relate to each person there individually. Public speakers (compelling ones) master or are trained to develop the ability to punctuate key claims, propose challenges, and invite for reflection or action. If you are doing some public speaking yourself, you might notice your line of sight dwelling on a particular person you might feel more comfortable with or consciously scanning the room around the group to make sure they are all understanding what you are trying to convey. Conversely, you might focus on a particular point in space (usually the exit sign) if you are very nervous or redirect focus to external stimuli, like audio-visual material (phone, notes, slides, etc.). Your movement preferences, situational factors, and comfort level/confidence with public speaking will have a profound influence in communicating with large groups.

Movement Break: Role Play on the Communication Stage

Take another short movement break and try out some of the communication explorations with a role play. Imagine you are making a speech, presentation, or performance to a large auditorium of people. Come up with a catchy sentence for yourself (like a slogan, affirmation, or a mantra). It can be a simple call to action like, 'You can do this!' 'This is what you're meant to be doing!' or 'This is what you are passionate about'. **Deliver these mantras out loud and try to not use any body language whatsoever.** Now use the Horizontal Plane consciously while you speak using your upper torso. It might feel uncomfortable to picture yourself public speaking in this way, and if that is nerve-racking, you can picture a different scenario – perhaps telling a story to a small group of friends at dinner. See if you can engage your core, and practice using gestures or full arm movement activating your full body, moving in ways in which you show you are inviting, connecting to, and encompassing all the (pretend) audience. What is important is that this feels natural and comfortable to you – try not to overthink it! **Have a go at practising attention with your whole body but also your voice.** Can you articulate your voice with Directness? Indirectness? Can you project your volume so that your words spread out and fill the space? Or can you direct your tone to enclose the people in the room?[22] Repeat this a couple of times even if it feels a bit silly – we might need much more practice for these to feel like 'us'. Make notes/ drawing/body responses for yourself to see what your breadth and range is for the Attention stage.

Attention Stage in Decisions and Life Transitions

Oftentimes some themes, situations, and/or aspects of our lives align with this stage. In your personal life, let's say, for example, you might want to go on a big holiday. You keep researching places to go but without making any concrete plans or figuring out what is needed/wanted. The search for all the enticing places you could travel to might feel like a dream. Every place seems equally exciting, with lots of potential for a great vacation. Down the line, there might be some limiting factors that will help narrow the search criteria: how much time you have, accessibility, weather conditions, and budget are some examples. If you were to progress into the Intention and Action stage, then you might connect to what you really would enjoy most, could afford, and could fit within the time frame. But if you remain persistent on the Attention stage, you just might keep searching for options without narrowing down. And many weeks/months/years later . . . no concrete plans for a holiday.

Conversely, you might be fixated on a particular aspect (or mesmerised by something to the point nothing else exists). In the aforementioned holiday example, you have chosen one option and have decided to go full on research mode of everything there is to know about this specific holiday destination. Nothing else might exist, and you might be holding on too tightly. You might not entertain other options or deviate from your original choice. Hyper-focusing is a behaviour that has risen in public awareness recently, particularly related to neurodiversity. It is often described as an "intense state of concentration; where external stimuli do not appear to be consciously perceived or there is a diminished perception of the environment"[23]. Hyper-focus (with flexibility around space) can be both constructive when you need to get a task done and need to buckle down, but conversely it can be problematic if you shut everything and/or everyone out in the process.

When we are stuck in the Attention stage, we are often endlessly looking for alternatives. We might gravitate towards one option but then hop on to another. We might be always searching for something better and not committing to anything just yet. However, the Attention stage also has many beneficial aspects. This might be the stage where you are putting feelers out there. In research, you might be searching different sources for one of your research questions or trying to explore various directions for procedures you want to follow. This is a key stage where a scoping of the environment tends to happen. This might be the time you are deciding on a topic or figuring out the key questions about what you want to find out. It is often the searching stage and highlights how we establish and foster communication. However, as Lamb cleverly stated, no one can action something by just giving attention; one needs to traverse all the stages to get there[24].

Almost everyone in their life has encountered a manager who prefers the Attention stage, which might be very frustrating when we need to get something approved or need a strong stance to be taken on a particular situation. Or we could be working in a group which just prefers to keep exploring options rather than to make a plan of action. If our preference is to stay in the Attention Plane, we might delay actions, keep researching, procrastinate, or not feel like it is time to look at our needs or make the plan. We might feel more comfortable trying to lay out all the options first before deciding. In some cases, we might need to ask further questions or consult more people to weigh in.

Participant themes that were reported in my sessions were feeling "ungrounded", "having too many options", or contrastingly "not having much choice" in the transitions they were contemplating. Accompanying movement experiences gathered statements such as being "stuck between a rock and a hard place", "unable to see a way out", and "difficulty reaching out for help from others". Some of the overall themes and patterns related to this stage will be discussed in Chapter 8. Worksheet 8.1 provides an overview of the themes that have emerged as a result of this research.

A priority in applying the decision-making through movement model is to allow the physical components of a particular stage to take on multiple layers: physical, cognitive, emotional, social, and cultural. We will see these themes emerge when we look at the whole system and examine the general patterns across all stages. It is important then to reflect on how we are using this stage, and whether it is serving you and the task at hand. If it is, then keep exploring. If it is not serving you, then you might need to move to exploring another stage in the decision-making through movement process.

Culture and Caveats

The Attention stage and its associations with community, communication, and inclusion have many cultural ramifications. In some cultures, particularly those that value communal engagement over individual, this might be the preferred plane. It is important to critically engage with the delicate balance between nature and nurture, as these factors all contribute to individual and societal movement preferences. This will also mean that stages and effort qualities will often be put into a hierarchical relationship. However, when analysed according to movement analysis, there are pros and cons for each stage, and all are essential to operating on a daily basis. For example, the Attention stage will inevitably be affected due to new societal patterns of social media, quicker pace, and multifocus/multitasking pressures in Western societies. These sections on cultures and caveats suggest further questions and some contraindications when appropriate, but by no means can I include all the cultural nuances despite my best efforts. What I can invite us to do is look at how each of the stages can be viewed critically and reflectively. It is important to note that, in terms of inclusivity, for people who have difficulty in the regulation of attention, this stage might be more challenging, and I strongly suggest being gentle and empathetic with oneself (and others) if this is the case. This might be different in rural communities and spaces with less access to (or cultural importance placed on) the internet.

Not only are there caveats in terms of our physical functioning, but there are often different values allocated to these in each environment, which will be evidenced among cultural norms and societal roles, which emanate from your experience like the rings of a bullseye. Each community might place different values on each ring: from your closest friends/family to your workplace, where you live, geographical region, and your culture(s) as a whole in all its domains.

What other cultural nuances do you find in your experience of the Attention stage so far?

Chapter Conclusion

In movement, the Attention stage involves Direct and Indirect Efforts, which are enacted through actions in our body. When we move with Directness, we have specific goals or intentions in mind. We use Direct Efforts, for example, when we tap our phone, grab a book from the highest shelf, push a heavy shopping cart into the cashier lane, hammer down a nail, point towards someone we know, or hold a specific yoga pose.

Indirectness is needed to take in a full landscape or the sea, scattering some leaves across a field or invite a group of people to gather. For a side hug, we might reach out and encompass someone's shoulders or waist and pull them into our side (Enclosing). A farmer might spread seeds across a field, or we might open our arms really wide to tell someone how much we love them. Movement explorations on the Horizontal Plane in this stage involve observation and searching and closing in or widening with our extremities[25]. This plane can be used to engage with groups and remain aware of multiple perspectives and our environmental context.

When we traverse this stage too quickly though, we might miss alternative points of view or act quite impulsively without considering others. We might also miss out on connecting to our needs (which is a different stage altogether) or somebody else's needs. Represented as a Body Question, attention to alternatives allows possibilities to be activated for situations that feel open-ended or where more investigation is needed. In workplace environments, the Attention stage is where an individual/group organisation takes time to consider the options available for a decision and investigating what is out there: it is the "researching stage". We need the Attention stage to explore, to play with options, to listen to other people.

REVIEW POINTS ON THE ATTENTION STAGE

- The Attention stage is related to the developmental task of regulating focus during infancy:
- It involves Enclosing/Spreading Shaping, Indirect/Direct Space Efforts, and front/back + side-to-side direction.
- Attention occurs with all the senses.
- It is the key stage for investigation of options and alternatives.
- Getting stuck on this stage might trigger feeling lost or without a purpose.
- The Attention stage is linked to communication and assessing the environment.

SKIP, BOOKMARK, OR CONTINUE

- If you have decided you want to continue in the order of the book, you can continue on to Chapter 3 "Intention Stage: Needs and Priorities". Often having too many options (or one strong option) prompts the need to consider jumping into the Intention stage to establish priorities and needs.
- You might have enough information to make a plan of action, set more of a timing/pacing of mapping out these options, or need to consider not act on the decision at all (skip to Chapter 4 "Action/Non-Action Stage: Timing and [Non] Commitment").
- If you are feeling the need to connect to your body if the options are overwhelming or if there is a sense of Tension building, skip to Chapter 5 "Flow/ Tension Stage: Bodily States".
- You might want to have a break and figure out your own movement style and your preferences before you go any further. (Skip to Chapter 6 "Movement Styles".)

Notes

1 Butterworth, George, and Nicholas Jarrett. 'What Minds Have in Common Is Space: Spatial Mechanisms Serving Joint Visual Attention in Infancy'. *British Journal of Developmental Psychology* 9, no. 1 (1991): 55–72. https://doi.org/10.1111/j.2044-835X.1991. tb00862.x; Moore, Chris, Maria Angelopoulos, and Paula Bennett. 'The Role of Movement in the Development of Joint Visual Attention'. *Infant Behavior and Development* 20, no. 1 (January 1997): 83–92. https://doi.org/10.1016/S0163-6383(97)90063-1; Rizzolatti, Giacomo, Lucia Riggio, and Boris M. Sheliga. 'Space and Selective Attention'. In *Attention and Performance XV: Conscious and Nonconscious Information Processing*, edited by Carlo Umiltà and Morris Moscovitch (MIT Press, 1994).

2 Ruff, Holly Alliger, and Mary Klevjord Rothbart. *Attention in Early Development: Themes and Variations* (Oxford University Press, 2001).

3 Cuevas, Kimberly, and Martha Ann Bell. 'Infant Attention and Early Childhood Executive Function'. *Child Development* 85, no. 2 (March 2014): 397–404. https://doi.org/10.1111/cdev.12126.

4 Proske, Uwe, and Simon C. Gandevia. 'The Proprioceptive Senses: Their Roles in Signaling Body Shape, Body Position and Movement, and Muscle Force'. *Physiological Reviews* 92, no. 4 (October 2012): 1651–1697. https://doi.org/10.1152/physrev.00048.2011.

5 Foglia, Lucia, and Robert A. Wilson. 'Embodied Cognition'. *WIREs Cognitive Science* 4, no. 3 (2013): 320. https://doi.org/10.1002/wcs.1226.

6 Gallagher, Shaun. *Embodied and Enactive Approaches to Cognition* Elements in Philosophy of Mind (Cambridge: Cambridge University Press, 2023). https://doi.org/10.1017/9781009209793.

7 Foglia and Wilson, 2013, 320.

8 Gallagher, 2023.

9 Schmais, Claire, and Elissa Q. White. 'Introduction to Dance Therapy'. *American Journal of Dance Therapy* 9, no. 1 (December 1986): 23–30. https://doi.org/10.1007/BF02274236.

10 Clement, Evelyne. *Cognitive Flexibility: The Cornerstone of Learning* (John Wiley & Sons, 2022), x.

  Clement calls this cognitive flexibility and makes a connection to how adaptability plays a key role in attention: cognitive flexibility allows us to adapt to a constantly changing environment, to discover solutions in new and/or unexpected situations, to transfer knowledge learned in one context to a new context, to select the relevant stimuli in the environment to achieve a goal, to switch our attention from one stimulus to another according to the constraints of the situation, to alternate between two possible forms of processing stimuli, and to change our representation of the goal we are pursuing.

11 Acarón, Thania. 'Shape-in (g) Space: Body, Boundaries, and Violence'. *Space and Culture* 19, no. 2 (2016): 139–149.

12 Gray, Amber Elizabeth Lynn, and J. Ryan Kennedy. 'Marian Chace Foundation 2022 Lecture & Introduction from the 57th Annual American Dance Therapy Association Conference, Heartlines: Gathering Wisdom from Many Streams; Montreal, Canada'. *American Journal of Dance Therapy* 45, no. 1 (June 2023): 88–108. https://doi.org/10.1007/s10465-023-09384-7.

13 Moore, 2005.

14 Csordas, Thomas J. *Embodiment and Experience: The Existential Ground of Culture and Self* (Cambridge University Press, 1994); Csordas, Thomas J. 'Somatic Modes of Attention'. *Cultural Anthropology* 8, no. 2 (1993): 135–156; Tantia, Jennifer Frank. 'Mindfulness and Dance/Movement Therapy for Treating Trauma'. In *Mindfulness in the Creative Arts Therapies*, edited by L. Rappaport (London: Jessica Kingsley Publishers, 2012), 96–107.

15 These are capitalised because they are part of the category of Action Drives, which combine three Effort Qualities – one of each: Space, Weight and Time. More on this in Chapter 6.

16 Ashinoff, Brandon K., and Ahmad Abu-Akel. 'Hyperfocus: The Forgotten Frontier of Attention'. *Psychological Research* 85, no. 1 (February 2021): 2. https://doi.org/10.1007/s00426-019-01245-8.

17 Robinson, Aisha Bell, kyla marie Gilmore, and Charla Weatherby. 'Embodied Cultural Competence Framework: A Body-Based Method to Examine Cultural Identity Development and Bias'. American Journal of Dance Therapy, March 2024. https://doi.org/10.1007/s10465-024-09399-8.

18 Robinson et. al, 2024

19 Kestenberg Amighi et al., 1999, 24.

20 Dell, 1977, 3.

21 Kestenberg Amighi et al., 1999, 166.

22 There is a book about applying BESS qualities to the voice if you are looking to do some voice training: Bloom, Katya, Barbara Adrian, Tom Casciero, Jennifer Mizenko, and Claire Porter. *The Laban Workbook for Actors: A Practical Training Guide with Video* (Bloomsbury Publishing, 2017). An additional resource for actor's training: Selioni, Kiki. *Laban – Aristotle – Ζώον (Zoon) in Theatre Πράξις (Praxis): Towards a Methodology for Movement Training for the Actor and in Acting* (Athens, Greece: Ellinoekdotiki, 2020). https://ellinoekdotiki.gr/gr/ekdoseis/i/laban-aristotle.

23 Ashinoff and Abu-Akel, 2021, 2.

24 Lamb and Watson, 1979.

25 Lamb, Warren, and Eden Davies. *A Framework for Understanding Movement: My Seven Creative Concepts* (London: Brechin Books Ltd., 2012).

3
INTENTION STAGE
Needs and Priorities

INTENTION

DOI: 10.4324/9781003360957-4

> ### Body Questions to Consider in This Chapter
>
> - What do I need?
> - What does my body need?
> - What are my priorities right now?
> - What is at the core of the issue?
> - What is essential?

In Development

Lamb and Turner[1] describe Intention as the movement decision-making phase in which priorities, needs, and wants are evaluated and assessed, ideally before a commitment to an Action/Non-Action decision is made. In 'typical' progression in development, the movement qualities for Intention correlate to the task of establishing verticality. After negotiating crawling and moving horizontally in the space, an infant begins to negotiate transfers of weight to pull up to standing, coming to their feet and balancing their own weight before walking (Figure 3.1). I am sure you have witnessed infants clinging to many objects (or humans) to help them establish their own balance. This inevitably involves many falls and stumbles, and within this struggle, a relationship emerges to the development of the self[2] and the dynamism of weight and gravity.

Body metaphors arise out of this relationship to verticality – like 'giving in', 'feeling low', 'with a spring in our step', or 'feeling the whole weight of the world on our shoulders'. Fans of all ages at a sport event will gesticulate upwards with excitement and encouragement. Even the famous stadium wave actions have a vertical moving of the arms. We might observe a two-year-old throwing a very loud, enthusiastic tantrum stomping the floor and thrusting their fists down in frustration and then change to complete lightness and laughter in seconds. Verticality is a 'typical' development task we carry throughout our lives both literally and symbolically – finding our own two feet, negotiating the wobbles, falling, and getting up again.

Additionally, we need to be mindful of assuming verticality from an ableist perspective. Verticality will take on a very different meaning with someone who is

FIGURE 3.1 'Typical' Developmental Stage – Crawling and Standing Up

Crawling

Standing up

in a wheelchair or bed bound. Please be aware of this when you go through some of the activities here and remember everyone will have a different perspective on verticality/horizontality.

In this book, I offer some movement examples of this relationship to the body and gravity and how this stage can help us clarify an intention or purpose behind a decision. I will use a similar structure as the Attention stage to go through the BESS elements of Intention; we will get a chance to move through some of these elements and look at real life applications for these movement qualities.

Movement Components of the Intention Stage

Plane: Vertical (Door)

Two Dimensions: Up Down and Left side   Right side

Effort Category: Weight/Force

Effort Qualities: Strong and Light

Shaping Qualities: Rising and Sinking

Movement Break: Vertical Plane 🎧

Suggested Music

Track Title: Intention

Duration: 05:11

Music Composer: Ross Whyte

<Link for QR Code: https://youtu.be/2GKq5MWCrHE?si=u5PtATaeHIO_-UXQ>

🎧 Link for audio description playlist: www.youtube.com/playlist?list=PLtGm4q
Ym5yBQZqgY5_PFpJHa4jgs2R6Cw

The Vertical Plane in BESS, as previously detailed, combines two dimensions:

Up ←→ Down and Left side ←→ Right side. To trace this trajectory in 2D, **raise your arms with your biceps by your ears, fingers reacting upwards as far as you can reach. Trace a half circle to each side (like doing snow angels)** with your fingertips until your hands rest next to your thighs or chair (Figure 3.2). The Vertical Plane is often called the Door Plane (which helps with visualising the plane). Imagine you are drawing an arc-like doorway which you are standing or sitting under. Engage with this 'door sensation' stretch up and down and side to side while trying to avoid too much front/back or forward/backwards motion. **Imagine you are a clock, and your hands are the clock-hands marking 3, 9, and then 6 o'clock.** Repeat that tracing one more time.

Many examples of movements occur on this plane – from exercise star jumps (called jumping jacks in the United States), cartwheels, stadium waves, the typical cheerleading poses with pompoms going up or down, the John Travolta trademark disco dance, or the concert audience wave with hands in the air swaying from side to side to an incredible tune. **Take a moment to play with this directionality – up and down, plus side to side – what other movements can you come up with?**

FIGURE 3.2 The Door or the Vertical Plane

Body metaphors related to the Intention stage and the self also describe an 'affinity' between how often our body shows attitudes towards gravity, reflected through our emotions. Often certain emotional states have an affinity to go 'up' (e.g. happiness, excitement, anxiety), while other states might have an affinity with 'downward' motions (e.g. sadness, disappointment, hopelessness). From a different perspective, if we are feeling energetic or anxious, we describe the internal sensations often as 'bubbling up'. When we are feeling dejected, in some countries, the body metaphors often used are 'dragging our feet' or feeling like we are 'giving in'; we often feel 'let down' by an action someone else took that disappointed us. This relationship between the self and verticality therefore transcends across the lifespan[3].

Shaping Qualities (Rising and Sinking)

Movement Break: Rising and Sinking

Suggested Music

Track Title: Rising/Sinking

Duration: 05:11

Music Composer: Ross Whyte

Link for QR Code: https://youtu.be/2GKq5MWCrHE?si=GpLo-KuJ0yr6vNkn>

Let's consider the Shaping elements – Rising and Sinking. If you are standing up, make sure your feet are hip width apart, and **give your knees a gentle bounce up and down and your hands a shake**. I often use the image of feeling like you are standing on memory foam, with your knees available, rather than locked in. **If you are sitting/ lying down, use your hands to guide your knees side to side.**

Notice your relationship to the ground beneath your feet (standing) and/or underneath your bottom (sitting). **Shift your weight from side to side either by alternating sit bones on your seat or your feet on your ground.** Then try shifting your centre of gravity in different directions by using either your torso, your hips, or a combination of both in a circle. **Shift forwards, towards the right, backwards, towards your left, and then come to your centre**.

Play with this task of rising and sinking involving your whole body. Use this concept as the premise of all your movement. Perhaps it feels good to start with your arms, and you can play with raising them and then letting them drop in gravity with a 'plunk!'. **Notice if you can release the tension in the arms to allow a natural drop rather than controlling them down**; this is what is called in BESS *passive weight*, which is letting gravity take its course. Resume your exploration – trying this with other parts of the body. **Enact different variations of Sinking gently, Sinking with more force, and rising lightly and rising while exerting more pressure/tension.**

After working with our whole body, we will shift our focus to working with our spine, letting our head drop down gently, then rolling down, rolling up. Once you are back to vertical, trace your name with your nose in the space in front of you. Notice how the different postures affect your body: arching, having a straight spine, holding, and letting go (Figure 3.3).

Take some time to experience Rising and Sinking using your own movement vocabulary. What do Rising and Sinking evoke in you? Are there any sensations, images, emotions, and/or words that come up for you?

FIGURE 3.3

Effort Qualities (Light and Strong)

Lamb claimed that in decision-making the Intention stage offers a relationship to the amount of pressure applied in a situation or circumstance[4]. In BESS movement analysis, the Efforts of Strong or Light application of Force (Weight) relates to verticality and rising/descending Shaping of movement[5]. How do these movements begin to answer the Body Questions in the beginning of the chapter?

Weight is the main Effort category associated with Intention. For those new to BESS, Weight is not about how much something weighs, but about the dynamic relationship between our body and gravity. In movement analysis it has also been termed Force[6]. Using this term has made it much clearer to my workshop participants, so I will alternate between the Weight and Force. We apply different types of Force to actions, situations, events, and interactions: we might prefer to have a light touch on certain subjects where we need to be more diplomatic or go full Force when stakes are high. Body Questions in this stage also look at the amount of pressure we put on ourselves (and others) and our movement attitudes towards it. The next sections will break down the Effort components and the Shape components respectively.

Effort Qualities: Light Weight

Let's begin with movements with Light Weight Effort. "Lightness creates springy motions and a buoyant attitude. . . . It is used in humour, tact, and expressions of happiness. Joking and laughing often promote a light attitude towards weight"[7]. Some examples of using Lightness in everyday situations: being discreet about a tricky situation or brushing away a disdainful comment or a stressful aspect of the day. Sometimes you could 'lighten the load' of tasks at work or need to move to lighten your mood. People might tell you to 'lighten up' when the mood is getting gloomy, or you might feel a little 'lighter' after confessing something that has been weighing on you. Body metaphors are everywhere! Can you think of any other body metaphor phrases about the Weight factor that are common in your culture?

Movement Break: Lightness

Suggested Music

Track Title: Weight Efforts: Lightness

Duration: 7:44

Music Composer: Ross Whyte

Link for QR code: https://youtu.be/MA9dt62tcnw?si=orLRdj2XSDmDiS3J>

Let's have a movement break to explore Lightness in movement. **Begin exploring with your first association with the word Lightness.** What moves first? Engage with the Efforts from the previous stage, try Lightness and Directness for a bit, focusing on certain objects around your space. You can also play with the timing or rhythm in this movement. **Start by engaging again with the Floating feeling in movement, taking in the room at a leisurely pace with no particular purpose in mind**, let your full body experience that sense of weightlessness. Explore for some time, then shift your focus to a particular direction or object in the room. **Approach the object and Dab its surface** with light tapping of your fingers or your feet. Notice the texture, temperature, and colour of the object you chose. **Shift from Dabbing to a light stroke or brushing.** Start moving the brush outward in lots of directions (Flick). Feel the discharge of energy outwards as you keep shaking things out. **Slow**

things down to turn this into a Glide. Engage with your feet/ wheelchair to find a clear direction to move towards. You will skate your feet or glide your wheelchair towards that direction – almost like moving in slow motion.

Explore that directional intent with a sense of weightlessness as you reach towards various spaces that call your attention. Discover Lightness while moving, and then travel your arms upwards until you reach out as high as you can and go on the balls of your feet if you are standing. **Take some time without a particular task in mind to listen to what your body wants while engaging with Lightness.** Engage with different levels if you are able (high, middle, low) – as in Figure 1.6 on page 34. Revisit these actions, alternating body parts or perspectives (facing other directions in the room). Then have some time to reflect on this exercise.

Effort Qualities: Strong Weight

Strong Weight is on the other side of the spectrum of this Effort category. This involves a more forceful relationship with our application of pressure with our movement. An important misconception is that Strong Weight refers to our personality, or strength of character.

This will become crucial when we talk about our movement preferences in our Movement Styles chapter section. Within BESS, Strong Weight is expressed in movement when we need more of an 'oomph' for situations, actions, tasks, and interactions. Strong Weight usually has an affinity with downward motions, but we can execute Strong Weight in a variety of directions.

We use Strong Weight in actions traditionally classed as 'aggressive', such as punching, hammering, and kicking, but this is not a universal application of this Effort Quality. We engage with Strong Weight when we need to deliver a big report with a short deadline, or when we need to push a very heavy piece of furniture across the room. We can also observe Strong Weight when athletes celebrate their big wins with fists punching the air or superheroes punch the ground and create earthquakes. Martial artist Bruce Lee combined the greatest combination of Light Weight and Strong Weight in his disciplined renditions of training and fight scenes. These are only some examples of Strong Weight being applied to different instances.

It is important to keep in mind that all the spectrum components of these effort factors are always fluctuating, and rarely people's movements remain static on one end of an Effort quality spectrum (Figure 3.4). However, we can reflect on our tendencies, the types of Efforts we are applying to situations and take a deeper look at constructive/unproductive patterns we engage with. In later sections we will explore how Lightness and Strength combine to express different aspects of the self. Body Questions emerge: What do I need? What is essential? What is at the core?

FIGURE 3.4 Weight Effort Continuum

Light   **WEIGHT**   Strong

Movement Break: Strong Weight/Force

Suggested Music

Track Title: Weight Efforts: Strong Force

Duration: 7:49

Music Composer: Ross Whyte

Link for QR Code: https://youtu.be/grT4rxZa5V0?si=YTdZpF5tythVKfVt

The exploration of Strong Weight is one that consumes a lot of energy, and therefore be mindful of the time spent in this exploration. **We will start with the most well-known motions of Strong Weight associated with Quick time – punching, hammering and kicking**. Take as much time as you need at that speed, to then begin to slow these motions down while keeping that sense of pressure/Strong Weight. Then you can **slow down and direct your focus, as if pulling something heavy towards you** or pushing something with lots of effort in any forward direction (Press). We can then play with Indirectness – slowly wringing your hands and squeezing the space around you (Wring). You might want to twist your torso to experience the wringing sensation in your core muscles.

Experiment now with keeping that Indirectness but quickening the pace of the movements. This will turn the movements into Slashing or Whipping motions. What do Strong Weight actions feel like?

After exploring for a while, take some time to write down some impressions – a word, feeling, descriptor, or image that helps you remember your embodied sense of Strong Weight. Notice the qualities of this movement and refer to them as you need.

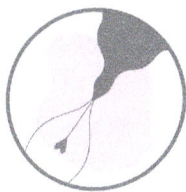

Reflexive Exercise: Weight Effort Spectrum

The following reflexive Body Question will help you to look at your own preferences and 'default settings' in terms of the Weight Effort Qualities. There are 'stereotypical' cultural associations with Strength/Lightness associated with being strong vs. weak in terms of our personality. I want to challenge these cultural associations as lightness does not mean weakness, or Strong Weight does not mean being strong. For example, one can engage with Light Efforts and still be a strong person. Despite there being affinities between movement qualities and internal states, clarifying what you need is what is important to reflect on. Does using Strong Weight or Light Weight feel comfortable or does it make you feel uneasy? You need both skills to operate in daily life – but you will have a preference, and it might suit or not the situation at hand.

As we move through these Body Questions, in Chapter 2 (Figures 2.4 and 2.5) we looked at your range and preference regarding the Attention stage. Peek at your spectrum for that one (Figure 2.6 on page 69 and then have a go at filling in your range and preference in the Weight Effort (Figure 3.5).

FIGURE 3.5 Weight Effort Spectrum Reflection; Please Fill Out Your Weight Effort Preferences

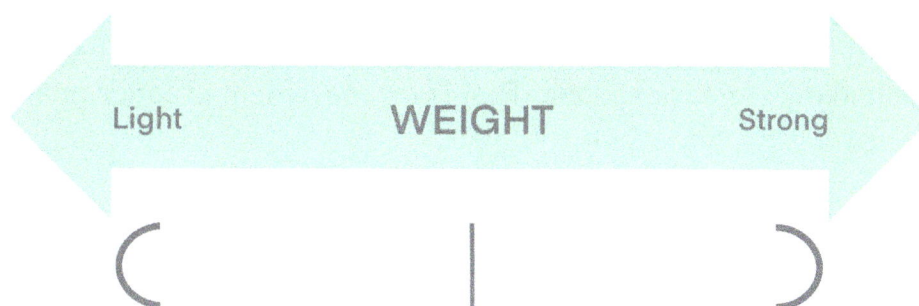

Light   WEIGHT   Strong

FIGURE 3.6 Weight Effort Spectrum (Thania's Example)

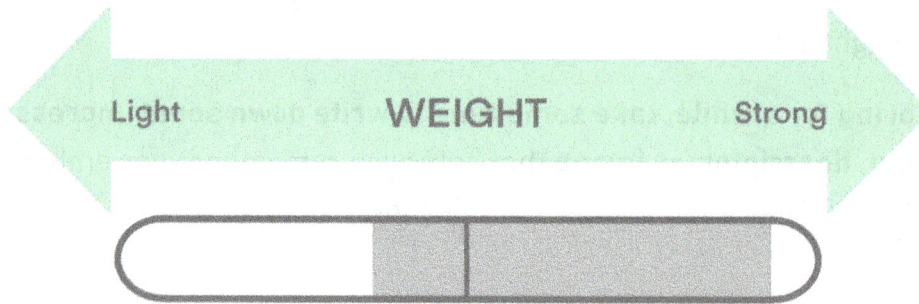

I will keep adding my examples to offer a more contextual explanation when we combine the stages in later chapters. Figure 3.6 reflects my preference (Strong Weight vs. Light Weight) and my range (which expresses the extent to which I feel comfortable exerting those qualities).

As you can see, I often feel very comfortable in moving with Strong Weight and applying more Force into things. I even took up boxing because that space allows me to access my full Strong Weight spectrum in a focused and engaging manner! When I move in Light Weight (despite ballet training), it feels less preferable for me, albeit quite soothing. Movement training has helped support this Lightness, and I have been able to reflect on this preference and how it connects to my upbringing, my profession, and my environment. As my career has veered more into facilitating large professional development groups, I am able to keep this Lightness, particularly through the use of humour. I find that sometimes laughter at the appropriate times can help people feel more at ease. I also find that by activating my Lightness I draw upon the warmth of my Puerto Rican culture and its sociocentric values (community/family/belonging) to hold safety in spaces and build relationships with people. I use Lightness in my voice during more open-ended explorations when I want to invite people to experiment more. I would like to keep working on Light Efforts more in my personal life, as I sometimes gear more towards them in my professional one. That is my movement practice goal – what would be yours?

In connection to decision-making, as we will explore in more detail later, understanding your use of weight can also help you assign the type of Force needed in the decision/transition. Does it need a gentle touch? Or stronger pressure? Do you need to assert yourself more in this situation?

Vertical Plane in Daily Life: Asserting Our Needs

As I discussed earlier in this chapter, in 'typical' development, we are engaging with building, rebuilding, finding our weight, and their inevitable falls and recoveries. In my PhD research, I also found some links to asserting our own voice, defending our stance, and exploring the development and declaration of our identity[8]. If we engage with the framework that this stage relates to identity formation and how we relate to ourselves, then we can look at some of the tasks we will be facing when engaging in this stage. The Intention stage in this current context can bring up a lot of pain and challenge, but also many stories of overcoming.

The Body Questions in terms of the Intention Plane ask us – What is closest to our core? This stage offers individuals an opportunity to also pick out the priorities of a given situation and distil a decision into its essential elements. In the decision-making through movement model, the information gathered from the alternatives identified in the Attention stage is brought into the Intention stage to be sifted through, prioritised, and integrated in order to be actioned. Or in the same sense we have a need that requires more research to see what options are out there. Or there is an alternative that immediately stands out and we action it. This is what makes this system so dynamic. Depending upon the decision question, there might be lots of back and forth between the stages until clarity on the issue is reached. It can sometimes remain as a dance between needs and options.

To clarify a need, however, we might need to build up some strength in our voice and unique outlook on life. Research in the field of embodiment in sport[9] claims that "there is the sense of affirming or insisting upon one's rights; protecting or vindicating oneself; maintaining or defending a cause". Developing assertiveness (when appropriate and safe) in movement involves interventions that allow an individual or group to be able to establish their own concerns, needs, and wants without resorting to aggression.

Assertiveness is a quality that involves self-reflection into one's position and training in assertive communication[10]. However, each culture will have its own view of assertiveness. "Assertiveness connected with certain cultural identities are at times mislabelled as aggression"[11], which goes hand in hand with racism and the assumption that violence occurs more within certain cultural/socioeconomic circles. Dance movement therapist Lenore Hervey[12], in her model of embodied ethical decision-making, exposes some of the movement activities in classes and workshops where "participants found themselves creating an imaginary space and boundaries for themselves and others through movement, and found that moving in the Vertical Plane supported respect for their own autonomy". DMT Bonnie Bernstein[13] associates verticality to assertiveness in her work as a dance movement psychotherapist for female survivors of sexual abuse, referring to the process of accessing "strength, voice and verticality" through the body in her practice. Bernstein affirms that assertiveness was key to her clients' process of healing and, in the case of one client, allowed her client to confront their aggressor[14]. However, confrontation and healing from sustained trauma needs resourcing through support networks, therapy, protective factors, and inner resilience.

Many participants in my workshops often expressed feeling uncomfortable in voicing their needs. However, this is understandable, given that an individual's needs are often entangled with family/friend/social circle obligations and many other demands. For people who are in a caring role within their life, being able to carve out time and space for self-care is often very difficult. I therefore devised some Movement Breaks for saying NO, and also working on asserting identity, which we cover on page 110. We discovered, through movement exploration, that at times saying NO and boundary-setting were also a challenge, as some participants felt they would 'hurt other people's feelings', or they felt guilty taking time from their other commitments.

In those cases, I often invited the group to practise moving in the Vertical Plane: up and down and side to side in preparation for the Vertical Plane Activities on page 96. In this exploration, I often encouraged them to notice that since the Vertical Plane doesn't have the forward/back motion often associated with aggression or retreat, that we could just focus on standing on our own two feet and embodying our own 'neutral' stance.

Working on the Vertical Plane helped many participants start differentiating setting boundaries from impinging or being pressured by other people. This felt like an embodied component that needed reiterating and practising to understand the role of the Vertical Plane in the assertion of self and unpin assertion from aggression or passivity.

In corporate workshops, embodied exploration was very stimulating to some participants who identified the struggle to find a professional voice and sense of agency within the workplace. A common theme across workshops with different communities was a concrete connection to the role of inner resourcing in resilience and wellbeing[15]. This provides an important rationale to focus on and invest in protective factors across all decision-making stages. Some participants also related this plane to emotional states, such as excitement, depression, anxiety, lack of motivation, stubbornness, nervousness, disappointment, gratitude, and acceptance. The relationship between the Planes and Emotions across cultures would be an incredible area for future research.

Body Questions open the space here to understand your relationship to this plane and the larger systemic structures you are encountering.

- What emotional states can you connect to while in the Vertical Plane?
- Is it safe to embody your needs?
- How are you able to express your priorities?
- What support systems do you have in place to do this?

We return to the ongoing question of each stage: Is your current use of Weight fulfilling a particular function? Is it sustainable?

Coming back to honouring the developmental aspects of this system leads me to a fun yet confronting improvisational exercise: the tantrum. If we analyse how tantrums first come about, we often visualise a toddler engaging in the full spectrum of their Strong Weight, which is not fully developed yet at a muscular level. In the KMP system, this is regarded as *Vehemence* – engaging with High Intensity but not yet acquiring mastery over engaging with the effort qualities of Strong Weight[16]. I have often felt that as adults, we are often 'denied' our tantrums, and often our frustrations are therefore expressed in other behavioural patterns, particularly, when participants need more support in engaging with Strong Effort Qualities or need a full-body discharge of emotions. In my practice, I have often experienced that we need to engage our body-voice to enact an intention or give light to a core issue which is causing us some strife.

I will therefore invite you to engage with an activity where we can allow our body to experience the elements of a tantrum. I offer an important caveat here: This activity might feel uncomfortable, or you might not be ready for it at this time. This is completely okay, and you might want to revisit this later. On the same note, it is often important to acknowledge our uneasiness and engage with being outside our comfort zone. Trying out new patterns of moving, as Hackney[17] often reiterates, can help us foster change. We can therefore approach this activity with a sense of curiosity, play, and not taking ourselves too seriously.

Movement Break: Tantrum Exercise 🎧

Suggested Music

Track Title: Tantrum Exercise

Duration: 2:20

Music Composer: Ross Whyte

Link for QR Code: https://youtu.be/xw3DXVn2g0A?si=pceLH1nGqxAz2BpB

🎧 Link for audio description playlist: https://www.youtube.com/playlist?list=PLtGm4qYm5yBQZqgY5_PFpJHa4jgs2R6Cw

---

This activity can be done individually or in pairs. An alternative to working in pairs is videotaping yourself and being your own witness. I have found that, when able to view myself without self-judgement, watching my own videos can help me reflect on my movement from a different stance. I will explain the exercise first as an individual and then with a witness (more on these roles shortly).

Stand with your feet a bit wider than your hips, or if you are sitting, try to leave a bit of space from the back of the chair to allow the spine some flexibility to move if this is possible. Close your eyes as we will do a brief body check-in first. **Connect to your breath and try to visualise your head and your feet at the same time.** If you are sitting, place your hands on your knees and bring awareness to them. If you are standing, bending your knees slightly. Once you sense your whole body has become more present, you will **try and connect with a source of frustration in this moment**. Remember, that when trying this for the first time, please choose something significant to you, but not transcendental (yet).

We will then practise representing the intensity of movement regarding this source of frustration. **The task is to escalate the movement of your choosing and then deescalate it in intensity by engaging with the use of the Weight Factors (Strong/ Light Force)**. You can choose the same movement and take it to its extreme, or you can vary the movement and just experiment with higher intensities, as your comfort level allows. Intensity could be embodied by taking up more space, repeating movements more, or increasing speed. **We will start small and then increase to full body if you are feeling up to it.** First, we will try by using percussive movement – either by 'drumming' lightly on your thighs or on a surface (drumroll) – or use your feet to do stomping movements while sitting if this is possible.

Remember: Tailor this activity according to your own mobility needs to make it your own.

Take your time in intensifying the movement – increase force, tension, and speed. You can use sounds if those come naturally and bring it to the highest level of intensity you can muster at this moment. Then bring it down in intensity/decelerate the movement. **Have a couple of tries at increasing and decreasing escalation** if you need it.

Drum or tap slowly, quickly, varying the speed. Notice the difference between fluctuating intensity and sustaining intensity over longer periods of time (for guidance, follow the bottom left image on Figure 3.7).

Next challenge: We have introduced this repertoire into our body, and now we will make it bigger, taking up more space. This exercise has brought up some strong emotions for some of my participants, and while we have been able to hold that safely within the groups, **be mindful that you are feeling resourced enough to try this at full intensity**. If you are not ready for this step just yet, you can repeat the steps of the aforementioned exercise again.

After taking some rest, if needed, try picturing something else that is frustrating you at the moment – something that you want to throw a full-blown tantrum about. It can be the same issue from the previous exercise or a new topic. **Start again**

with a repetitive movement like the drumming before but expand it through your whole body or give it more forceful intention. Gauge where the highest threshold of the intensity is and take this into crescendo (more and more intensity) without self-judgement (or overdoing it). When you are ready, deescalate the intensity of movement, slowly taking the movement back towards a neutral stance, which is usually stillness. Deescalating the intensity might look like: making the movement slower, smaller, and/or with less tension. Everyone has a different threshold for interpreting intensity. The important aspect here is that you see where your comfort level is right now. All Body Questions and somatic information is welcome and valid.

After this, you will verbalise the following phrase out loud:

"I need _____"

Let the need come naturally (try not to overthink it). **Voicing the need should be connected to the body and to the movement.** If your body expresses this experience and there is no need for words, that is fine as well. Notice what you discovered about this process. **Draw or journal about what this experience was like.**

If you want to try this out with a partner, a witness can offer a containing, non-judgemental space for you. After the activity detailed next, witnesses and movers can then change roles (please refer to Figure 3.7).

The Role of the Witness

The term 'witness' here relates to a method of dance movement therapy called Authentic Movement (AM), which is connected to Jungian psychotherapy and was developed by Mary Whitehouse[18] and expanded by Janet Adler[19] and many more colleagues. I will explain more about this method later.

While primarily used in therapeutic contexts, Authentic Movement has been used in theatre, contemporary dance, and other nontherapeutic realms. Two components of this method are called *inner listening* (listening to our body's impulse to move) and the role of *witness* to others' experience. In movement we can connect to joy, pleasure, and confusion and mediate difficult and celebratory aspects of life.

FIGURE 3.7 Intention Stage – Tantrum Exercise

In Authentic Movement, there is often a mover and witness. The mover cultivates a practice of moving in silence and with eyes closed, attuning to their own body and developing inner listening[20]. A witness is someone who will hold someone's experience for them without judgement. This role differs from being an audience member because the witness is never trying to figure out what the mover is experiencing. For witnessing to feel safe, there are a couple of tasks and 'rules' for the witness. They need to only pay attention to what their body is experiencing while witnessing someone else move. The witness is one of the most important roles in movement work[21]. It is about experiencing, being present, and modelling a safe space for other people to be. It is an ongoing practice that takes some time.

In this exercise, the witness needs not to feedback anything to the mover and should try to maintain neutral body language, especially before and after witnessing. The witness will face them at the same level (either sitting or standing) as the mover is as detailed in Figure 3.7. They will listen and be there for them as the mover goes through their tantrum, without reacting, and remain as neutral as possible. When the mover states the need, the witness and mover thank each other. In our workshops, we use the gesture in the Body Questions icon to start and finish the experience. This was particularly helpful when conducting sessions online to signal beginnings and endings of an exercise to the witness.

Movers can offer what that experience was like while the witness listens. Useful frameworks from Authentic Movement suggest both mover and witness can reflect on[22]:

- Sensations (senses, movements, body parts, energy level, intensity, temperature, movement qualities, etc.)
- Images (that came up during/after movement, metaphors, symbolic content)
- Thoughts (+ memories, self-talk, phrases, etc.)
- Emotions (feeling states that arise).

Worksheet 3.1 will give you a space to do this.

The witness will ask the mover if they want feedback (full consent is always best). Movers can always say no at any point (this is okay). Witnesses can then either offer one word or where they felt it in their body.

Witnesses will always try not to project[23] their own stuff (make it about them) or have an interpretation of what they saw. Interpretations can often be received as judgements and sometimes can make people feel insecure about their movement experience or feel judged, which might thwart creativity. One of my Authentic Movement and DMT training teachers, Danielle Fraenkel, always told us to go deeper, stay in the present moment (when speaking as a mover and witness), and to be patient with what our bodies are trying to say. It might not come out immediately, but it is important to trust the information as it emerges. Witnessing is a form of listening that allows a separation of the experience and makes it okay for the mover's experience to be enough and something that is only for themselves and not for others.

Authentic Movement methods have specific ways of providing feedback to movers, which will take some practice[24]. My preferred mode of feeding back to someone is in first person – I talk about myself moving even if I was watching someone else.

For example, if I witnessed someone do the movements in Figure 3.7 (bottom half), I will offer this feedback to the mover:

> As a witness, I am sitting in my chair. I feel a tension in my chest as I clench my fists. I feel my jaw tighten and as I use my fists in agitation and with tension in to pulsate in the air. I get this image of feeling powerful and energised.

I must admit, when I was training with dance movement therapy trainer Danielle Fraenkel, I really struggled with first person feedback. But then when I was the mover and heard the witness speak in first person, it really helped to separate the witness' experience from the mover's and helped me be more receptive to the feedback. There is an interesting connection to making decisions with others and how witnessing could potentially serve as a bridge to communal decision-making in future research.

Another safer, quick way to feed back is through somatic feedback – I comment as a witness what it felt like in my body, without any mention of the content of the other person (and whatever feels useful to share). That way this stays in the body, and a sense of safety is generated. As a witness, I also only feed back after the mover speaks and ONLY if they want to hear the witness. It is always okay to say no – you can say "I don't need feedback at this time". It's alright!!

There are many ways in which this way of communicating can be cultivated. It takes a bit of practice and feels somewhat weird at the beginning, but it separates the mover's experience from my own as witness (or vice-versa). Therefore, if you are beginning your practice, start small. It is also always important to ask if feedback is needed since the movement expression is sufficient. It helps in the decision-making process to connect to your own needs and to clarify your path through inner listening. Having a witness, however, is also very gratifying because you can feel seen and acknowledged (if that is what you need).

Other Authentic Movement practitioners have different ways of doing this, but this is a way I have found useful in my sessions both as a practitioner and as a mover myself.

WORKSHEET 3.1 Embodied Journalling (Sensations, Images, Thoughts, Emotions)

Sensations

Emotions

Images

Thoughts

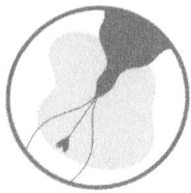

Reflexive Exercise: Embodied Journalling

What did expressing a need after frustration feel? Was it stronger in movement or in words? What sensations did you experience in terms of verticality? How did you feel witnessing or being witnessed? Have some time for yourself to reflect through drawing, words and/or movement.

In Professional Practice

My doctoral research explored links between the Intention stage and oppressive power structures[25]. These can occur at micro-level (e.g. your immediate environment) or at a macro-level (wider political, social, and cultural contexts). For example, in your workplace, when you voice something that you feel is important, you may get rejected, excluded, ignored, silenced, or ghosted[26]. This pervading feeling of powerlessness can really take a toll on your own self-worth and impact productivity, motivation, and the drive to action. These experiences could occur because of direct dynamics within the work hierarchy (managerial stratification) at a micro-level, which might also be impacted by the policies and organisational culture within the workplace at a macro level.

Professions that I have found are attracted to the Intention stage are ones that prefer policies and procedures. These are people who prefer to stick to the norms, love structure, and may look at compliance. Some examples of departments that come to mind are Human Resources, Health and Safety Officers, Compliance, Evaluators/ Assessors, and Surveyors, amongst many more. Which other professions do you think might prefer the Intention stage?

If we often hold our Intention position and verticality rigidly, we won't necessarily be able to engage in understanding other alternatives (Attention), execute Actions when needed, or decide not to act until we have a safety assessment or more information. Sometimes this happens when we are clinging too closely to a particular issue or are feeling immovable in how we are approaching this issue. Inflexibility might also evoke feelings of stubbornness, and others might consider we are being relentless or rigid. Remember that being fixated and/or feeling stubborn about the core issue might be serving a particular purpose.

Activism

In the context of activism, it takes interminable strength to combat social injustice. Often the responsibility of standing up and protesting relies on very few people. Community groups who rally together and support each other can help 'lighten the load'. Resourcing both Force and Lightness become crucial in these types of battles. For example, in an equality/diversity/inclusion context, combating existing structures and ways of doing/operating things will often be a challenge. Standing up for what you believe in is sometimes tricky. At times, defending ourselves and our rights will involve withstanding pressure, stumbles, and recovery, rising despite these events and finding our voice and our own two feet in terms of our position and priorities. Activism can also be the link between Intention to Action, as the next chapter will discuss.

From a non-judgemental stance, the Body Question then becomes:

- If I could express my stance in terms of this issue – what movement or shape would represent it? What level of Force am I adopting/introducing into a situation when I execute this movement/shape? What quality of breath am I adopting while I move?

It is beneficial to acknowledge our current position and whether it is allowing the need to surface in a way in which it can be properly resourced. We might need to reflect on why we are holding on so tight. Where are the possibilities of movement which don't completely sacrifice the need but also allow new ways of accessing it? Rigidity involves binding the flow of things which perhaps serves to strengthen our stance, and stages need to remain dynamic for things to evolve.

Movement Break: Intention Stage and Identity: 'Here I Am'

If we are giving in to the pressure and forgoing our own needs, the burden from outside structures might feel too overpowering. This will impact our ability to generate the Weight Effort necessary to counteract this pressure. This means we might need to resource our movement repertoire to engage in a way that helps us resource and expand our capacity. The other stages in the decision-making process often allow us to either reconnect with the source of frustration/joy (Flow/Tension), look at viable alternatives (Attention), and decide on whether this is the right time to be prioritising this core aspect (Action/Non-Action). In the Intention stage, the crystallisation of the issue is the essential task. Then we must look at all the other Body Questions, resources, environment, and timing to enact this need accordingly.

Some of these examples are from my practice in the United Kingdom and are therefore embedded in that context, and I recognise that this experience might be different from your own. I approach this next exercise with my own environment in mind, being a Puerto Rican who spent eight years in New York but has been working in the United Kingdom since 2011.

Case Example: Finding Your Walk Workshop

During a workshop with trans youth in Scotland, I was engaging with exercises around the Intention stage, as the overarching theme was exploring our identity. Often, when working with marginalised communities, I begin with exploring movement in the Vertical Plane since I have found that grounding and centring first allows possibilities in other planes to come into play. We did some work by feeling our feet, noticing where we stood, and shifting our weight between the feet (Modification: shifting between sitting bones while sitting). This often helps stimulate the vestibular (inner ear – balance) system and helps participants establish their own relationship to their centre of gravity. This is usually the axis in the centre of our body into the ground/surface which maintains us in balance. Off centre might mean we are leaning a direction and likely to feel off balance or fall. Later in the workshop, we asked the participants about what challenges they were facing in terms of their own identity.

One participant said,

> I really want to say good morning to the bus driver. But I am afraid they might misgender me and that would crush me as I want to be seen as how I am. I feel that I am being impolite and rude by not saying good morning. It affects my whole day.

This felt so important to the group, and therefore I engaged with the following activity to help participants practise voicing who they were with pride and assertion. I was very aware that this voicing might have difficult consequences for them, and they might feel unsafe amongst other people in the wider society who target trans people, which is so painful for them and heart-breaking for me. This made me feel increasingly powerless and sad in terms of how this group of young people would face these challenges. However, as a facilitator, all I felt I could do in those moments is resource the Vertical Plane in voice and body to encourage more confidence in their presentation of themselves. Resourcing the strength needed to also cope with how others would react felt crucial since we cannot control other people's reactions.

The exercise firstly involved practising our walk. We explored walking with different movement concepts: Fast/Slow, Direct/Indirect. Then I added tasks regarding feeling states: walk/locomote around while feeling confident, unsure, resistant, bold, and many other feeling states they felt were appropriate.

We explored walking from one end of the room to the other and stopping at a fixed point and planting our two feet in a neutral stance: feet a bit wider than hips with accessible knees and connecting to our breath. Then we practised voicing the phrase: "I AM".

We played with the varying cadences of saying 'I AM'. We discussed how we felt about who we are and these qualities being enough. The next day (it was a weekend workshop), the young person announced: "I said 'good morning' to the bus driver! And it was okay!" This felt so significant, and I was grateful that who they were was acknowledged and respected by the bus driver. Another participant had approached a clothing store clerk and asked for assistance for the first time in years, which was another source of celebration for the group. This acceptance from others might not always be the case with all my clients, which deeply impacts me, but I take the small wins when I can.

This is something you can also explore. **This activity can be done with someone else as a partner, in front of a mirror, or in your own space.** If doing this activity with a partner – **set a piece of masking tape or a mark to stop at a reasonable distance that is agreeable to your partner** (arm's length or the distance you and your partner both feel comfortable with in terms of interpersonal space) (see Figure 3.8). They in turn will witness your walk from a neutral stance. Be mindful

FIGURE 3.8 I AM – Exercise

that interpersonal distance varies depending on culture, upbringing, height, and other physical markers we possess and our previous experiences with personal space.

Walk/move your wheelchair towards the person/mirror/object/mark. Close your eyes and tune in to your body briefly. Connect to an aspect of you that you feel is your strength or your source of pride. **Once you find this, open your eyes (make eye contact with your partner if you are doing this in pairs) and say, 'I AM'.**

Repeat this various times – with different attitudes in the walk or in movement. **Vocalise 'I AM' in varying ways.** Play with pitch (lower/higher), tone (e.g. stern, questioning, etc.), speed, volume, inflection (going up or down with the words).

Body Question: What shape or movement symbolises a key part of your identity at this moment in time?

Variation: You can try this exercise with different statements, mantras, to foster positive self-talk. I use this in workshops at my university on Embodied Skills in Public Speaking. I ask participants to add their 'short elevator pitch' about their professional identity. It helps people build confidence in approaching clients or in networking events which can often be anxiety provoking.

For example, my pitch is:

> I AM . . . a dance movement therapist and researcher developing movement-focussed wellbeing programmes about decision making and burnout prevention for the caring professions and marginalised communities.

Ideally, your pitch will be short but specific and offer a clear image of what you can offer the other person (e.g. a funder, employer, collaborator). Pitches might change over time or adapt to the audience we are pitching to.

I am aware that this is a very significant activity regarding the Plane of the Self as explored within the Intention stage. Later in this chapter, we will explore this activity in terms of saying NO – assertion and boundary-setting – and you'll notice the difference. Every time I enact this activity, even my own sense of 'I AM' varies. This signifies that exploring these aspects of movement will change throughout our lives. It becomes a practice that helps us connect with what we need and give it the platform that it deserves.

Grounding and Anxiety Management

There is a whole body of literature which refers to 'grounding' or centring as tools for anxiety management. I often work with groups who identify with having high levels of anxiety. Anxiety, in an embodied sense, is often described in affinity with rising, 'bubbling feelings' that have an upwards motion. Other qualities of anxious feelings involve feeling frozen, shaky, and with an accelerated heartbeat. People often describe having 'butterflies in the stomach' or feeling very much in their head. Our bodies provide somatic information indicating when we are feeling anxious, often before we cognitively code these body feelings as anxiety. There are some affinities that occur naturally in the body, while sometimes the movement and feeling state might be in disaffinity and provide contrasts in movement qualities[27].

There is an overwhelming amount of attention on coping techniques for anxiety management in both the research and self-help arenas. One of the primary interventions has traditionally been breathing techniques which help regulate autonomic nervous system responses. This makes complete sense in terms of regulating Flow/Tension to be able to introduce varying degrees of containment of these 'rising' feelings (more on this in Chapter 5). Yoga and other somatic approaches have also brought in a wide gamma of interventions to help us find our feet and work on balance, which contribute to a sense of grounding. Metaphors about having 'anchors' are often useful – what are the aspects that keep you present and remind you of what is important? All these factors have an intrinsic relationship with the Intention stages' movement qualities. Body Questions emerge here regarding what aspects, activities, and support systems help you stay present and/or resilient?

These tools often refer to the connection back into the ground or something that offers stability. However, a Cultural Caveat here: As I was reminded in a conference, the ground might not be the universal symbol for stability in countries who have been affected by hurricanes and natural disasters. It is important to consider how verticality is regarded across cultures[28].

Movement Break: Saying No and Setting Boundaries

Avoiding confrontation is a human coping mechanism. Although some people thrive when confronting others, this type of assertion might not be as easily accessed by everyone. The reasons behind this are myriad – our upbringing, socio-cultural context, background, gender identity, personality, and sense of agency are some factors that influence our ability to assert our needs and confront others when needed and if it is safe to do so. Some cultures and contexts will encourage confrontation and assertiveness. In other contexts, individual dissention might be silenced or under resourced, so that there is less confrontation or other more indirect mechanisms will be employed. Providing a universal approach to these exercises is futile – as I want to encourage you to examine your own context through your own lens. Please note there is no music set for this Movement Break, but you are welcome to use any of the music provided or your own if you feel you need it.

Think of a situation where you need to say NO about something in your life. As I often say in workshops and have said before in this book:

Pick something significant, but not transcendental.
Some transcendental decisions might need additional support.

Examples of significant situations might be setting a work boundary or saying no to an extra favour someone might ask of you, an event you don't want to go to, or any request you feel needs more limit-setting.

We will repeat the same process as we did in the previous I AM exercise, but here we will practise stating "NO" with your body. Walk towards a particular object or place in your room, plant your feet a bit wider than your hips. Try not to tense up your knees or shoulders. **What comes up? Now try saying it out loud – say it differently each time** (as we did with "I AM"), and then say it in connection to an issue you need to set boundaries to. **Go back and forth from the specified point in space (or a partner/mirror) as many times to get different senses of each NO.**

Options for changing the voices of NO: Play with pitch (lower/higher), tone, rhythm, volume, or elongating or shortening the sounds of the letters. Reflect on the embodied sensations this NO provokes and journal this if you need it. This might need revisiting later, as boundary-setting is an ongoing practice. **Let's combine body and voice with the next suggestions.** Remember – this is a reflexive exercise. Keep yourself and others safe. Here are other suggestions:

[NO???] Try saying NO as if it is more of a question. Notice if your chest tends to shift a tad towards your back in your stance and your upper body gets curved slightly (it might be small). Contemplate how this NO communicates a boundary to others. Are you being clear about the NO? Are you backing away from the NO? Is it negotiable? Does it feel ambivalent? Are you fidgeting with your body?

[NO.] Explore saying NO from a neutral stance. There is no forward movement, and no backwards movement. You feel your verticality fully and have a complete sense of your spine, your head, and your feet. Your knees are a bit bouncy and available. It is a NO that is a statement of what you need – which might be space, time, relaxation, and/or Lightness. Notice if you need an arm/hand gesture to go with this to reinforce this – try as much as you can to stay in the Door Plane.

[NO!!!!] There are some 'NOs' which feel a tad aggressive and/or abrupt – and have a stance that is moving forward into the space. These might be needed for more forceful situations or defence-type situations, where we need to protect ourselves. Try saying NO with a big explosion. Does it feel out of control? Does it feel unsafe? Does it serve the situation?

How does saying NO feel? Often this NO will have a movement equivalent. These are three movement stances, all related to both the Vertical Plane. These also involve the Action/Non-Action stage/Sagittal Plane, which we will explore later, but here's a sneak peek.

All these stances (forward/backward/neutral) have a reason for being there. Asserting this NO might be beneficial if you are establishing some boundaries with others. Some NOs will require more strength, some NOs might need more support. Other NOs might need involvement from a group (as it happens in protest, network, unions, or looking at changing policies). There will be some NOs, particularly if someone is infringing our human rights, where this NO might be non-negotiable. The essential question remains: How can we find a NO where we don't cause harm to ourselves or others? What are the effects/consequences of saying NO?

Reframing these assertions and saying NO in the Vertical Plane helped participants practise their own ways of voicing and embodying what was important and what they needed. Explaining these stances in terms of all the three planes became very helpful in understanding how communication has movement equivalents that help us reflect on how, what intention, when and where we need to stand.

At times identifying between your many priorities might be difficult. There might be too many factors at stake within your decision. Draw out how these factors interweave and whether there is a clear sequence of importance (even if it fluctuates). An idea here is to make a list of these factors and then assign a value to how important this is in your life and start differentiating within your priorities.

You can also use the Intention stage to prioritise items by combining movement, writing, or drawing. Pick a situation (significant but not transcendental) with two options or follow up on the situation you chose for the previous NO exercise.

For example: You might be deciding on moving to a new place. You have researched all the alternatives and must choose between two spaces: one near the countryside, and one close to the city centre. There are many factors to decide here: price, proximity, access to protective factors (e.g. gym/classes/friends/support network/family), size of the space, access to a garden/outside, etc. You might also consider whether being closer to nature or having cafes and places to eat nearby is more important. There is also transportation to consider, amongst many other variables, which might make this decision difficult.

So far this feels like a decision made solely cognitively with our mind. Now let's incorporate movement. Here is where the movement Intention stage qualities will be useful. If you were to offer a movement or still shape (gesture/posture) to represent all the variables/factors within that decision, what would emerge in movement?

Would there be factors in this decision that involve Strong pressure, Light pressure, none? Is there an embodied response to any of these factors? Do you feel heavier or lighter with some factors vs. others? We can get creative with our prioritising, assign a colour/movement/shape to each factor or go with numbers if you are more math oriented. Hopefully there will be a pattern that emerges. Reflect on why these variables are important. When we transition into the next stage (Action/Non-Action), we can look at timing/plans and potential commitment.

Culture and Caveats

Identity is such an overarching theme that it would ideally deserve its own book. I learned how cultural context was so important when introducing the tantrum exercise in my workshops. I grew up in Caribbean Latinx Puerto Rican culture, where high strong emotions hold high cultural value and expressing these externally was something I experienced as commonplace. This might not have been the same for everyone in Puerto Rico, but it was my frame of reference. It wasn't until I travelled that I realised this release of emotion, while cathartic for me and socially accepted where I come from, was increasingly difficult for some participants – especially those whose cultures tended to discourage overt displays of emotional expression. They communicated in those groups that expressing a full-blown tantrum was something they had grown up as taboo in their culture.

Although our bodies hold those developmental patterns when we experienced tantrums as 1–3-year-olds and maybe even later, as adults we might feel societally discouraged from expressing High Intensity Free/Bound Flow. I realised how much my own cultural assumptions were playing a role even in the facilitation of the groups, and this is why I designed some 'preparatory' exercises to begin introducing the movement principles of escalation of intensity to support group members who might have more of a challenging time accessing these Efforts. There are so many factors surrounding agency and identity and the embodiment repertoire to express that. If you are working with other people, I recommend you engage with these discussions with your participants/groups to discover the nuances within our movement possibilities.

There is often a cultural prerogative, particularly in Western cultures, to 'stand up for yourself', 'empower', and 'stand your ground'. We often hear these statements thrown around. Although assertiveness is a factor in Intention, understanding the socio-cultural context in which it takes place is an important ethical consideration. "Asserting", "voicing", or declaring one's needs might not be socially accepted or, in some contexts, may be dangerous without the appropriate social support within a particular region. Introducing cultural distinctions between an embodiment of assertion vs. what could be perceived as aggression is also crucial. Being mindful of procedures for expressing grievances within a workplace or a community context is also something to reflect on.

It is also fundamental to revise the "Western" prerogatives and models, such as storytelling, and "voicing" personal stories[29]. There has been an increasing trend in sthealth systems about patients "telling their stories". While it is important to recognise the power of storytelling in health contexts and how impactful it is to hear those voices, it is equally valuable to examine the agency of each person to be able to embody and express these stories, and process them. Clients/participants need to be able to feel resourced to tell their story to prevent retraumatising themselves or vicariously traumatising others. We also need to be mindful that trauma is not stored logically, sequentially, and in a cohesive manner. Coming to terms with our own trauma and feeling supported and safe enough to communicate these stories (verbally and/or nonverbally) is crucial to promoting constructive and participant-responsive or co-created storytelling.

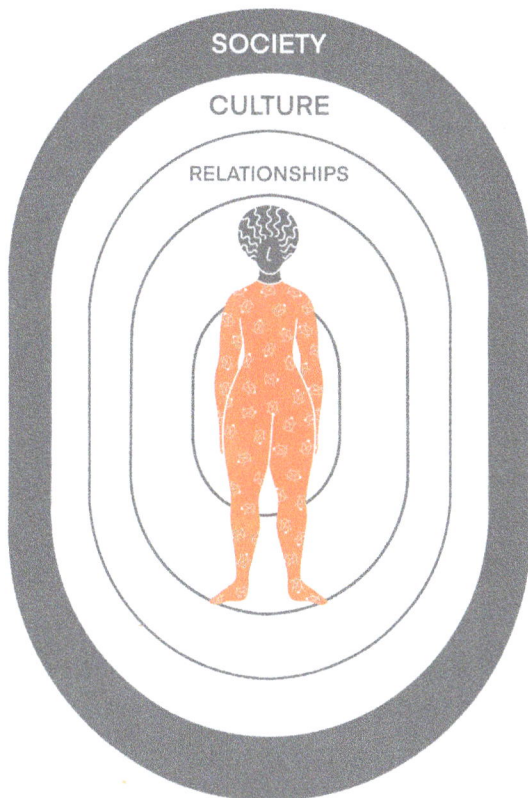

Cultural Background and Values

If our decision is impacted by or impacts other people, priorities will need to be negotiated. The rings of the bull's eye continue to expand as priorities are in constant change according to personal, communal, and collective demands. Body Questions regarding the Intention stage might be influenced by whether we live with or come from cultural values on the individual vs. the collective. The terms *individualistic cultures*, as those cultures which prioritise the individual vs. the community, and *sociocentric cultures* in which the community has priority over individual goals have been used by scholars to introduce nuance into the relationships between an individual and the society[30]. Peacebuilding sociologists Shank and Shirch[31] describe individualistic cultures as employing more "direct, formal, rational and individualistic" ways of engaging vs. sociocentric cultures where there is a preference for "indirect, informal, relational and collectivistic" cultural norms. According to social psychologist Geert Hofstede, sociocentric cultures prioritise the family unit, the community needs, and values over an individual's needs[32]. Individualistic cultures prioritise independence, personal realisation, and individual trajectories[33]. In situations where there is a conflict of needs and priorities, considering multicultural differences might be a useful variable of insight into how this gets mediated. This might influence how you perceive a decision and which factors within it might take precedence.

For example, in one of my academic collaborations, sociologist Sandra Milena Ríos Oyola conducted fieldwork in Bojayá, Colombia, and we analysed (from an interdisciplinary point of view) funerary rituals in the aftermath of a massacre which occurred in 2002. We examined the Afro-Colombian dances that took place, and the difficult negotiation between sociocentric pressure of remembering the atrocities of the massacre, while balancing the individual effect on the bodies of the community who went through this traumatic series of events and felt compelled to repeat it, for it to be remembered[34]. The book chapter Dr Ríos and I wrote offers an examination of the complexity of memorialising difficult events and the role of grief and ritual in Afro-Colombian cultures. There are many impactful examples of difficult decisions which are impossible to capture with the respect they deserve within this book. These examples are just the beginning of understanding the impact of decision-making on the body at both individual and collective levels.

Chapter Conclusion

The analysis of the Intention stage corresponds with the following themes: practitioner's own voice, both in the literal and symbolic sense: voicing/embodying concerns, asserting needs, and identifying the strengths in our own identity. In this stage we might need to connect back to what is important and/or express a frustration (as we did via a movement tantrum). Decision-making through movement interventions in this stage create a correlation between the identification of needs and cultivating resources in the body to support voicing and enacting priorities and needs.

REVIEW POINTS ON THE INTENTION STAGE

- Involves Rising/Sinking shaping, Strong/Light Weight Efforts, Up/down + side-to-side directions.
- Stage related to 'typical' developmental task of negotiating weight, pressure, and balance.
- Vertical Plane in dance movement therapy research is linked to the sense of self.
- Key stage for identification of priorities and needs.
- Getting stuck in this stage might trigger feeling stuck, stubborn, or hold on too tight.
- Intention stage is linked to assertiveness and identity.

SKIP, BOOKMARK, OR CONTINUE

- If you have decided you want to continue in the order of the book, you can continue on to Chapter 4 ("Action/Non-Action"). Often focusing too much on one's needs without a plan can leave us frustrated. Looking at a specific (sustainable) timing to action things or not acting at all might be the way to go!
- You want to research more on potential actions now that you have clarified a need. (Skip to Chapter 2 "Attention Stage".)
- You are feeling the need to connect to your body if the tantrum activity activated some core tension that might need more emphasis. You might want to figure out how to Flow more in order to explore your decision more. (Skip to Chapter 5 "Flow/Tension Stage".)
- You need a break from the stages and want to figure out your own movement style and your preferences before you go any further. This might align very much with the exploration of your identity. (Skip to Chapter 6 "Movement Styles".)

Notes

1 Lamb and Turner, 1969.

2 Kestenberg Amighi et al., 1999; Hackney, 2002, 100–109.

3 Naess, Joan. 'A Developmental Approach to the Interactive Process in Dance/Movement Therapy'. *American Journal of Dance Therapy* 5, no. 1 (December 1982): 43–55. https://doi.org/10.1007/BF02579540; Kestenberg Amighi et al., 1999; Hackney, 2002, 100–109.

4 Lamb and Davis, 2012; Moore, 2005.

5 Lamb and Davis, 2012; Laban, 1966; Laban, Rudolf. *Principles of Dance and Movement Notation* (Brooklyn, NY: Dance Horizons, 1970); Laban, Rudolf, and Frederick Charles Lawrence. *Effort: Economy of Human Movement* (Macdonald and Evans, 1974); Laban, Rudolf, and Lisa Ullmann. *Choreutics* (Macdonald & Evans, 1966); Laban, Rudolf, and Lisa Ullmann. *The Mastery of Movement*, 4th ed. (Plymouth: Northcote House, 1988).

6 Lamb and Davis, 2012.

7 Kestenberg Amighi et al., 1999, 95.

8 Acarón, 'The Practitioner's Body of Knowledge', 2015.

9 McNamee, M. J., and S. J. Parry. *Ethics and Sport* (London: Routledge, 2002), 298.

10 Anderson, Cheryl, and Linda Rouse. 'Intervention in Cases of Woman Battering: An Application of Symbolic Interactionism and Critical Theory'. *Clinical Sociology Review* 6, no. 1 (January 1988). http://digitalcommons.wayne.edu/csr/vol6/iss1/17.

11 Robinson, Aisha. Personal communication, 2024.

12 Hervey, Lenore Wadsworth. 'Embodied Ethical Decision-Making'. *American Journal of Dance Therapy* 29, no. 2 (December 2007): 91–108. https://doi.org/10.1007/s10465-007-9036-5.

13 Bernstein, Bonnie. 'Dancing Beyond Trauma: Women Survivors of Sexual Abuse'. In *Dance and Other Expressive Art Therapies: When Words Are Not Enough*, edited by Fran Levy, Judith Pines Fried, and Fern Leventhal (New York: Routledge, 1995), 54; Bernstein, Bonnie. 'Empowerment-Focused Dance/Movement Therapy for Trauma Recovery'. *American Journal of Dance Therapy* 41, no. 2 (December 2019): 193–213. https://doi.org/10.1007/s10465-019-09310-w.

14 Bernstein, Bonnie. 'Dancing Beyond Trauma: Women Survivors of Sexual Abuse', 2019.

15 Ogden, Pat, Kekuni Minton, and Clare Pain. *Trauma and the Body: A Sensorimotor Approach to Psychotherapy* (Norton Series on Interpersonal Neurobiology) (New York: W. W. Norton & Company, 2006).

16 Kestenberg Amighi et al., 1999, 81.

17 Hackney, 2002.

18 Adler, 2002.

19 Adler, 2002.

20 Pallaro, Patrizia. *Authentic Movement: Moving the Body, Moving the Self, Being Moved: A Collection of Essays*, vol. 2 (London and Philadelphia: Jessica Kingsley Publishers, 2007).

21 Hess, Kyra. 'Witnessing Another, Witnessing Oneself'. *Dance/Movement Therapy Theses* (May 2018). https://core.ac.uk/download/pdf/217287591.pdf.

22 W. Wyman-McGinty, 'The Body in Analysis: Authentic Movement and Witnessing in Analytic Practice'. *The Journal of Analytical Psychology* 43, no. 2 (April 1998): 239–260. https://doi.org/10.1111/1465-5922.00023.

23 Projection is a term used in psychotherapy and rooted in a method developed by Sigmund Freud called psychoanalysis. It describes the process where someone attributes or assigns their own feelings/emotional states/attitudes to someone else as if the other person were experiencing this. It is quite common, as we as humans tend to 'split' the parts that cause us harm or are incongruent with our self-image. However it also may "present itself in areas of artistic creation, play" and through our beliefs. Reference: Novick, Jack, and Kerry Kelly. 'Projection and Externalization'. *The Psychoanalytic Study of the Child* (January 1970). www.tandfonline.com/doi/abs/10.1080/00797308.1970.11823276.

24 Adler, Janet. 'The Collective Body'. In *Authentic Movement: Moving the Body, Moving the Self, Being Moved: A Collection of Essays*, edited by Patrizia Pallaro, vol. 2 (London and Philadelphia: Jessica Kingsley, 1999), 190–208; Tina Stromsted, 'The Dancing Body in Psychotherapy: Reflections on Somatic Psychotherapy and Authentic Movement'. In *Authentic Movement: Moving the Body, Moving the Self, Being Moved*, edited by Patrizia Pallaro (London: Routledge, n.d.), 202–220; Pallaro, 2007.

25 Acarón, 'The Practitioner's Body of Knowledge', 2015; Acarón, 2018.

26 A colloquial expression meaning when someone stops responding to your messages and attempts at communication without an expressly offered reason.

27 Studd and Cox, 2013.

28 Li, J. 'Verticality, Horizontality, and States of the Self: Cognitive Metaphors for the "Spatial Self" in Chinese Autobiographical Writings'. *Metaphor and Symbol* 26 (2010): 68–95.
   Li makes reference to similar spatial body metaphors of horizontality and verticality in Eastern philosophy in relation to the self and, specifically, to verticality as related to development of a sense of identity.

29 Thompson, James. 'Questions on Performances: In Place of War?' *Applied Theatre Research* 1, no. 2 (2013): 149–156; Thompson, James. *Performance Affects: Applied Theatre and the End of Effect* (Basingstoke: Palgrave Macmillan, 2009); Thompson, James. *Digging Up Stories : Applied Theatre, Performance and War* (Manchester: Manchester University Press, 2005).

30 Shweder, Richard A., and Edmund J. Bourne. 'Does the Concept of the Person Vary Cross-Culturally?' In *Cultural Conceptions of Mental Health and Therapy (Culture, Illness, and Healing)*, edited by Anthony J. Marsella and Geoffrey M. White, vol. 4 (Springer Netherlands, 1982), 97–137. http://dx.doi.org/10.1007/978-94-010-9220-3_4; Hofstede, Geert H. *Culture's Consequences: Comparing Values, Behaviors, Institutions, and Organizations Across Nations* (Thousand Oaks, CA: Sage Publications, 2001); Minkov, Michael. *Cross-Cultural Analysis: The Science and Art of Comparing the World's Modern Societies and Their Cultures* (Thousand Oaks, CA: Sage Publications, 2013).

31 Shank and Shirch (2008, 234) term sociocentric cultures as high context cultures and individualistic cultures as low context – these don't necessarily mean that they don't have context, but that they have more to do with whether the context takes more of a priority. Full reference: Shank, Michael, and Lisa Schirch. 'Strategic Arts-Based Peacebuilding'. *Peace & Change* 33, no. 2 (2008): 217–242.

32 Hofstede, Geert. 'Dimensionalizing Cultures: The Hofstede Model in Context'. *Online Readings in Psychology and Culture* 2, no. 1 (2011): 8.

33 Harris, David Alan. 'The Paradox of Expressing Speechless Terror: Ritual Liminality in the Creative Arts Therapies' Treatment of Posttraumatic Distress'. *The Arts in Psychotherapy* 36, no. 2 (2009).

34 Ríos, Sandra, and Thania Acarón. 'Peacebuilding and Dance in Afro-Colombian Funerary Ritual'. In *Peacebuilding and the Arts (Rethinking Peace and Conflict Studies)*, edited by Jolyon Mitchell, Gisselle Vincett, Theodora Hawksley, and Hal Culbertson (Palgrave Macmillan, 2020), 395–413. www.palgrave.com/gp/book/9783030178741.

4

ACTION/NON-ACTION STAGE

Timing and [Non] Commitment

ACTION / NON-ACTION

DOI: 10.4324/9781003360957-5

Body Questions in Practice

> ### Body Questions to Consider in This Chapter
> - What can I commit to?
> - What timing does this need?
> - What actions or next steps can I take/not take?
> - Is Non-Action an option?
> - Do I need to move to a different stage?

In Development

The Action stage is where we reflect on our relationship to the timing of a decision – whether we are committing, retreating, deflecting, anticipating, or just going for it. In 'typical' development, we see this reflected in toddlers as they negotiate the process of learning how to walk. Most caregivers will describe the time when the child negotiates the developmental task to regulate their acceleration and deceleration. Stumbles, running into objects, and losing balance usually occur at this stage. We may observe some children moving too fast, approaching tentatively, and learning how to retreat from situations (walking backwards is yet another skill to master). In their body, children are typically learning to bind the flow of movement and regulate their muscle tension to decelerate. Core muscles need to engage in a different way to propel the body forward. Their bodies navigate stability and mobility in their core and pelvis. The same might occur in the negotiation of using a wheelchair for the first time or a mobility scooter – one will need to negotiate the timing and intricacies of directionality and regulate timing, proximity and redirecting and making a stop.

The task of regulating our bodies in terms of advancing or retreating requires many micro decisions in the body. Some people experience variations of this stage across our lifespan. For example, it might be difficult to accelerate and motivate ourselves towards a goal. Other times we might be accelerating forward too quickly (in body and mind), which makes us feel out of control. We might be too impulsive in our decisions without giving them much thought. At times we could feel more comfortable retreating from situations rather than acting on them. We might retreat, or take too much time to retreat from a situation we know is not good for us. That sense of advancing and retreating is what gets typically negotiated developmentally (Figure 4.1), which later in life translates into negotiations in the Time Effort (BESS). Let's break this down into their movement components:

122

FIGURE 4.1 'Typical' Developmental Stage – Learning to Walk and Balance

Movement Components of the Action/Non-Action Stage

Plane: Sagittal (Wheel)

Two Dimensions: Front

Back and Up   Down

Effort Category: Time

Effort Qualities: Quick   Sustained

Shaping Qualities: Advancing   Retreating

In BESS, this is called the Wheel Plane (Figure 4.2) or Sagittal Plane. Sagittal is a word often used in anatomy, which refers to a suture on the top of the skull, which divides it into left and right halves[1], and this slice projects forward and back. Extend your arm up and then trace a curved line with your fingertips as far forward as you can reach without bending your arm (see top half Figure 4.2) Keep drawing an arc moving downwards, then keep moving upward towards the back and close the circle by moving up over your head again.

Some images that come to mind when thinking of the Sagittal Plane are a hamster wheel, rolling pin (baking), bicycle or a steam roller, a front roll, or swimming in freestyle/front crawl. A funky way to try the Sagittal Plane is to roll your forearms forward and back (like the 70s style dancing) (Figure 4.2 – bottom half).

FIGURE 4.2 The Sagittal or Wheel Plane

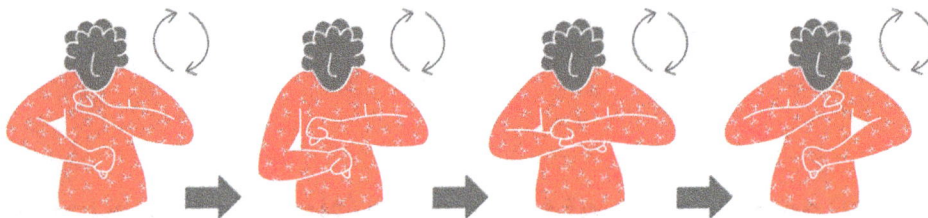

The Sagittal (Wheel) Plane

The Sagittal Plane: 70s Style Movement

What other movements can you do in the Sagittal Plane? They can be full-body movements or gestures.

Of all the Effort Qualities, Time is the one we are most used to addressing explicitly, fluctuating between sustained and quick time (Figure 4.3). The interesting point of reflection here is how we engage with advancing and retreating – combining the acceleration and deceleration of time, which forms rhythms and gives us insight into pacing and planning.

FIGURE 4.3 Time Effort Continuum

Sustained TIME Quick

Movement Break: Advancing and Retreating (Shaping Qualities)

Link for audio description playlist: www.you-tube.com/playlist?list=PLtGm4qYm5yBQZqgY5_PFpJHa4jgs2R6Cw

In the other stages, we explored each element separately, but here we will do a combined exploration of Effort and Shape regarding the Time Effort. In decision-making, this correlates to the dynamic rhythm and pacing you will encounter. You can do this sitting or standing, and remember you can activate any body part and move in any kinesphere level with these qualities.

We will start with a check-in with some energising movement. Close your eyes and start bringing awareness to your toes. Please remember that if you have any mobility issues, you can adapt this activity as you need and pick different body parts to engage with. Shrug your shoulders with small movements or take big shrugs, tensing the shoulder muscles and releasing them. Do that a couple of times, inhaling and exhaling. Then move your elbows, arms, and hands. See if you can keep accelerating the beats/rhythm and decelerating them. Involve the head and be mindful of the breath. Take some moments to move on your own time. Notice what needs shaking off or a stomping out. Open your eyes (if you haven't done so already) and start taking in the space around you.

In the next stages of the movement, you can continue the same sentiment of the warm-up, but then let's add attention to the space. We will start advancing and retreating. **Advance towards an object in the room or a point in space** (Figure 4.4). Try different ways of approaching this object. If you are walking around the room, you can try different paths towards an object or point in the room (same if you are in a wheelchair). Here are some illustrations for ideas of paths you can engage with going forward or backward: **straight, curvy, spiral, zig zag, meandering, circular paths** (see Figure 4.5).

An alternative is to draw the paths or use different body parts to trace different shapes in the air. Change objects or points in the room when you feel you have explored them sufficiently.

Explore accelerating and decelerating as you advance towards something. Then experiment with retreating. **Try different attitudes** now: advancing with curiosity, doubt, tiredness, excitement, or any feeling tone you feel fits. Notice the timing each of these involves. If you have a partner or movement volunteer with you and want to try that in pairs, feel free to explore this. Approaching someone (something), retreating away. Notice the differences between certain objects in the room, or when you visualise certain people. If you work with groups, you can try this activity in a circle, in small groups or pairs.

FIGURE 4.4 Shaping Qualities – Advancing and Retreating

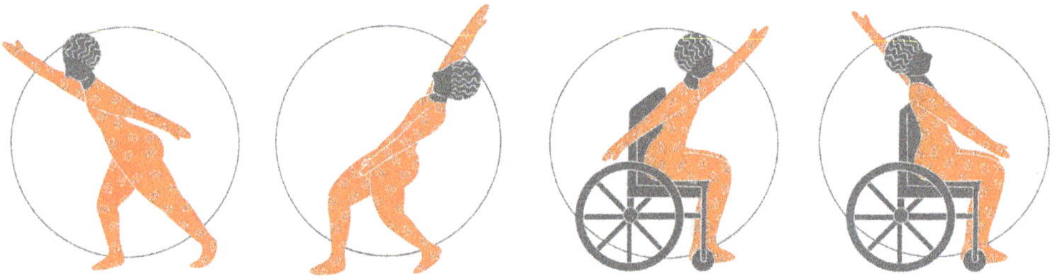

FIGURE 4.5 Paths Across the Space in Movement, Words, Art, and Thought

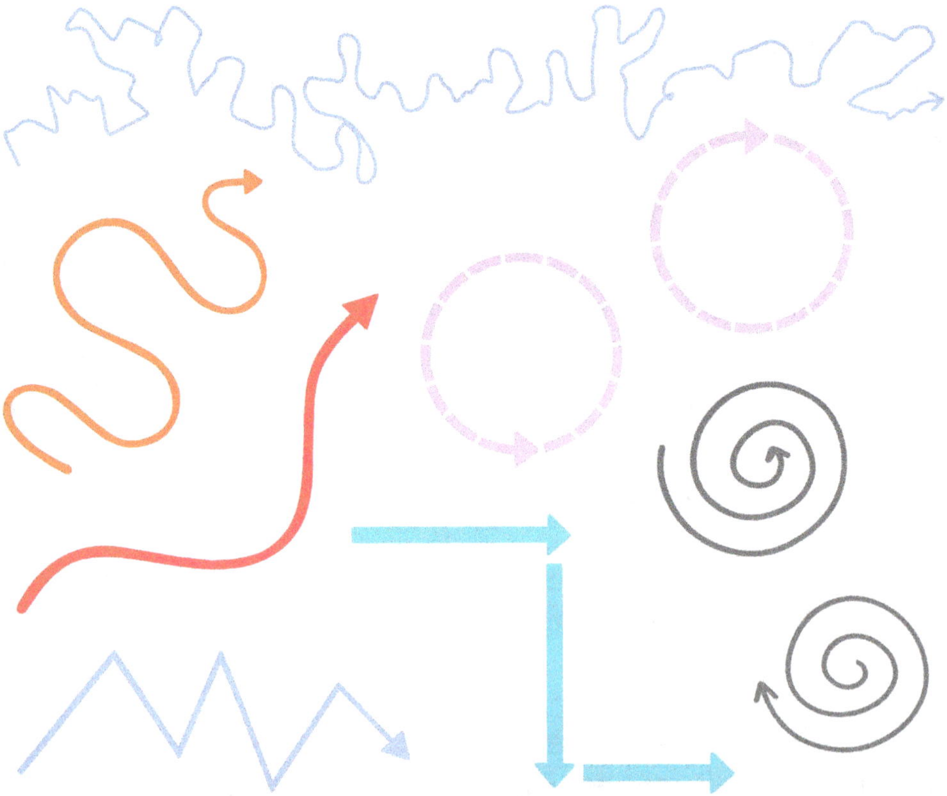

Effort Qualities: Time (Quick vs. Sustained) – Movement Break Continued

Suggested Music

Track Title: Action / Non-Action

Duration: 04:22

Music Composer: Ross Whyte

Link for QR Code: https://youtu.be/HjeKC6o8264?si=dia0HEABxp4uUzOm>

Now, we will pay more attention to the Effort Qualities here – Try just playing with Time on its own – **explore sudden movements, delay transitions, and move abruptly between rhythms**. Create different rhythms that accelerate and decelerate. Notice what happens in your body as the quickness increases, then vary advancing and retreating. What does your body do? Does it increase pressure or become Light (Weight Effort), or does it become expansive in the space or more focused (Space Effort)? Do you notice the level of tension in your body when you become faster or wind down (Flow/Tension)? Which types of movements do you prefer?

We are combining Efforts now to see how that might start to influence your decision. Timing might feel rushed, too slow, changing too gradually, or too abruptly. How is this linking to potential ways of actioning a decision? Is non-actioning an option?

Reflexive Exercise: Time Effort Continuum

Here is music for both Quick and Sustained Efforts. If you are curious about your relationship to Time, have a go at exploring these separately and attaching the timing to current situations in your life.

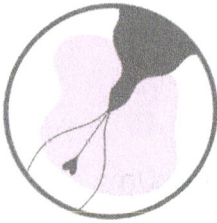

Suggested Music

Track Title: Time Efforts: Quickness

Duration: 7:54

Music Composer: Ross Whyte

Link for QR code: https://youtu.be/Hwx-tKeSsMc?si=NdxSTSBpZt2d3tZ5>

Suggested Music

Track Title: Time Efforts: Sustained

Duration: 7:47

Music Composer: Ross Whyte

Link for QR code: https://youtu.be/9ZsTf9S8zng?si=JoCKMEXvoRLZBKqm>

In terms of Effort Qualities, before we move on to applications of Time, we should stop and reflect on our own preferences for time. Of course, your ability to accelerate/decelerate or approach situations with a particular rhythm or pace will vary. How flexible are you in terms of our own uses of time to accommodate other people's rhythms or pace in a situation? Do you shift quickly, or do you struggle with matching quicker paces? Are you easily influenced by others' uses of time? Or do you maintain your pace no matter what happens? This might be a more complicated reflection since it often is situation specific. But in general, what is your preference in terms of Time? How easily can you access the ends of the spectrum (breadth) before you start to feel uncomfortable?

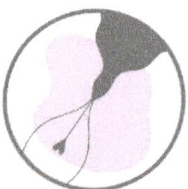

Carve out a reflexive moment to colour in your preference and breadth in Figure 4.6. Remember, these may change throughout your life depending on what is happening. Nevertheless, keep reflecting on your propensity for time. Perhaps there could be several spectrums here you can draw out: one for your default (left to your own devices), one for stressful situations, one for engagement with others? Any others you can think of?

FIGURE 4.6 Time Effort Spectrum Reflection

Please fill in your preferences below:

Thania's Example

In Figure 4.6 (bottom half), you can see my sense of timing is the Effort category I feel most comfortable with and have the most breadth. However, I know I prefer Quick time – I often want things done quickly and get impatient with bureaucratic delays or inefficiency. In my workshops, timing has slowed down for me as I have gotten more experienced and seen the value of processing, marinating, and digesting experiences. I also cram less things into sessions to allow for more time for reflection. Everyone has a category that they feel most comfortable with. I feel Time is mine – what is yours? Space? Weight?

Action/Non-Action and the Sagittal Plane in Daily Life

Most interactions with others and the environment often entail a negotiation of time. The pace of our lives at times differs from how we would want it to be. If life is going at a quicker pace, we might be rushing between things, have fast turnarounds, do (too much) social media scrolling, and be exposed to much more stimuli for our body to sift through. This might be quite different if in this stage in your life, the pace is slower, there is less stimulation and it is a quieter period. Many coping mechanisms come into play here to help us self-regulate when encountering overwhelming stimuli. We often adapt to other people's rhythms, level of energy, and negotiate these in group settings, which can become overwhelming. We might need to retreat away from our body, cognitively rationalise a situation, seek out isolation, shut down, want to distract or numb ourselves, or escape.

> Body Questions explored here can help us understand how our body is coping with the pace of our work/personal life/relationships:
>
> - Are your preferences in Time aligned with what you are doing in life?
> - Is the pace and timing of things in your life serving you?
> - Are these qualities sustainable?

The Sagittal Plane correlates to advancing or retreating from a situation, person, conflict, object, etc.[2], combined with quickness/acceleration or sustained uses of time (Sustained Effort, deceleration). When we are making decisions, once we have clarified what the options at hand are, ideally, we will need to decide the appropriate timing when this decision can be actioned. This framing allows many other questions to flow: if the timing is not achievable or realistic – is this the path we need to take?

Unfortunately, as you have gauged from the types of the questions I have been asking – ascertaining the adequate time for a task/path is challenging. If the task is too huge, breaking it down into manageable mini tasks might help. Determining whether this is a short-term, mid-term, or long-term decision can clarify what is needed. Lamb's framework within managerial settings describes the Action stage as Commitment, which requires the body to begin "mobilising to implement both tactically and in longer term [decisions], staging what has been intended initiating and pacing action adroitly to attain goals and avoid pitfalls"[3].

In the Action stage, we examine the potential outcome of a decision through our body. We envision its possible pathways and the consequences of our decision (through reflexivity). If a decision is only left at the Intention stage, one might feel stuck in our own needs and priorities without clarifying ways of actualising what was identified. Too much emphasis on exploration in the Attention stage might incur a delay, procrastination, or higher anxiety around a deadline. Examining pacing, timing, retreating, and advancing towards a particular option in a decision might help support people in understanding their own approaches, patterns, and cycles within a decision.

Many environments place severe importance on action as the ultimate goal. Placing sole emphasis on Action becomes problematic when there is no time dedicated for introspection, assertion of priorities and needs and a connection with the impact of a decision on the body. However, it is also important to consider that perhaps this might not be the right time for you to make a decision (Non-Action). You might need to spend more time in other decision-making stages, or perhaps the Action is not acting on it! Unlike solution-focused models, the Decision-Making Through Movement framework presented here is not intended to put pressure on the individual to enact or 'fix' a problem. Exploring what you can commit to and work towards is a way to begin tying in the priorities and needs identified in Intention to pathways towards a particular goal/decision.

In Professional Practice

There are several professions that come to mind when I think about the Action elements of this stage: salespeople, executive assistants, occupational therapists, physical therapists, performance technicians – the 'Doers'. People who are oriented towards 'getting things done' and usually assess and evaluate quickly have a tendency towards this stage.

In the workplace, there might be additional pressure to act quickly on difficult decisions or to act on things constantly without having enough time to assess/ evaluate them. This can make employees feel they have little control of their actions, and the pressure might increase stress or lead to impulsive actions or employees making errors. On the other hand, perhaps the workplace is not action oriented, perhaps managers spend too much time on the evaluation or surveying of issues, which means action plans take very long, are circumvented, or thrown through more bureaucratic processes. This in turn can demotivate employees since they might not feel their considerations and suggestions are being taken seriously.

Equally, a workplace might be stuck in the Intention stage, reiterating its core needs but not assessing options and not taking any action. This might cause employees to feel that the organisation is not valuing them or that it is inflexible. Many workplace dynamics have a particular positioning in terms of the Action/Non-Action stage. It then becomes important to understand our role in the dynamic. What is your embodied experience of the workplace dynamic? What aspect of the decision-making process do you feel is being prioritised? How does your preference line/not line up with these? This can also be considered in terms of your personal life as well.

Coping Mechanisms: The Pros and Cons of the Action Stage

When you think about commitment and action in your life in general, what comes to mind? Where in your body do you feel it? What qualities emerge? Before we explore the full movement qualities of a particular situation/decision, we can begin by inquiring into the following Body Question: What are my embodied coping mechanisms for taking Action?

We will explore a movement task related to the three most common ways we could engage with the Action stage: avoiding, procrastinating, and acting impulsively. The idea is to explore what this coping mechanism is and understand them from an embodied perspective. These mechanisms are usually there for a reason, and we can then identify and reflect on how these are resonating with you at present.

Movement Break: Journey Maps for Action

Suggested Music

Track Title: Journey Map (Eve)

Duration: 2:36

Music Composer: Ross Whyte

Link for QR Code: https://youtu.be/T7T6UKJ0ywQ?si=5oPQa5lW1q-d7lHx

---

Journey Maps is an activity I have adapted from dance movement therapy and dance education practitioners, and I have applied different configurations tailored to each client group I have worked with. I first came across this activity as part of the audition for my Dance Education master's degree at New York University since it helped the facilitator, dance movement therapist Dr Miriam Berger, get a sense of how we were able to reflect on our professional identity. This activity is often used in creative movement, drama, drama therapy, dance, and dance movement therapy since it helps break down a complex process into manageable parts. The therapeutic application makes the connection between the movement aspects and reflecting on our daily life or representing our situation via movement, as we discussed in Chapter 1.

Begin by finding a neutral position and do a brief scanning of your body and your breath. Find some movements that feel nice in your body – explore what feels pleasurable in movement.

Create a movement phrase to represent you and where you are at the moment. A phrase is a short sequence of one to three movements that you can repeat and remember. It can be anything that says something about how you are feeling now or how your day has been! You can create a series of small gestures or big shapes (frozen postures). They might use your full range of movement or very minimal movement: All contributions are valid! If you need some inspiration to create the phrase, you can think of your own identity/personality. These movements can represent who you are at home, with friends, or at the workplace. If this is hard at the moment, just embody the movements that you first come up with. There is no pressure to create anything aesthetically pleasing, just a movement that expresses something. If one to three movements are too little, try three to five movements. You can also start with just one movement or shape. Repeat this sequence of movements a few times and remember it (you can also take a photo/video on your device just in case).

1. **Pick three points on the floor of the space** (see example in Figure 4.7) which are further away from where you are standing/sitting now, and then pick a starting point (a total of three places). If you are sitting/laying down, you can do these next steps in one place. If you can ambulate, then give a name or label the three points:

   Point A: Starting point
   Point B: The situation you are currently in
   Point C: Short-term goal

FIGURE 4.7 Journey Map Example – Three Key Points

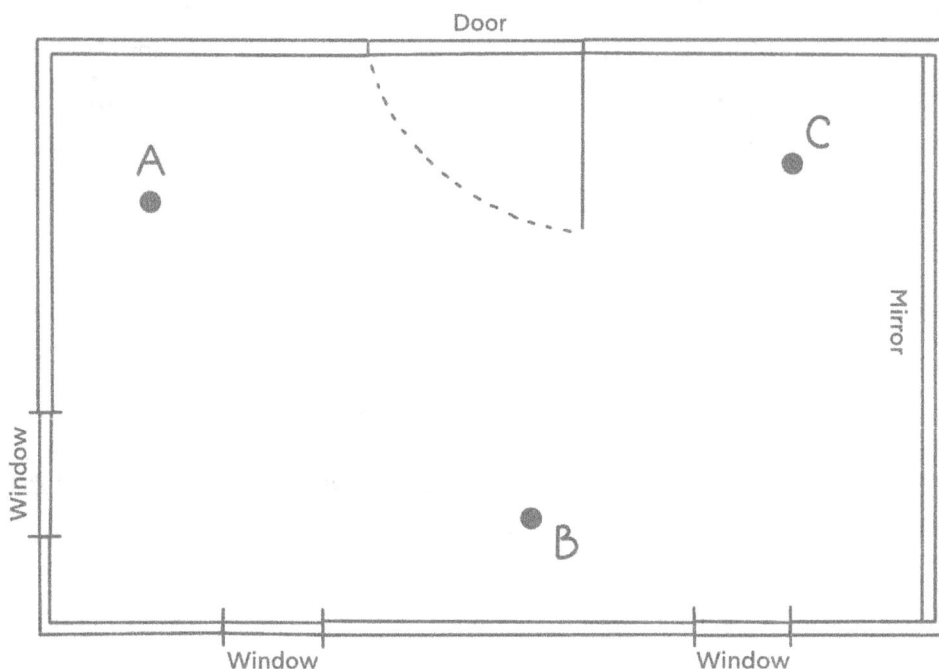

2. **Think of a short-term goal** or something you would like to do or achieve. It can be something quite concrete, for example: a weekend away, taking a class, learning something new, going to the gym, or meeting friends. In the workplace, it can be a target you want to reach or completion of a task or a position you aspire to. These are just some ideas – make the goal achievable and manage expectations. Remember you can always modify this task and make it your own. I have many variations of this exercise with reflections on journeys and paths – I picked a goal this time but there are many possibilities: strengths/blocks, past/future, among others.

3. **Choose a shape or movement to represent this goal for Point B. Connect to the qualities that this goal represents for you.** There is no right or wrong movement for this. Try not to overthink it – I always say there are no accidents in movement: Even the most unconscious of choices can have a lot of meaning down the line. But for now – just choose a still shape or short movement that you are reminded of when you picture your goal. Remember our deal from the beginning: No Judgement!

4. **Let's look at the relationship between your Self and the Goal.**
   Standing version: Explore a trajectory between Point A and Point B as we began exploring in Figure 4.7. A trajectory is another word for direction of travel. In

creative movement, there are several ways in which we locomotive across the floor, which practitioners and researchers have called paths[4]. We explored these paths earlier in Figure 4.5. We can use these paths as our movement vocabulary to represent our ways of approaching the goal.

Sitting version: You can create movements that represent these trajectories while sitting. You can involve your torso, arms, and any body part you are able to enact this or represent these via drawing.

5. **We are creating a map now, which includes**

- a starting point (A) with movement phrase or shape
- a path between Point A and Point B
- a shape or short movement phrase at Point B
- a path between Point B and Point C
- an ending movement phrase or shape.

Another alternative is to draw this out first on paper as a map (see Figure 4.8) and then recreating the map by moving in the space.

6. **Exploration of Trajectories:** Start with your movement phrase, and then let's try different trajectories from Point A to Point B to Point C. This is going to be your Journey Map. Notice if the original movement phrases change or need some changes. Figure 4.8 is an example drawn by Eve, which we will come back to later.

FIGURE 4.8 Journey Map Example (With Paths)

Now we will give these paths a feeling/attitude state (sort of like a role play).

Let's start with a trajectory between point A and point B. You can try walking, moving, dancing, or a particular move that represents this relationship. Remember you don't always have to walk forwards, you can try moving sideways, backwards or change direction, as long as you keep yourself safe.

Try Going from B to Point C. Now try the whole journey or segments with confidence, calmness, excitement, procrastination, and other attitudes you feel you want to try out. Does it change your original intention? Does it offer a new perspective?

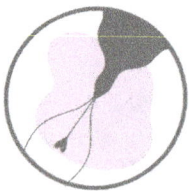

Reflection – Take a moment to draw, write, or move how this experience may translate into your orientation towards Action/Non-Action and commitment. What effort and shape qualities did you embody?

As part of the book's process, I sent a prompt to Eve (Figure 4.8) to use the *Journey Maps* exercise to represent past, present, and future selves in her professional life. Then I asked Ross to generate some music to respond to Eve's journey. We sent it back to Eve so that she could suggest modifications to the music, as a sort of visual art-music-movement postcard. Eve had never done this before and never explained to us what her journey was in the end. This is an important aspect of the work, which underlines the importance of symbolism, and how it doesn't need words. It is amazing to have a piece of Eve's life represented here, which you can also witness by playing the music as you follow the journey drawn in Figure 4.8. Going back to your own journey map, you can add as many points and perspectives as you want to. I like to sometimes even travel backwards across the points (C-B-A) to reflect on whether this changes some of the qualities of reflection. I enjoy creating shapes for each point because shapes help crystallise a situation and offer some anchor points. I often video tape these journeys to watch back and use them as a reflection tool, which you can try as well.

Representing things through the arts help us 'get out of our head'. I am hoping you can make your own versions down the line if you find this approach useful.

Movement Break: Abrupt vs. Gradual Transitions in the Action/Non-Action Stage

A movement aspect which is valuable to be explored within this stage is the quality of transitions: Abrupt or Gradual. Take a moment to experiment with these two concepts. Make a repetitive movement and keep it consistent for a while. Try changing it quite abruptly and notice how that feels in your body. Then go back to the original movement. Change little things about the movement: the timing, the direction, the Weight of it; you can play with changing a minor aspect of its shape. Bit by bit it can morph into a completely different movement. Go back to the original movement again. Try an abrupt transition. Change everything about this movement. You can give this a go with a partner and practise different transitions. Which ones were easier or harder to follow? Which transitions felt more satisfying? Frustrating?

Adapting, negotiating, or effecting transitions occur consciously or unconsciously. Sometimes we exert the transitions, or these are enforced upon us by external factors. The potential impact of a decision often involves reflecting on the type of change involved. Does it need an abrupt change? Or a gradual one? Do we need to accelerate? Decelerate? Approach, retreat, or redirect? As any transition brings varying degrees of anxiety, it is important to consider the feelings, thoughts, images, and/or sensations that abrupt or gradual shifts provoke.

Case Example: Sagittal Plane in the Caring Professions

In the early days of The Body Hotel, before it was a formalised company, I was asked to lead a workshop for occupational therapists in Puerto Rico for a private company which focused on supporting children with additional support needs. As we explored the different planes, I noticed their readiness for the Sagittal Plane. I thought that this perhaps had to do with working with children. The usual propensity for action and energy level required for this client group is very high, and so I didn't think twice about this. However, as we started exploring the Horizontal Plane in more depth, the mood in the room shifted. This intensified when moving between Horizontal to Vertical Planes in movement. Some participants became very reflexive, and one of them burst into tears. Any emotional expression in the group is always welcomed, and I wanted this feeling to feel contained and the participant to feel seen, as these themes could potentially be triggering for people. I approached the participants in the debrief, asking the feeling states evoked throughout key moments in the group. Most participants mentioned they rarely felt they had the time to slow down and consider themselves and their needs. They often instinctively were on an Action paradigm, due to the high demands of their work and client group. In having the space to explore options, they noticed that their whole profession and life were always geared towards acting. They began to identify that they needed to carve out space for the other stages, to replenish and gather energy for the work with the children. Actioning all the time meant for this participant that other aspects of self-care, rest, and reflection were sacrificed.

This is important when we reflect on the decision-making through movement system as a whole, and particularly when we analyse our own propensities towards action or non-action. This stage brings some interesting Body Questions as to how commitment shows up in our body. This stage enables us to understand how our body processes action and actualises intention and whether this commitment/lack thereof has an impact on our life, work, or relationships.

Culture and Caveats

Every chapter has needed an injection of cultural subjectivity, and this one is no exception. At the risk of sounding political, capitalism has motivated an Action-first paradigm which wires us as humans to always strive forward to compete. However, this is not true of all societies as their own cultural values will be different. There will be some cultures where the greater good of the community will supersede individual success. Some microenvironments might also put less pressure on outcome/performance objectives. For example, artistic residencies offer the space to explore a work-in-progress without the pressure of a performance. The arts therapies also prioritise the therapeutic process over aesthetic outcomes.

There are other areas where process is valued over product and some cultures where this is true as well. This is why I valued including Non-Action as a possibility, which hasn't really been talked much about in earlier discussions of this system.

Other cultures/environments might also want to curb actioning or challenging the status quo, which can also disrupt processes of change. The importance of dance/movement and its role in activism and social justice, plus its cultural significance, became evident when I was researching violence prevention and interviewing practitioners based around the world for my PhD. We have seen in history whole regimes suppress individual characteristics, dissent, and community voices. Examples of these can be found in my doctoral work – with historical instances such as the tango dancing protest to preserve Taksim Gezi Park in Türkiye in 2013. There are numerous historical incidences where even dance has been complicit in this process of suppression of action, as well as in the voicing of social justice[5]. For example, dance was used to perpetuate political affiliations for President Seko in the 60s and 70s in the Democratic Republic of Congo, then called Zaire, or used by Khmer Rouge soldiers to march and wipe out cultural heritage by prohibiting dances that were not part of the dominant regime in Cambodia between 1975–79[6]. Rhythm is the universal organiser[7], which helps us find our flow and direction and helps us coordinate and organise. These two sides of the coin need to be acknowledged as dance isn't always a panacea, and Action is not always benign. This is why it is important to consider the themes that emerge out of reflecting on the proportion of time and energy spent at each of the stages, which we will examine in Chapter 8.

It is important to resource the other stages at times to also prevent impulsive actions and violent actions or repair relationships after ruptures have taken place[8]. The ability to view one's culture critically with positives and flaws within their context is a contributing factor of ongoing reflexive practice.

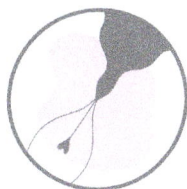

- What does your culture/environment/microculture value in terms of this stage?
- How do you feel in relationship to the pressure to act?
- Does this align/misalign with your environment?

Chapter Conclusion

In this chapter we have been exploring your movement relationship to commitment and action. In this stage, we negotiate the timing and concretisation of the decision. We might want to delay or make the matter urgent. We reflect on whether we are anticipating the timing of decisions, or whether it feels like the appropriate time to act or review other stages. We explore how much commitment a decision or transition will involve – and whether this is sustainable within this period.

Our relationship to how adaptable we are, and how flexible we can be with the timing of a decision, underlies the Body Questions asked during this stage. Resourcing our Time Effort Qualities is a fundamental resource in the process of analysing a decision, and how we engage with the possibility of committing to an outcome is the basis of all movement exploration.

REVIEW POINTS ON THE ACTION/NON-ACTION STAGE

- Action/Non-Action is linked to commitment, planning, and transforming ideas into concrete tasks/goals.
- Stage is related to the 'typical' developmental task of regulating acceleration and deceleration.
- Movement Qualities: Involves advancing/retreating shaping qualities, quick, and/or sustained effort qualities, and up/down + front/back directions.
- Getting stuck in this stage might mean we are placing a lot of importance on acting, and not a lot of reflecting on options or deciding what is important.
- Non-action is always an option. Evaluate the pressure needed to act.
- This stage looks at Commitment, while also inviting the option of Non-Action or revisiting other stages
- It involves the negotiation of Time and deciding whether the time allocated is reasonable, sustainable, and appropriate for the decision or transition
- Research links the Action stage to activism and social justice.

SKIP, BOOKMARK, OR CONTINUE

- If you have decided you want to continue in the order of the book, you can continue on to Chapter 5 "Flow/Tension Stage". It might be important that you reconnect to the source of tension/joy before proceeding to a commitment to a decision.
- You might have realised that your plan might not be feasible just yet, and you need to research more options and assess your environment. Your Non-Action might involve more consideration (skip to Chapter 2 "Attention Stage").
- Your plan might have been unsustainable, unrealistic, and/or not connected to what you need. Or you might need more clarity into what is essential (skip to Chapter 3 "Intention Stage").
- You might want to dig deeper into how your Movement Style might be influencing your attitude towards Commitment or Non-Action (skip to Chapter 6 "Movement Styles").

Notes

1 Kapit, Wynn, and Lawrence Elson. *The Anatomy Coloring Book*, 4th ed. (Pearson, 2013); Calais-Germain, Blandine. *Anatomy of Movement* (Kagaku Shinbun Sha, 1993), 2–3.

2 Laban and Lawrence, 1974.

3 Brenda L. Connors and Richard Rende, 'Embodied Decision-Making Style: Below and Beyond Cognition'. *Frontiers in Psychology* 9 (2018): 3. https://doi.org/10.3389/fpsyg.2018.01123.

4 Hutchinson Guest, Ann. *Your Move: A New Approach to the Study of Movement and Dance / Teacher's Guide* (Taylor & Francis Ltd., 1983).

5 Acarón, 'The Practitioner's Body of Knowledge', 2015, 49–51.

6 Jackson, Naomi, and Toni Shapiro-Phim, eds. *Dance, Human Rights and Social Justice: Dignity in Motion* (Plymouth, UK: Scarecrow Press, Inc., 2008); Shapiro-Phim, Toni. 'Dance, Music and the Nature of Terror in Democratic Kampuchea'. In *Annihilating Difference: The Anthropology of Genocide*, edited by Alexander Laban Hinton (University of California Press, 2002), 179–193; Acarón, 'The Practitioner's Body of Knowledge', 2015, 41, 49–51, 190–192.

7 Schmais, Claire, 'Healing Processes in Group Dance Therapy'. *American Journal of Dance Therapy* 8, no. 1 (December 1985): 17–36. https://doi.org/10.1007/BF02251439.

8 Eddy, 2009, 93–143.

5

FLOW/TENSION STAGE

Bodily States

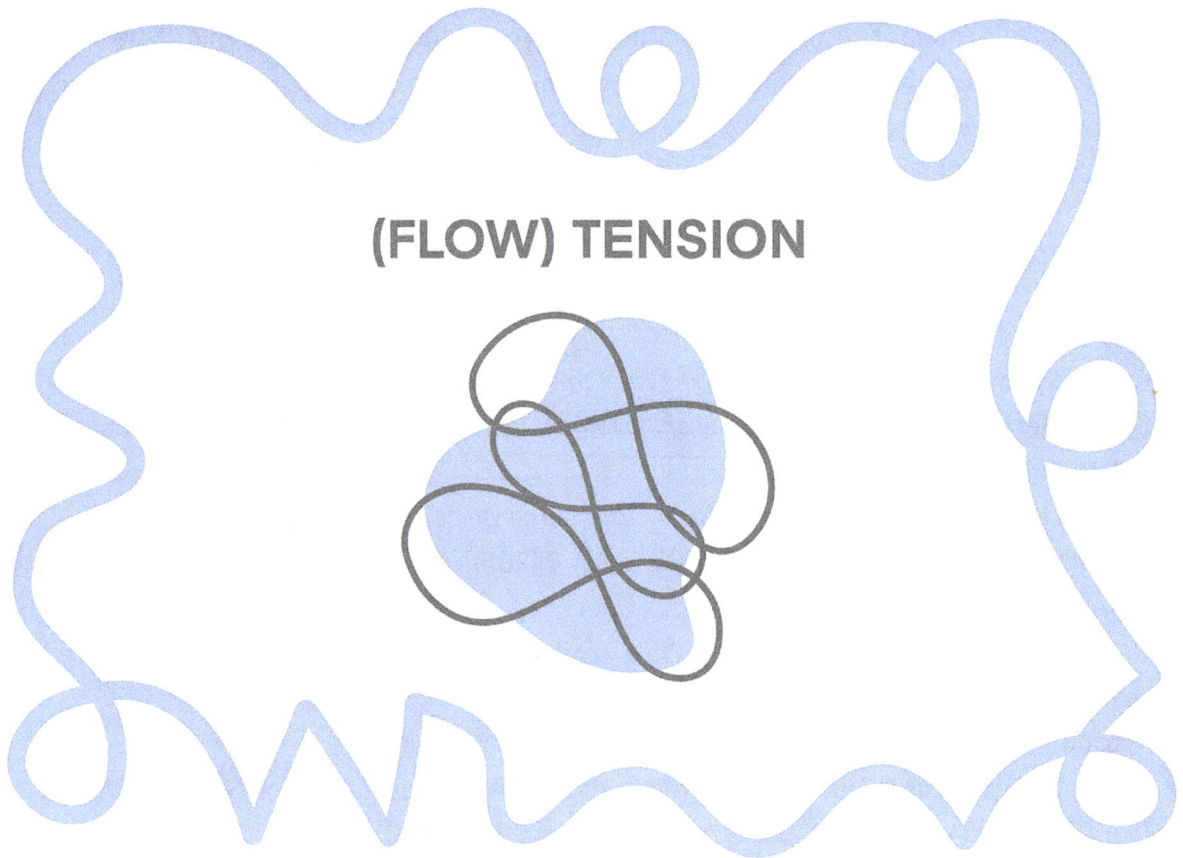

(FLOW) TENSION

DOI: 10.4324/9781003360957-6

Body Questions to Consider in This Chapter

- What tensions exist?
- What sparks joy/pleasure (Constructive Tension)?
- What produces annoyance/discomfort and/or curiosity?
- Where do I feel this in my body?

Flow/Tension is found in all organic systems in our bodies. Motion is key to our internal and external functioning, and the acknowledgement of held tension in our bodies underlies all body awareness. Unfortunately, the way the body usually comes into consciousness is when there is pain, injury, or illness[1]. Movement practices can help re-establish this connection with the body and foment a new relationship with the information it may provide. The general Body Question that is asked when exploring this stage is, "How is tension reflected in my body?"

In Development

Flow/Tension relates to internal processes of contraction and release that occur in our muscles and inner organs. In its most basic form: Flow (within the BESS system) is composed of two elements: Bound Flow (tension or holding) and Free Flow (release). Our months in utero are spent primarily using Flow/Tension. Lamb and Davies comment that, "the concept of Flow is most easily explained by imagining the amoeba-like movements of an infant before any social interaction has required it to discipline its actions". In the womb, babies kick, move, and stretch, which is essential to the development of joints, muscles, and bones[2]. They will be exposed to all the sounds of the inner workings of the pregnant woman/person's body and will engage with tactile stimulation and exploration (Figure 5.1)[3].

Giving birth involves the highest expression of tension and release as muscular contractions expand to encompass a small human. From our muscular system to digestive system to respiratory system, our body is engaged in a constant state of fluctuation between Bound Flow and Free Flow.

> The flow factor varies between the qualities of binding and freeing. Binding the flow results in controlled or even tense actions that can be readily arrested. On the other hand, freely flowing actions are relaxed, easy-going and hard to stop immediately[4].

FIGURE 5.1 Developmental Stage – In Utero

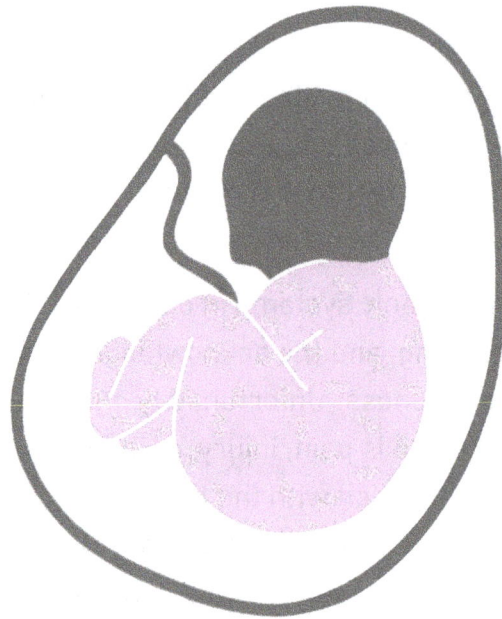

Flow is therefore engaged in a constant state of negotiation across our whole body, and as our body is made up of anatomical systems of tension and release, Flow/Tension is the most basic element of how we are alive. Our autonomic nervous system, for example, which is connected to breath, muscle tension and internal organs in humans and some species of animals, has an evolutionary connection to our survival instincts. When human beings perceive themselves as being threatened, the body triggers survival responses, commonly known as Fight, Flight, or Freeze responses[5], which recently also includes the Fawn response, which is the attempt to appease[6]. These survival body mechanisms are regulated by the body's sympathetic nervous system, which activates the body in stress. Your body will react, for example, by having an accelerated heart rate and breath, increased sensory awareness, hormonal release, sweating, and – in extreme cases of defence – urination/defecation. These responses may also occur in minor degrees of perceived threat. The parasympathetic nervous system (which helps relax/calm the body) works in tandem with the sympathetic nervous (system that activates the body) system, helping to regulate these responses into more relaxed or regulated states[7].

Experiencing a traumatic event or a series of traumatic events can impact our sense of how we perceive and interact with the world. Body-based trauma research has been dedicated to understanding how trauma has an impact on the body, and how intervening with the body can help with dysregulated responses. Some well-known theorists who focus on the effects of trauma on the body are Peter Levine[8], Babette Rothschild[9], and Bessel van der Kolk[10], among many others. There is also exciting new research on multicultural lenses of trauma and dance/movement therapy, as DMTs have long been in the trenches of the trauma-body relationship since the 1950s[11]. The main issue discussed by DMTs Rivera, Furcron, and Beardall is the importance of also understanding underrepresented voices within trauma research and the link of these analyses to social action and social justice[12]. It is crucial to understand the cultural nuance of the body to include Global Majority perspectives within the literature which has historically prioritised White, Western, heteronormative bodies.

There has been a rise of research in neurophysiological interventions in the treatment of trauma which we can link to the Flow/Tension stage. Polyvagal theory, explored by psychologist Dr Stephen Porges, researches the role of our neural circuits in self-regulation, attachment, and social interactions. The theory explains how the vagal system can be disrupted by trauma[13]. The vagal nerves are the main nerves of the parasympathetic nervous system, which help control our digestion, heart rate and immune responses, and even your mood[14]. Porges particularly emphasises that we are often not aware of many of these processes, and that in the "neural circuits located in and near the temporal cortex . . . our brain has the capacity to detect the intentionality of biological movement including body movements, gestures, facial expressions, and vocalisations"[15]. Polyvagal theory in practice suggests that by understanding how these systems interrelate, we can therefore design interventions which address post-traumatic stress[16]. This is helpful for decision-making, as stress is a major factor in decisions and life transitions. Many of the polyvagal theory exercises involve/suggest movement, which has contributed to the wealth of evidence base for DMT and other somatic therapies[17].

In decision-making, we start to understand our resistance to change, self-sabotage patterns, and how to self-regulate to face challenges and opportunities. Porges further suggests that movement in social interactions can play a positive role in communicating cues of safety, which can help us shift our mood and emotional state[18]. I introduced a taster of polyvagal theory here to help us understand that this work is part of something larger and correlates well to current research on the delicate and co-dependent relationship between body and mind. This research continues to contribute evidence to what movement specialists have known in practice for years.

Shifting back to decision-making through movement, the importance of the Flow/ Tension stage is to cultivate the practice of listening to the body and understand the cues it is offering. The Body Questions also open up questioning how the external environment might have an impact on your situation. In this stage, we will be looking at the role of breath, muscular tension/release, resistance, and/or joy of movement.

Movement Components of the Flow/Tension Stage

Flow is regarded as the "relative degree of control in a movement"[19]. Kestenberg and colleagues claim that movement is endlessly oscillating between the Bound Flow and Free Flow[20]. The quickest way to understand Flow/Tension is to try some short exercises.

Movement Break: Flow Effort Qualities (Bound/ Free Flow)

Suggested Music

Track Title: Flow/Tension

Duration: 01:08

Music Composer: Ross Whyte

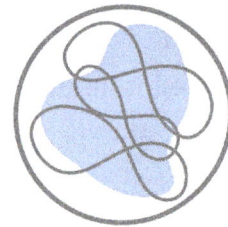

Link for QR Code: https://youtu.be/-LnCGS-dPh0?si=z2m0hPkUOM7p2cuj

---

Hold your arm in front of you and gently grab your bicep (upper arm muscle) with your opposing hand (see Figure 5.2). Place your top four fingers on the top of the bicep and your thumb below the arm to feel the triceps muscle (the muscle running from your elbow bone to your shoulder on the back). **Bend your elbow a couple of times by flexing** (bodybuilder style). What do you notice?

The action of extending the elbow needs the opposite reactions to happen. To bend the elbow, the biceps muscle will need to flex/bind (called the *agonist muscle*), and the triceps muscles will need to release (*antagonist muscle*) making up the basic actions of Bound/Free Flow. The combinations of agonist/antagonist muscles help you sit, stand, raise your arms, and do most actions.

FIGURE 5.2 Arm Flexing Exercise: Flow

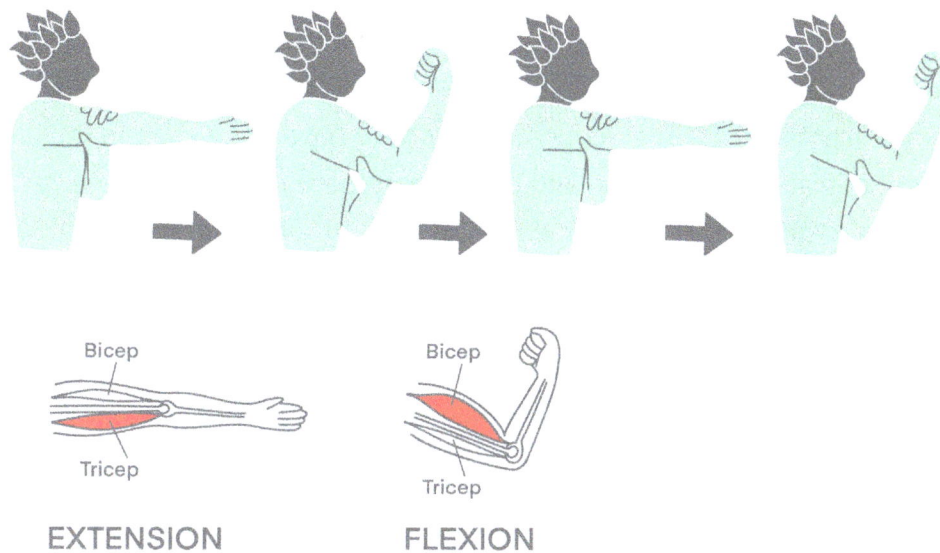

You will often feel Bound Flow more in your body as you notice the tension. Free Flow, however, is difficult to understand at times since it is very difficult to observe in its purest essence. Breath is sometimes the constant reminder of Free Flow, but in my workshops, the quickest way to access Free Flow was to spin as fast as safely possible and notice what their arms do naturally when they are relaxed while spinning. If you are sitting down, you can try and shake your hands. You see the release in the fingers as the tension is reduced. Free Flow is also experienced when we get enough momentum just before we apply tension to slow down or stop. I was taught that the moment when runners are mid-momentum in a race before they need to slow down showcases Free Flow. What other ways have you found you can experiment with Free Flow?

Flow/Tension in Decision-Making – Ongoing Connection to Our Body

Lamb initially excluded Flow from decision-making frameworks, stating it should be analysed independently and needed more careful consideration, stating it was an "element in its own right, rather than a separate category of the three Effort qualities"[21]. Movement analyst Judith Kestenberg and her colleagues, however, dedicated most of the Kestenberg Movement Profile (KMP) system to the study of Flow. They observed and researched children (originally child survivors from the Holocaust) from birth to six years old. They noticed different patterns of fluctuation of the Flow Effort which they noticed formed some rhythms according to each developmental stage (termed Tension-Flow Rhythms).

The KMP team originally bridged the system with developmental psychoanalytic theory and psychodynamic orientations, but these have been now expanded into wider developmental frameworks. The applications of KMP have been used in the diagnosis and treatment of trauma in children and the development of "trust, attunement and attachment" with caregivers[22]. However, KMP is an "observation system and not dependent on self-reports"[23]. Lamb and Kestenberg influenced their work simultaneously. While Lamb suggested Kestenberg's notation was "linked to changes in flow rather than in effort" as she originally believed, Kestenberg offered Lamb a more comprehensive view of how Flow could be analysed in adults[24]. In later research, the Flow Effort was re-integrated into decision-making by Martha Eddy[25] in her movement education work within school contexts. Eddy applied the decision-making stages as categories with which to analyse and evaluate school curricula. She made explicit links between these stages and used them to evaluate whether specific activities for school children would target bullying and violence in schools[26]. Eddy believed children needed to engage with the movement qualities in all the decision-making stages to build coping skills, prevent bullying, and foster empathy. In my thesis, I extended Eddy's inclusion of Flow, as Flow/Tension, considering it an essential part of decision-making, but rather placed it at the core of embodied practices and the key factor in listening to our body[27] (Figure 1.1 on page 5). To not confuse the terms Flow (Effort), day-to-day usage of the words flow/flowing with Tension-Flow (KMP), I applied the term *Flow/Tension* in my doctoral work[28] to describe the decision-making stage and its implications for self-reflexivity in violence prevention work. As I have progressed through this system and because of the experience of running many workshops on this material before and during the writing of this book, I have shifted Flow/Tension to the centre of the system. You will see Flow/Tension in a quadrant in many of the worksheets, as this maximises the space in the paper, but it should be considered as central to the system.

Lamb and Davies concurred how important Flow/Tension was, stating, "Flow links all other components of movement to give them balance, flexibility and grace"[29]. Flow/Tension, for me in my practice, has shifted to be the vehicle through which we begin to maintain, repair, and address our relationship to our body.

Movement Break: Invisible Cord Approach

Suggested Music

Track Title: Serious - Pensive

Duration: 01:51

Music Composer: Ross Whyte

Link for QR Code: https://youtu.be/IfaV-TYeX3A?si=dDb0vvn3yf7ONlj0

Oftentimes Flow/Tension is equated with resistance – both in terms of the muscles required to engage with Bound/Free Flow, but also internal (psychological) resistance which you might see represented through your movement. Resistance to change is completely natural, as we are progressing into the unknown. You might be taking risks on something new or different, which will activate some uncertainty in your body-mind. The amount of Flow/Tension in our body in any given circumstance will be an ongoing Body Question you tackle.

I will now use the metaphor of an invisible cord to illustrate this concept in the body. For this exercise, please start with a quick body check-in exercise from the beginning of the book, grounding yourself (page 26) and taking notice of the key anchor points in the body: feet, knees, hips (only if this feels okay), belly button, shoulders, head, hands, and spine. You can be sitting or standing for this. If you are working with a partner or a group, stay tuned for the second version of this exercise.

Once you feel more present and grounded, **visualise an invisible cord starting from your sternum** (Figure 5.3), which is the bony plate on the front-centre of your chest where your ribs meet (Figure 5.4), and connecting to an object you love or a point in the room.

There are some neat features to this visualised cord: It will have the mechanism of a retractable dog lead – it will expand, and contract as needed (see Figure 5.4). I will then invite you to experiment more with the push and pull of a situation. You can engage with advance/retreating, or if you are sitting down, you can do the same principles but initiating from the core.

FIGURE 5.3 Sternum

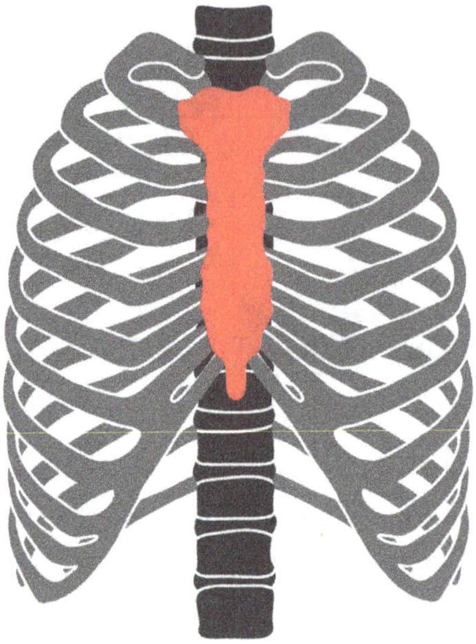

FIGURE 5.4 The Invisible Cord Exercise

Add your own meaning – you can enact Flow/Tension in your body and/or you can add the emotional component of this push and pull. Sometimes this may translate into decision-making when you are unsure about which step to take. **Represent a situation that involves a tension/release and push/pull.** Notice what happens to the invisible cord, and to your body as you engage with distance and proximity. Which distance feels comfortable? Uncomfortable? Are you expressing resistance, control, release? Where is it in your body?

Ideally, you want to negotiate the relationship between Free/Bound Flow in a way which is constructive to your wellbeing:

> The ratio of the free to bound movements used by individuals offers an indication of how restrained or how unrestrained they are. Too much restraint inhibits. Too much Free Flow signals a deficiency in control[30].

The Flow/Tension stage in decision-making offers insight into what we are holding on to, and what needs letting go.

Flow/Tension in Daily Life and Professional Practice

Flow/Tension is the stage where you listen to our body for its clues. You gauge how our body is engaging with the processes and/or people involved in your decision. In theory, the whole decision-making through movement process exists in four stages (Flow/Tension, Attention, Intention, and Action/Non-Action), but I keep returning to Flow/Tension as the baseline of all stages. If you are to connect back into the body, perhaps Flow/Tension is the way to interweave between stages and is a catalyst and grounding anchor for each aspect of a decision. Is Free Flow or Bound Flow dominating more? What's the ratio of Flow/Tension in this situation? Are you approaching this rigidly or are you being too *laissez-faire* or laid back?

This is what makes the decision-making through movement process so dynamic.

Decision-making through movement considers Flow/Tension as the connecting factor which you return to, to understand how the system is being connected to these fundamental experiences of Joy (Woo hoo!) and Frustration/Annoyance (GRRRR!), which I will explain next.

People usually associate tension with the 'GRRR!' feeling in our bodies that tells you might need a shift. You don't know quite what needs to change, how or why, but there is an internal signal that a transition is about to happen, has happened, or needs to begin. Unfortunately, it is human nature to desire change when something is going wrong. Often, you can pinpoint negative events in our lives that have forced you to make decisions. This is often the case with burnout, acute stress, health issues, or post-traumatic stress, which come into awareness when symptoms have accumulated for a while. Other circumstances in our lives which are out of our control could force a shift or change.

On the other hand, you might want to change something due to something positive happening in your life. This is what I term as constructive applications of Flow/Tension. I define constructive tension as the experience of joy and pleasure when experiencing something that inspires us to achieve or modify our behaviour. For the purposes of this book, it is an embodied feeling which prompts us to want to engage more. It is the source of motivation – that burst of goodness you need as an impetus for change. Now that we have covered all the stages and their movement components, you can take a look at Table 1.2 (page 41) to refresh everything you have learned.

I often witness this in workshops with newcomers to the field of therapeutic dance/movement and DMT: the 'aha' moment when participants get to connect to their sense of play, and they say: "Wow! I need to move more – this feels great!" Movement, play, and creativity are great sources of constructive tension. I personally experienced this during the pandemic, when an encounter with paddling in the sea had such a profound effect on my mood and overall wellbeing. I had such an incredible sense of being in the water – and I felt my whole body smile. The next day I still felt like this, and I redirected all my efforts to take on kayaking as a self-care activity, which remains a protective factor to this day. Kayaking continues to be an activity that is a protective factor in my life, as when things get really tense, I engage with the flow of paddling in the water, engaging with breath, core, and connecting my feet to the pedals inside the kayak. Kayaking is an activity I relate to Flow/Tension the most. This full embodied feeling of focused calm, along with the connection to nature, has made a profound impact in how I mitigate burnout.

Take a moment to reflect on the Body Questions related to a moment of constructive Flow/Tension:

- When in your life have you had an experience of joy/pleasure that motivated change?
- Did you follow through on that change? Was it temporary?
- Did you engage with that activity intensely for a while and then it tapered away due to other life commitments?
- Have you acted on it consistently? Where do you feel it in your body when you think of this activity?

We will come back to these Body Questions when we analyse the totality of the decision-making system.

I will present an example of body-based interventions that I used with workshop participants to analyse their own current level of Flow/Tension related to their professional identity. I suggested the participants represent a situation in the workplace. They were asked to reflect on the aspects of this situation which was affecting them. Then we represented these feelings by assigning the situation a rhythm. This rhythm could take any form – as long as it was a rhythm participants could repeat and, later, show their peers (without verbally needing to explain what it symbolised for them). Leaving something in symbolic form is a way to keep experiences at a nonverbal level, maintain group safety, and allow participants to process their own experiences safely.

The participants were asked to map and monitor the related bodily tension in their bodies related to this situation. This was done through the many tools I have included in this book, such as body scanning and tuning into the body. Then they represented this tension by enacting it through movement. They could use gestures, tapping, sound, or music related to this level of tension.

The group was asked Body Questions related to the movements they chose:

- How does this movement represent the level of tension at the workplace?
- What type of tension is it?
- Is it sustainable?
- What emotional states does this movement evoke?
- Does it need to change? How?

If you are curious about this, you can try this experimentation on your own. Quick representations (Chapter 1) of situations in terms of shapes, movements, or gestures can be an accessible way to get perspective quickly on what is happening nonverbally and acquire information from our bodies that you might not be able to cognitively process just yet.

Movement Break: Circular Flow and Resistance

Suggested Music

Track Title: Reflexive Style: Floaty

Duration: 2:16

Music Composer: Ross Whyte

Link for QR Code: https://youtu.be/EXpUKLvnB5Y?si=tGHGHn2OgR4ofTTX

(Adapted from Rena Kornblum)

Another activity in Flow/Tension consists of exploring muscle resistance both independently (as individuals), in dyads, and with objects and moving through various levels of intensity.

One of the DMTs that has incredibly influenced my research and practice is Rena Kornblum, who developed an impressive curriculum for bullying and violence prevention for children[31]. Although I stopped practising DMT with children in 2009, her exercises still influence my work with adults to this day. With Rena's permission, I have re-adapted one of her exercises called circular pushing[32].

The aim of the exercise is to make circles in the Sagittal Plane (one hand at a time) applying more Bound Flow/more Tension when you go forward and using more Free Flow or less Tension as you go backwards (see Figure 5.5). This exercise has been a crowd favourite over the years since it offers immediate feedback to your body on how you are mitigating, receiving, and co-creating Flow.

If you are working on your own for now, please grab a small towel, scarf, or sturdy piece of clothing that has a bit of give or stretch (Figure 5.5 – top image). Hold one end of the cloth with each hand. The idea is to notice the tension of the cloth as you trace the circles in movement. If you are sitting, make sure your body is positioned so that you can receive a small amount of resistance. Please sit up in your chair so that the back is not touching if it's possible. Alternate between pushing forward or pulling backwards, and explore how this feels in the context of making a circle. Notice where the resistance is and whether you can find a rhythm.

FIGURE 5.5 Circular Flow Exercise and Variations

Circular Flow Exercise

with a towel

in a pair

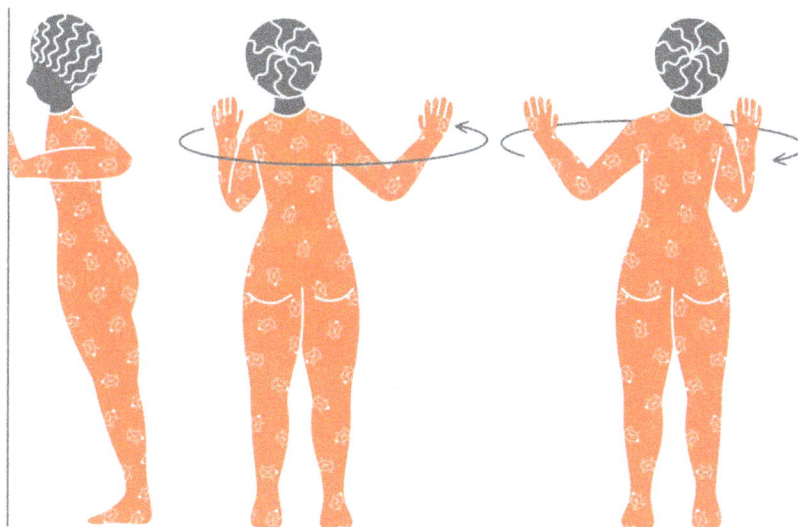

against a wall

You can also work on matching and negotiating Tension in partners and in groups. If you are doing this with a partner, please make sure contact is okay (always ask for consent before and during an exercise), face them and place the palms of your hand together (see Figure 5.5 middle image). (There is a no-touch variation described next in case this feels uncomfortable.) If you are standing, make sure that both your feet are underneath you (a hip's width apart), that your knees are soft. **After you get a flow going, you can change direction, speed, or slow it down.** Each of you should share a bit of each other's weight equally and feel comfortable with the varying degrees. Please make sure you are not exerting too much weight/pressure on your partner or receiving too much yourself. Communicate with your partner if this feels like too much. It is always okay to stop at any time.

No-Touch Variation

I devised a variation of this just in case touch does not feel okay at this moment. This is a variation which is important to introduce if you are working in groups, which has been particularly welcomed by participants with touch sensitivity. In this version, you can enact **the circle in the same fashion as the middle image in** Figure 5.5, **but with the distance between you and your partner's hands around 2–3 inches (5–7 cm) apart from each other**. It involves similar principles of body awareness and finding the Flow; but without the Bound Flow/resistance from someone else, it requires a lot more concentration and awareness (but is still effective). **Another variation which I have introduced is to use scarves or a long piece of cloth/sturdy string as an alternative modification to the exercise.**

Circular Flow: Wall Version

Another version of alternating resistance is to use a wall to experiment rocking side to side almost like a push up/press up but against the wall – playing more with the side-to-side and circular motions (see Figure 5.5 – bottom image).

Engage the arms in front of you and alternate between giving in your weight towards the wall and pushing back from it. First as a press up (push up) and then alternating bending on each side to create more of a circular motion. You can also do this exercise sitting or standing, noticing how Flow/Tension can oscillate and offer different kinds of feedback to the rest of your body. If it gets too tiresome – you can return to a neutral stance and do a short body check-in or some reflection on Flow/Tension.

Whether you are employing this activity individually, with a partner, or group, this leads very well to discussions on resistance/acceptance/willingness or being a listening leader or engaged follower who proposes new ideas. I do this activity a lot with leadership/management groups to get insight on nonverbal communication.

Body Questions to Consider

- What elements of Bound/Free Flow are you engaging with?
- What was challenging or interesting about this exercise?
- How did you negotiate the Flow?
- Was it hard to receive? Hard to offer more resistance?
- How did it feel to engage with the release aspects of Flow/Tension?
- What body sensations are you registering as a result of this exercise?
- What other Body Questions arise?

Culture and Caveats

The Flow/Tension stage connects us to our primal body responses and our internal relationships with tension, resistance, joy, and pleasure amongst many other instinctive responses to engaging with the body. There are many cultures in which touch might not be okay, and if you are introducing these exercises in those contexts, please make sure participants are okay with touch, and make sure to communicate that consent can be withdrawn at any time. An important caveat is to be aware of disability, injury, health, and mental health conditions (alongside age and other protected characteristics[33]) which might affect and be affected by Flow/Tension.

KMP offers some insights into our cultural context. For example, they relate Neutral Flow to restriction of expression[34], which might be of high cultural value in some contexts. Some cultures might exhibit more Animated Flow, or there might be cultural value associated with High Intensity (and this Animated Flow usually gets stereotyped as 'fiery' or 'feisty' in other cultures). Other cultures might prefer Low Intensity and foster behaviour that is detached and foster 'controlling' our emotions.

However, we constantly need to revise these cultural assumptions and reflect on what function they serve and what power dynamics emerge from these implicit and explicit preferences for certain movement elements. As Bound Flow is often equated with aggression, it is also important to be sensitive to your group/clients/ colleagues when you work with Flow/Tension. Please be mindful if you or the group you work with have a history of traumatic experiences, as the process of reactivating fight/flight/freeze mechanisms through the exploration of Flow Efforts might prove difficult.

You also need to be mindful that sometimes you might need to keep building up your body resources. If you had difficulty engaging with Bound Flow and were unable to exert more pressure by activating Weight Efforts, this might be something you might need more practice with. In the same turn, if the resistance was too much and it was difficult to relax and engage with Free Flow – doing more breathwork and engaging with body practices or other physical activities that feature tension release might help with introducing Free Flow more with Flow Adjustments in our body. As our primal responses might be hyper-engaged if you have experienced trauma, please be kind to your body and engage with more support if needed.

Chapter Conclusion

Flow/Tension provides an important aspect of somatic awareness that provides the base line stimulus for all decisions, meriting further consideration and unique implementation in the context of embodied reflexivity practices. Tension is commonly associated with negative experiences, stress, and illness, yet the awareness of the proportion and conscious engagement with Flow/Tension may serve as a catalytic motivator for change. Breath and muscular tension are examples of bodily actions that relate to the flux between constriction and release of organs, which exists to allow organs to function and the body to move. The body itself is a system of flows of blood, of hormones, of neurons. Breath and Flow are essential to living and are affected in stress responses. These primal movement qualities of life correlate to actions and aspects of lived experience.

Constraining or expanding Flow can indicate how an individual is coping with their own emotional states, situations, and living/working environments. Embodied investigations can help ascertain sustainability and long-term impact on self-regulation in professional practice.

A perspective I have seen in my practice is the understanding of constructive tension, manifested both as 'healthy' tension that provokes new insight and/or joy or excitement that stimulates curiosity into alternative paths. The point of reference for a 'healthy' amount of tension will vary with each individual. In many cases somatic expressions come before our cognitive responses in stressful situations. Primal reactions to perceived external threat, the fight/flight/flee response, involve autonomic body-based reactions. In a contrasting way, the body registers happiness, gratitude, and emotional warmth with corresponding movement indicators[35]. This can be experienced at a bodily level as a surge of endorphins, surge of breath, or a sense of muscular release. Flow/Tension can underlie an innate desire for something to change, despite not being able to consciously name the cause or situation. We can examine our ratio of Bound-Free Flow applied to our decisions and transitions. Movement experiences which target body-based stressors can promote a healthy connection to the body that can stimulate new modes of understanding.

It is a distinguishing aspect and essential contribution of dance movement therapy to use metaphor and symbolism to activate intersubjective knowledge (information gained from being in contact with other people). Although many somatic-focused therapies and stress-management programmes advocate the conscious activation of muscular tension and release, movement-based interventions that make a symbolic connection to current states/situations/issues can offer a deeper exploration into the self. I exemplified these concepts by using representation of a situation through Flow/Tension movement qualities and equally activating Flow/Tension in our bodies through the circular pushing activities. Additionally, there is much promise in continuing to share best practices through interventions that stimulate respite and release based on self-observation and body awareness. Ongoing bodily reflexive practice involves listening, understanding, and giving value to Flow/Tension, with an acknowledgement that this information and 'tuning in' underlies all stages.

REVIEW POINTS ON THE FLOW/TENSION STAGE

- Stage related to internal body cues that signal something might need shifting.
- Involves connections to tension, breath, and autonomic system responses.
- Getting stuck in this stage might mean you are either constraining or expanding Flow and therefore coping/not coping with your own emotional states, situations, and living/working environments.
- This stage might underlie all stages, or you might return to this stage often to 'check back' in with our body.
- Flow/Tension is linked to your ability to relax, resource, defend, and/or offer resistance when needed, or connect to joyful moments that enable change.

SKIP, BOOKMARK, OR CONTINUE:

- If you have decided you want to continue in the order of the book, you can apply all your knowledge of the Efforts and decision-making through movement stages to engage with your own movement preferences (continue to Chapter 6 "Movement Styles").
- You might have connected with the source of tension or joy of your decision and want to conduct more research on your own context and explore more options regarding your decision (skip to Chapter 2 "Attention Stage").
- It has become apparent that you want to understand the need this tension is representing and core aspects of the transition to prioritise some aspects of your decision (skip to Chapter 3 "Intention Stage").
- You now want to explore some action items connected to what you discovered in this chapter, and/or understand more your relationship to commitment (skip to Chapter 4 "Action/Non-Action Stage").

Notes

1 Leder, Drew. *The Absent Body* (Chicago and London: University of Chicago Press, 1990).

2 Trinity College Dublin. 'Why Babies Need to Move in the Womb'. *ScienceDaily* (2018). www.sciencedaily.com/releases/2018/03/180312104014.htm.

3 Kenner, Carole, and Welma Lubbe. 'Fetal Stimulation – A Preventative Therapy'. *Newborn and Infant Nursing Reviews, Fetal Therapeutics* 7, no. 4 (December 2007): 227–230. https://doi.org/10.1053/j.nainr.2007.06.013.

4 Moore, 2005, 58.

5 Dieterich-Hartwell, Rebekka. 'Dance/Movement Therapy in the Treatment of Post Traumatic Stress: A Reference Model'. *The Arts in Psychotherapy* 54 (July 2017): 38–46. https://doi.org/10.1016/j.aip.2017.02.010.

6 Merlo, Gia, and Steven G. Sugden. 'Trauma Considerations'. In *Lifestyle Psychiatry* (CRC Press, 2023).

7 Porges, Stephen W. 'The Polyvagal Theory: New Insights into Adaptive Reactions of the Autonomic Nervous System'. *Cleveland Clinic Journal of Medicine* 76, no. 4, supplement 2 (February 2009): S86–S90. https://doi.org/10.3949/ccjm.76.s2.17.

8 Levine, Peter A. *In an Unspoken Voice: How the Body Releases Trauma and Restores Goodness* (Berkeley: North Atlantic Books, 2010).

9 Rothschild, Babette. *Help for the Helper: The Psychophysiology of Compassion Fatigue and Vicarious Trauma*, vol. xiii (New York: WW Norton & Co., 2006); Rothschild, Babette. *The Body Remembers: The Psychophysiology of Trauma and Trauma Treatment* (New York: Norton, 2000).

10 Kolk, Bessel A. van der and Alexander C. McFarlane, *Traumatic Stress: The Effects of Overwhelming Experience on Mind, Body, and Society* (Guilford Press, 2012); Kolk, Bessel A. van der, 'Beyond the Talking Cure: Somatic Experience and Subcortical Imprints in the Treatment of Trauma'. In *EMDR as an Integrative Psychotherapy Approach: Experts of Diverse Orientations Explore the Paradigm Prism* (Washington, DC: American Psychological Association, 2002), 57–83. www.essentia.fr/blog/wp-content/uploads/2011/09/vanderKolk-Beyond-the-talking-cure.pdf; Kolk, Bessel A. van der, 'The Body Keeps the Score: Memory and the Evolving Psychobiology of Posttraumatic Stress'. *Harvard Review of Psychiatry* 1, no. 5 (1994): 253–265.

11 Dieterich-Hartwell, Rebekka, and Anne Margrethe Melsom. *Dance/Movement Therapy for Trauma Survivors: Theoretical, Clinical, and Cultural Perspectives* (Routledge, 2022).

12 Rivera, María, Charné Furcron, and Nancy Beardall. 'Embodied Conversations: Culturally and Trauma-Informed Healing Practices in Dance/Movement Therapy'. In *Dance/Movement Therapy for Trauma Survivors* (Routledge, 2022), 24–39.

13 Porges, Stephen W. *Polyvagal Safety: Attachment, Communication, Self-Regulation* (New York: WW Norton & Co., 2021).

14 Breit, Sigrid, Aleksandra Kupferberg, Gerhard Rogler, and Gregor Hasler. 'Vagus Nerve as Modulator of the Brain – Gut Axis in Psychiatric and Inflammatory Disorders'. *Frontiers in Psychiatry* 9 (2018). www.frontiersin.org/articles/10.3389/fpsyt.2018.00044.

15 Devereaux, Christina. 'An Interview with Dr. Stephen W. Porges'. *American Journal of Dance Therapy* 39, no. 1 (June 2017): 26. https://doi.org/10.1007/s10465-017-9252-6.

16 Gray, Amber Elizabeth Lynn. 'Polyvagal-Informed Dance/Movement Therapy for Trauma: A Global Perspective'. *American Journal of Dance Therapy* 39, no. 1 (June 2017): 43–46. https://doi.org/10.1007/s10465-017-9254-4; Porges, 2021.

17 Gray, 2017; Shafir, Tal. 'Neurophysiological Aspects of Dance Movement Therapy for Psychiatric Rehabilitation'. In *Arts Therapies in Psychiatric Rehabilitation*, edited by Umberto Volpe (Cham: Springer International Publishing, 2021), 117–120. https://doi.org/10.1007/978-3-030-76208-7_14; Girshon, Alexander and Ekaterina Karatygina, 'Psychological Re-Sources in Integral Dance and Dance/Movement Therapy'. In *The Routledge International Handbook of Embodied Perspectives in Psychotherapy* (Routledge, 2019).

18 Porges, 2021.

19 Laban and Ullmann, 1966; Laban and Ullmann, 1988; Lamb, 2012, 42; Laban, 1966; Laban, 1970; Laban and Lawrence 1974; Moore, 2005.

20 Kestenberg Amighi et al., 1999.

21 Kestenberg Amighi et al., 1999, 3; Lamb and Davies, 2012, 42.

22 Sossin, 1999 in Kestenberg Amighi et al., 1999, 266; Loman, Susan, Hilary White, and Melanie Johnson French. 'Kestenberg Movement Profile (KMP) Approaches to Working with Young Children and Caregivers in Dance/Movement Therapy'. *Journal of Infant, Child, and Adolescent Psychotherapy* 20, no. 1 (January 2021): 36–50. https://doi.org/10.1080/15289168.2021.1875703.

23 Kestenberg Amighi et al., 1999, 3.

24 Eddy, 1998; Moore, Carol-Lynne. 'On Flow, Lamb, and Kestenberg' (MoveScape Center, 2015). https://movescapecenter.com/on-flow-lamb-and-kestenberg/.

25 Eddy, 1998, 93–143.

26 Eddy, 2009.

27 Acarón, 'The Practitioner's Body of Knowledge', 2015, 163–166.

28 Acarón, 'The Practitioner's Body of Knowledge', 2015, 160.

29 Lamb and Davies, 2012, 24.

30 Kestenberg Amighi et al., 1999, 15.

31 Kornblum, 2002.

32 Kornblum, 2002, 176.

33 According to the Equality and Human Rights Commission in the United Kingdom, protected characteristics are age, disability, gender reassignment, marriage and civil

partnership, pregnancy and maternity, race, religion or belief, sex and sexual orientation. Reference: 'Protected Characteristics' (Equality and Human Rights Commission, 2021). www.equalityhumanrights.com/equality/equality-act-2010/protected-characteristics.

34 Kestenberg Amighi et al., 1999.

35 Shafir, Tal. 'Movement-Based Strategies for Emotion Regulation'. In *Handbook on Emotion Regulation: Processes, Cognitive Effects and Social Consequences* (New York: Nova Science Publishers, Inc., 2015), 231–249; Shafir, Tal, Rachelle P. Tsachor, and Kathleen B. Welch. 'Emotion Regulation Through Movement: Unique Sets of Movement Characteristics Are Associated with and Enhance Basic Emotions'. *Frontiers in Psychology* 6 (2016). https://doi. org/10.3389/fpsyg.2015.02030.

PART 2
APPLYING OUR BODY QUESTIONS

6

MOVEMENT STYLES

DOI: 10.4324/9781003360957-8

> ## Body Questions to Consider in This Chapter
> - How do I move in relationship with others?
> - How do I negotiate differences using my body (in myself and with others)?
> - Which movement qualities do I use at a 'default' state?
> - What is my comfort/discomfort zone in movement?

Picture yourself relaxing at the beach or your favourite landscape. What movement qualities would you need the most? Are these qualities that you feel most at home with? Or is it challenging to take in the whole landscape? Slow down? Not feel tense? Each situation and interaction with others and/or our environment often entail that we apply specific movement qualities.

Fun fact: Movement profiles have been created about infamous figures like Hitler! Movement analyst and DMT Martha Davis created a profile for profiling criminals and deception, which lends itself for an interesting read[1].

A movement style is your way of interacting with the world through movement. Understanding your movement style can help you reflect on what movement traits you tend to use in certain situations and how these are negotiated with others. In different movement analysis systems, trained movement analysis observers notate the frequency, repetition, and proportion of movement to create what is usually termed as a profile. In corporate applications of movement observation, Connors and Rende[2] were movement analysts who continued Warren Lamb's work on Movement Pattern Analysis, and alongside Ramsden[3] and Zacharias, notated repeated movement patterns to create what they termed as Action Profiles. As we are focusing on self-reflexivity and not on movement observation, we will reflect on our movement preferences and learn more about the theory of the movement styles we apply to life situations.

In this chapter, we will look at the combinations of Efforts and reflect on the movement patterns we might employ in making decisions. You will begin by exploring your tendencies in behaviour and examine how these actions, when understood in movement within BESS, apply these observations to decision-making.

In BESS, a Drive is a combination of three Effort qualities, which we introduced in early chapters. An Action Drive includes one quality pertaining each of the following effort categories: Space, Weight, and Time[4]. When we combine them, they form eight configurations with the following names: Press, Float, Punch, Flick, Dab, Wring, Glide, and Slash[5]. The illustration in the chapter 6 cover page 167 has some of these examples demonstrated in movement. You might have noticed that I snuck in these terms when we were doing many movement explorations earlier on to prepare our bodies for more layered explorations. I will go into detail into which Effort Qualities constitute each one, and we will explore them sequentially in movement.

Movement qualities are applied in very concrete actions needed for our daily routine as previously described. This is indeed different from our preferences in movement. In earlier chapters during our reflexivity breaks, we mentioned focusing on your 'default settings'. Even though we can use many Effort Qualities in other functional situations, we will focus here on what we defer to or where we feel most 'at home' as a starting point.

Look back at your reflections on each of the Effort spectrum exercises (Space – Figure 2.6 on page 69, Weight – Figure 3.5 on page 91, Time – Figure 4.6 on page 129). Let's combine them here all in one page. Use the spaces provided on Worksheet 6.1 to copy through the range and preferences you drew in earlier chapters, or if you would like a new point of reference, start a fresh reflection here (and compare them later). This will give us a starting point to consider which combinations of Efforts can describe our movement style(s).

NOTE: For this exercise, we will leave out Flow since, as I have covered in Chapter 5, Flow/Tension is in every other movement quality.

There are other Drives within the BESS system: Vision Drive (Flow-Space-Time), Passion Drive (Flow-Weight-Time), and Spell Drive (Flow-Weight-Space)[6]. Carol-Lynne Moore explains that these other types of Drives are more related to internal states, and Laban described these as "movement thinking" worlds[7]. In *Body Questions*, I will only focus on Action Drives since they are the most accessible and related to day-to-day activities. Then we will use this information to reflect on your movement style(s) in the sections that follow. Exploring the Drives in movement will help you understand how you operate in groups/with others, how our strengths are manifested in movement, and which movement qualities you can develop more within our practice.

Be mindful that your movement qualities/preferences might change over time and could fluctuate according to the stage you are traversing in life and/or the situations you are going through. (Please note the date of when you did this because you can potentially come back to this in the future.)

WORKSHEET 6.1 Spectrum Worksheet (Combined)

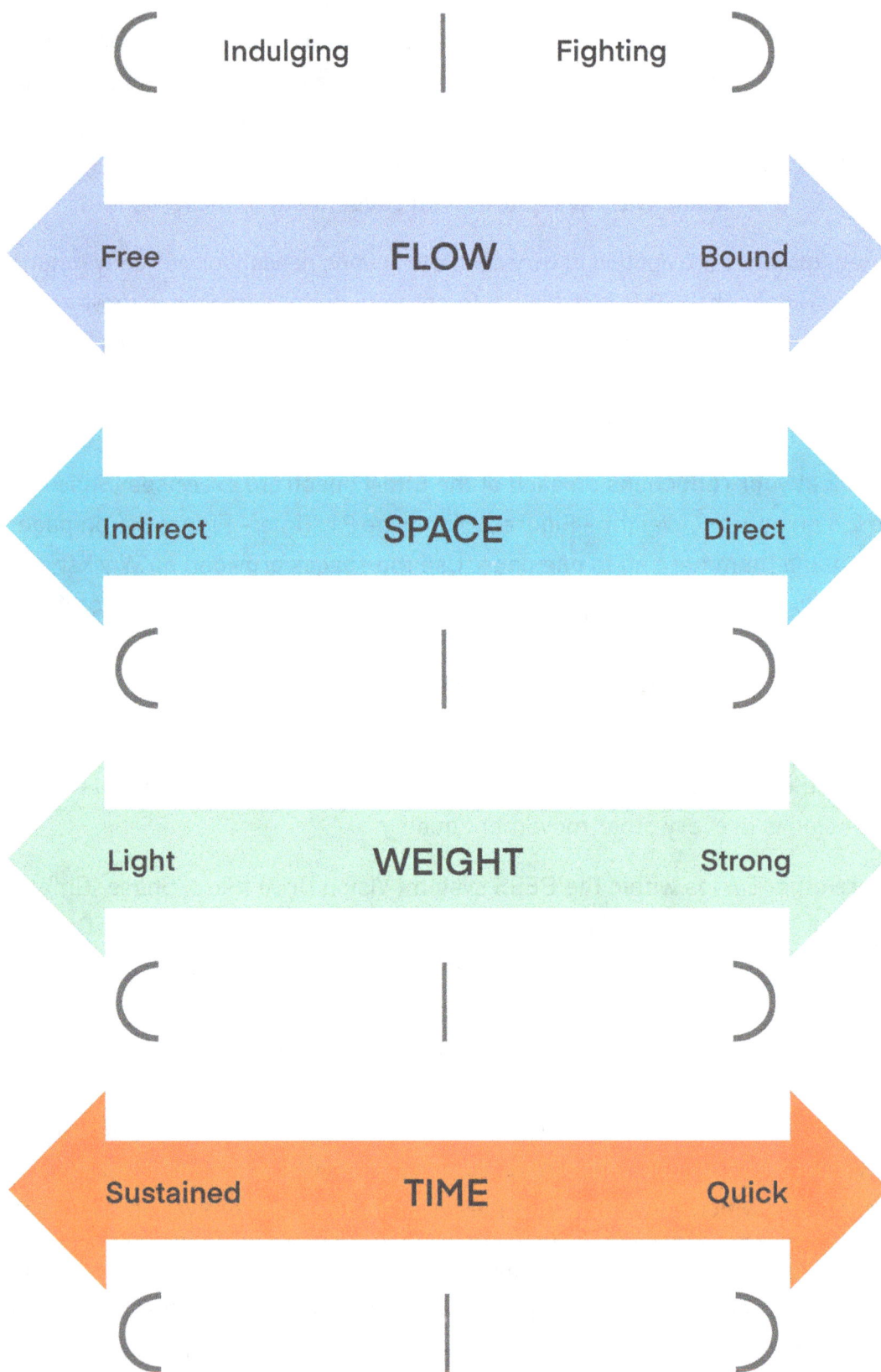

Indulging | Fighting

← **FLOW** →
Free   Bound

← **SPACE** →
Indirect   Direct

← **WEIGHT** →
Light   Strong

← **TIME** →
Sustained   Quick

We will review the effort qualities we have embodied in previous chapters to group them into Drives. Use the preferences you have compiled – are there some Drives that stand out to help you determine your dominant Drives?

As you can see from my preferences on Worksheet 6.2, I definitely have a tendency towards the Punch Drive. This helps me locate myself and figure out a point of reference for determining the areas I need to work on more.

WORKSHEET 6.2 Thania's Spectrum Worksheet Example

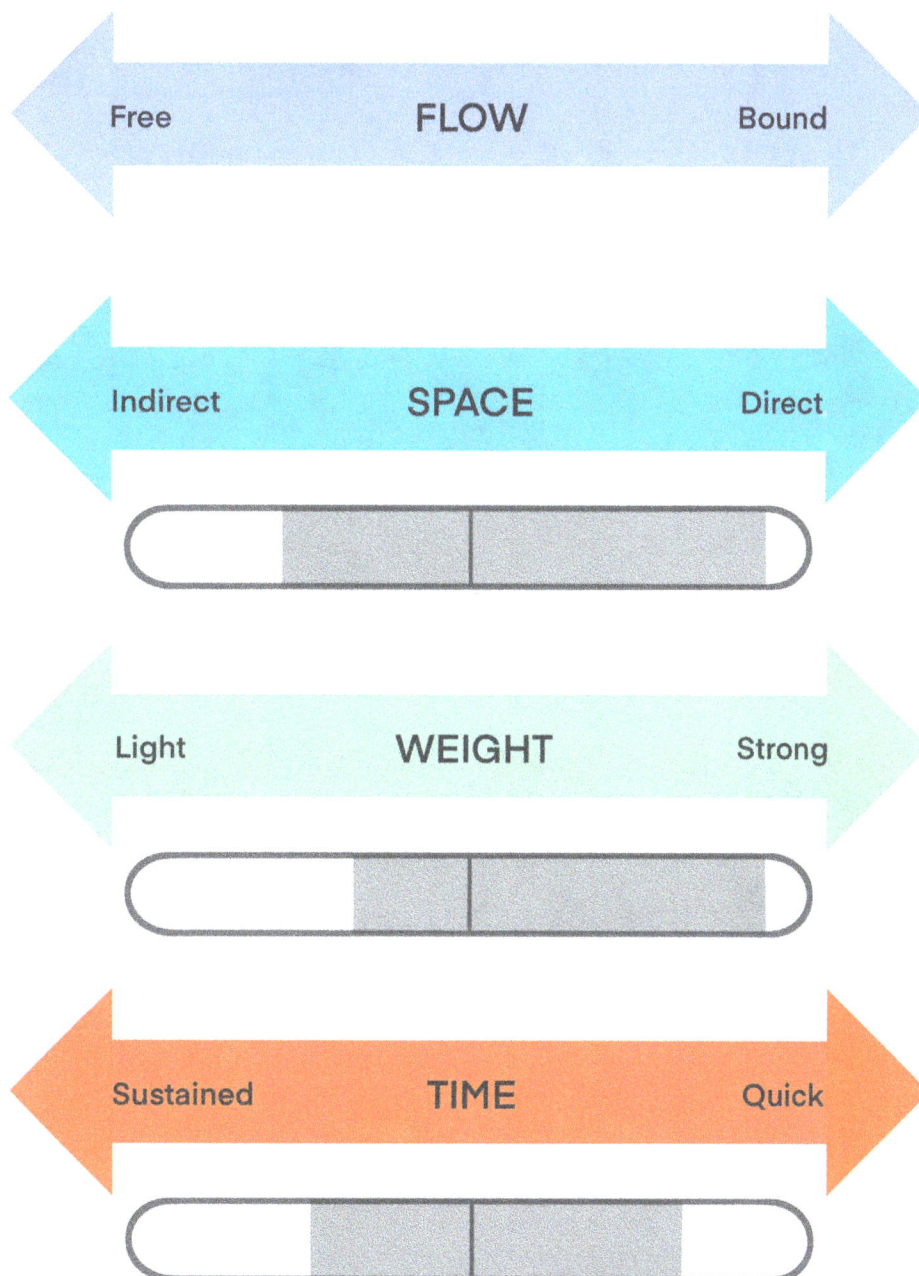

Copyright material from Thania Acarón (2025), *Body Questions in Practice*, Routledge

Figure 6.1 is a visual map of the Action Drives that we will explore, in order for you to get some visual images for the following exercises we will navigate.

FIGURE 6.1 Action Drives Icons

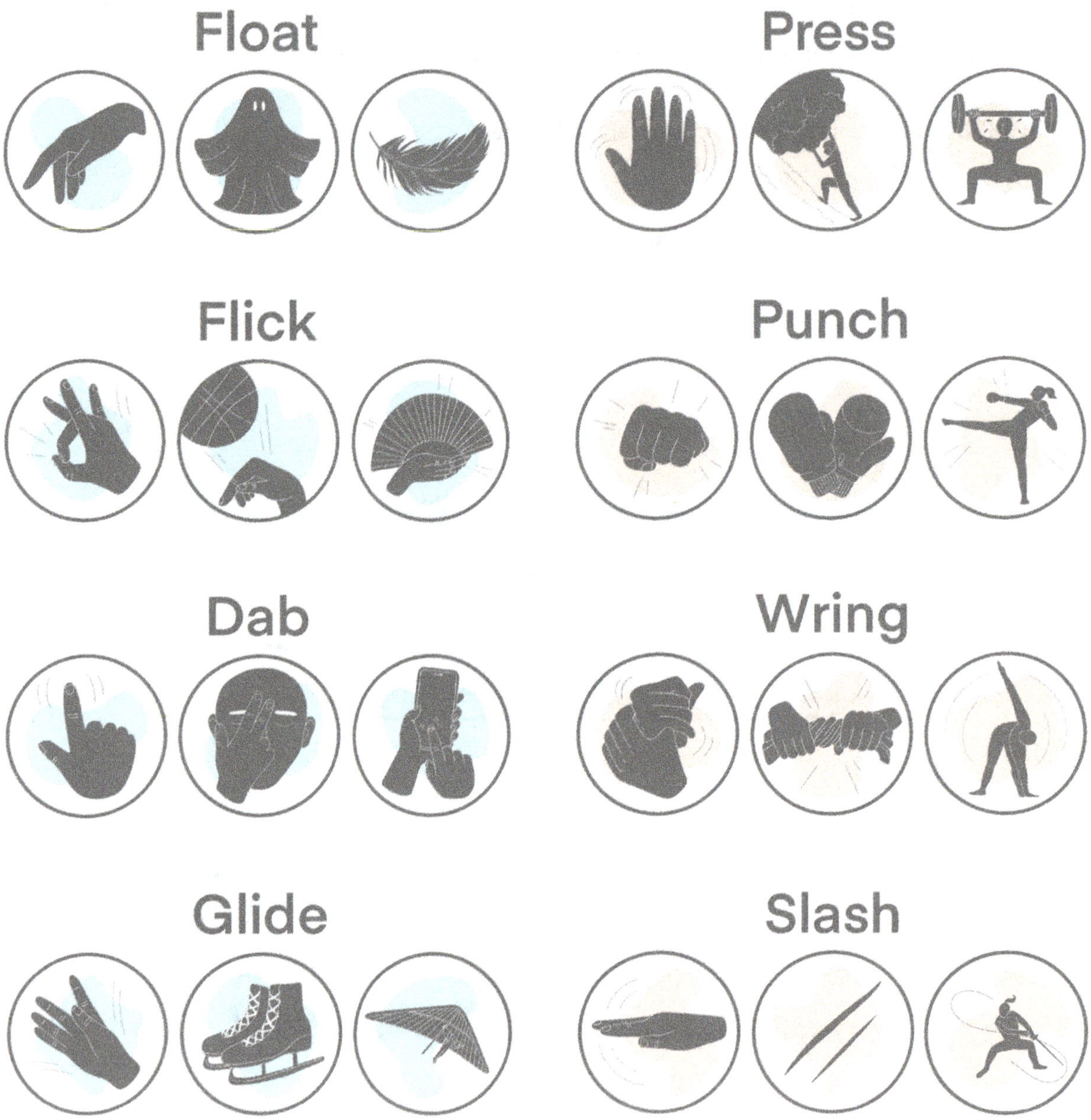

Figure 6.2 has a listing of each of the Drives with their effort qualities to support your movement explorations.

FIGURE 6.2 Action Drives: With Effort Qualities

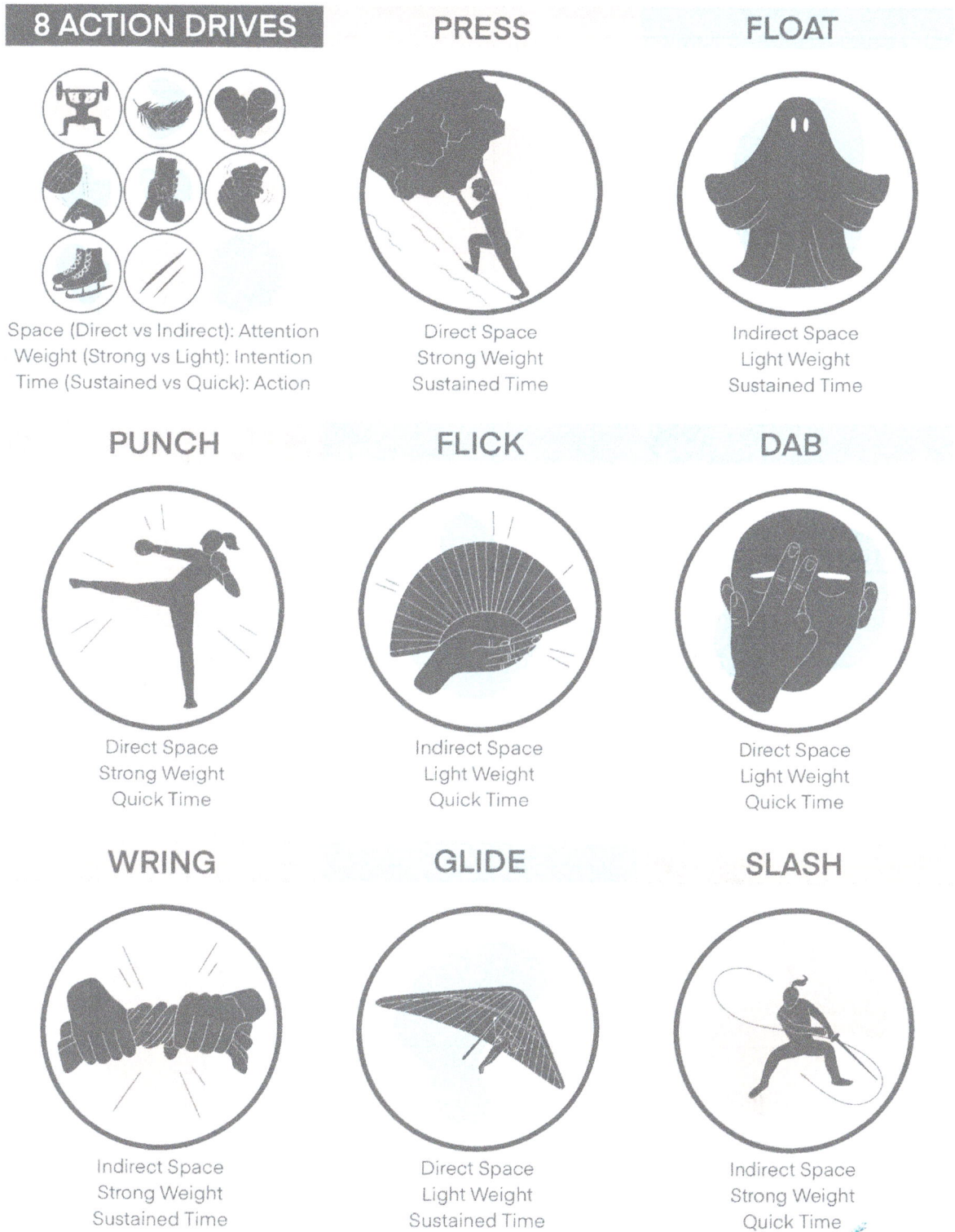

8 ACTION DRIVES

Space (Direct vs Indirect): Attention
Weight (Strong vs Light): Intention
Time (Sustained vs Quick): Action

PRESS
Direct Space
Strong Weight
Sustained Time

FLOAT
Indirect Space
Light Weight
Sustained Time

PUNCH
Direct Space
Strong Weight
Quick Time

FLICK
Indirect Space
Light Weight
Quick Time

DAB
Direct Space
Light Weight
Quick Time

WRING
Indirect Space
Strong Weight
Sustained Time

GLIDE
Direct Space
Light Weight
Sustained Time

SLASH
Indirect Space
Strong Weight
Quick Time

If you prefer a more word-focused map view of the Efforts, Table 6.1 has all the Effort Qualities for you to follow as we do the exercise. There is another combined view with the Effort Qualities which we will provide for our movement breaks.

TABLE 6.1 Action Drives With Movement Qualities (Word Map)

Drive (Suggested Music)	Space Effort (Attention)		Weight Effort (Intention)		Time Efforts (Action/Non-Action)	
Press Suggested Music Track Title: Press Duration: 02:21 Music Composer: Ross Whyte **Link for QR code: https://youtu.be/7g3 P39WWYGY?si=Gp2TTno0Tl8cZY8n**	Direct		Strong			Sustained
Float Suggested Music Track Title: Float Duration: 02:15 Music Composer: Ross Whyte **Link for QR code: https://youtu.be/ LAB-R6TGobo?si=huk3s2Kq-Zuyw5fX**		Indirect		Light		Sustained
Punch Suggested Music Track Title: Punch Duration: 02:00 Music Composer: Ross Whyte **Link for QR code: https://youtu.be/DSx K43Mu3t4?si=2JMi8EcHvZY4LIPs**	Direct		Strong		Quick	
Flick Suggested Music Track Title: Flick Duration: 02:08 Music Composer: Ross Whyte **Link for QR code https://youtu.be/ JhypU-vhTnU?si=IjN11M-1v0H0GWFp**		Indirect		Light	Quick	
Dab Suggested Music Track Title: Dab Duration: 02:04 Music Composer: Ross Whyte **Link for QR code https://youtu.be/J46L 1CEbaSc?si=0j6EcHExEmeE5sp3**	Direct			Light	Quick	

TABLE 6.1 Continued

Drive (Suggested Music)	Space Effort (Attention)	Weight Effort (Intention)		Time Efforts (Action/Non-Action)	
Wring **Suggested Music** Track Title: Wring Duration: 02:08 Music Composer: Ross Whyte **Link for QR code https://youtu.be/zB_zthWXZol?si=wA9jLmNlfaO-3b5h**	Indirect	Strong			Sustained
Glide **Suggested Music** Track Title: Glide Duration: 02:00 Music Composer: Ross Whyte **Link for QR code https://youtu.be/_JkGkPOHhbU?si=vAiCx3kiOubwUQUu**	Direct		Light		Sustained
Slash **Suggested Music** Track Title: Slash Duration: 02:04 Music Composer: Ross Whyte **Link for QR code: https://youtu.be/nNgCRwlTYoA?si=EBMmcUK4LXx7lksj**	Indirect	Strong		Quick	

Movement Break: Action Drives 🎧

Suggested Music

Track Title: Action Drives Combined
Duration: 17:04

Music Composer: Ross Whyte

🎧 Link for Audio Visual playlist: www.youtube.com/playlist?list=PLtGm4qYm5yBQZqgY5_PFpJHa4jgs2R6Cw&si=z1OtnV5Ml_io4ilK

Link for QR code: https://youtu.be/t1USwhrH8lQ?si=WN9Xw2sJqDAG3vMa>

We will explore each Action Drive in a sequence following the order of the first column of Table 6.1. You can also follow the icons in Figure 6.2 if you prefer a more visual outline of the Drives. The music tracks (QR codes) have been composed specifically for these movement qualities[8]. Action Drives provoke interesting reflections regarding their musical qualities – as these sometimes can be subjective. What types of music reflect each of the movement qualities?

Begin with the notion of **Pressing – which uses Strong Weight, Directness in Space, and Sustained Time**. Imagine pushing a big bundle of clothes into the washing machine very slowly. Or pushing a heavy wagon across a field. Notice the strong sense of pressure in your forward motion. Try to maintain this pressure for longer periods of time, with a sense of slowly moving with strength towards a place in your room or with a goal/intention in mind. **Move different body parts using this Action Drive.** If you are standing, you can try a very heavy squat. **If you are sitting, you can try pulling something gradually towards you,** almost like a tug of war or pulling a rope to bring a heavy boat to shore. **Explore Pressing in all directions** (towards the back, against a wall or flat steady surface, upwards, etc.) Remain in this movement for as long as you feel comfortable.

Keep this sense of sustained time, but now let the Attention/Space Effort become Indirect. Take in all the space around you – constantly shifting focus without a specific intention or goal. Allow your movements to become lighter. We are transitioning into the Float Drive. Engage different body parts in this floating sensation. You might explore feeling the weightlessness, like you are suspended in water or without gravity. Take some time to enjoy this sensation: **Try Floating while staying in one place or meander across the space**. Engage with your arms, legs, and head in this light, airy feeling – how many ways can you engage with Floating?

After taking some time in this Drive, **prepare yourself for an abrupt transition: Punch**. This Action Drive is the opposite of Float in terms of movement qualities, so take your time to transition each Effort factor separately. We will start with shifting the focus of your movements to Directness. Start zooming in on a particular aspect of the space you are moving in. For example, clarify the intention of the movement towards a specific point in the room or with specific shapes. You may switch your attention between places, but always have a clear intention of where you want to go with the movement. Then start quickening your pace and then, finally, engaging with Strong Weight, using more Force.

Punch involves Direct, Quick, and Strong actions. Try these out with all your limbs when possible and then varying direction: Slap your knee or bring it upwards with a jerk if you can. You can also try to Punch upwards, like the athletes celebrating a victory. Punch downwards and all around the kinesphere. If you are using only fists, try the movements with palms open or with elbows or with other body parts. The Effort Qualities are what matter. How else can we explore Punch? What feelings are evoked? Anger? Excitement? Focus? Notice how long you can sustain the Punch Drive. Be wary of overexerting – it is okay to take breaks.

The next two Action Drives use Quick and Light qualities, but they vary in terms of Focus/Attention. **We will keep the quickness from Punch but modify the Weight/Force of the movements to make them lighter.** We will move to try the Flick Action Drive (Indirect, Light, Quick). This Drive uses Indirectness, and therefore try Flicking away or Brushing towards – with hands, head, feet. Some images/actions you might want to try are the following: fanning, brushing, flicking fingers, shrugging off, brushing the floor with your feet, or flicking the feet up like they do in tango. Make it your own and explore for a while, and like the previous Action Drives, try also changing directions, levels, and body parts. Try exploring beyond the actions that we are familiar with – what else can you try?

When you are ready, we will shift focus to Directness: Dab (Direct, Light, Quick). The image that comes up the most: dabbing our mobile phone, or applying cream lightly to our face, typing, tapping your feet, pressing a button. How else can we Dab? Try movements like this on your own body and notice what that light pressure evokes. Notice if there are any feeling states that come up when doing Dab and Flick. How was it different from Punch, Press, and Float?

Move between Flick and Dab motions for a short amount of time to experiment with varying from Directness to Indirectness. Then prepare for a different transition. It is probably easier to go back to Flick to transition to Wring (Indirect, Strong, Sustained).

The **Wring Drive needs a lot of Indirect pressure and requires a lot of effort**. When you slow down the speed of the movement, gradually start applying more force to the Indirectness. Imagine squeezing water out of a very big, very wet towel. Or imagine a metal screw going into a thick piece of wood. How much strength is needed? How can you negotiate the Strong Weight involved with Indirectness? Involve your whole body in the Wringing actions and notice what happens as you exert this pressure.

Just two more Action Drives to explore! Take a break if needed. **From the Wring Action Drive, start easing up the pressure to go into Lightness** (you'll notice this becomes Floaty), then shift your intention to reach towards a specific point in your space. Choose a place a few metres/feet in front of you. **Clarify your movement towards a specific direction or goal in mind.** The Glide Drive uses a Direct focus, engages with Lightness in terms of its relationship with gravity, and employs a deceleration in time. Engage both the upper and lower halves of your body in this exploration if possible. Glide often evokes the sense of skating, slowly reaching for fruit from a tree branch, or sailing or paddling on a boat. Glide for a while in your own time – what other images come up? Notice the sensations in your body.

We will now prepare for the last transition (albeit an abrupt one): Slash! This will use more energy. We will begin by quickening the time of the movements (notice this will become a Dab for a short time) and then gradually engage with more Strong Force (Punch).

Slash is Quick, Indirect, and Strong. The image that I have used most often in workshops is trying to get through a very dense jungle with a long stick or a machete. Or moving in a whipping motion. I have also used the story/film *Alice in Wonderland*'s Queen, indiscriminately shouting: "Off with their heads!". Try letting the strong pressure and quickness be activated, but without a particular aim in the space. Careful you don't get too specific in terms of the Space Effort of these movements, otherwise it becomes a Punch Drive. Fluctuate between those two if it becomes unclear. Many people in workshops often have questions about Indirectness with Slash.

I often respond that when we engage with Indirectness, we can't really control/predict the 'end' of the movement.

How do we engage with Indirectness while keeping the Quickness and Strength present? Take a break if needed.

If you want to have some more time with the Drives, feel free to explore all the Drives in your own time through movement. Table 6.1 can serve as a 'score' (like in music) where you can follow the order of Action Drives or create your own.

Congratulations! You have enacted the whole system of movement styles. My participants found this quite full on but reported feeling quite energised. We also used these as warm-ups for my students and developed some mini choreography with the Drives, which was so much fun.

Action Drives and Voice

An additional idea here is to explore Action Drives in terms of voice. We can apply these Action Drives in the way we speak and communicate with others, which can be useful if you are doing facilitation, presentations, and/or performances. It will inevitably be useful for decision-making activities and analysing your own role in groups. I have included both movement exploration of the Drives, with vocal warm-ups when I taught within drama/physical theatre/dance programmes. For example, we would explore what cadences in the voice would reflect Weight and Space and look at pitch, inflection, and rhythm in terms of the Drives. Although we won't be able to delve too much into the uses of voice in this book, there have been several resources dedicated to Laban and vocal training you can refer to if this is an area of interest[9].

Our movement range can be also impacted by disability, injury, health, and age, amongst many other factors. Early research on movement analysis suggested that mental ill health and/or any type of health condition that is pervasive will often cause our movement repertoire to become smaller or feel stuck. One of the principles of dance movement therapy is to understand our repertoire, why and how it is serving us and investigate creative possibilities where/when we need them.

We have often referred to movement here in terms of expressing emotions or internal states, but movement qualities are also used for functional tasks, like tying a shoelace, or picking up a teacup. Lamb attempted to distinguish between *expressive actions*, which are those in which we apply movement to respond to others and our environments, and *functional actions*, which are the ones we apply to execute something concrete[10]. Lamb stated that the line between what is functional and expressive was very difficult to ascertain as these actions often blend into one another, or transition between functional and expressive quite quickly. Movement analyst Marion North determined that there will be movement that "is at the service of a practical or external functional action, without any particular stress of mental or emotional significance"[11]. North also determined there would be movement which has an "inner-emotional or mental function"[12] associated with a goal or aim. Therefore, movement will not always have an expressive component, which is often why practitioners usually distinguish between dance and movement.

Please remember, as we move through these, that we will reflect on our 'default settings' – what qualities we *usually* revert to when left to our own devices. Many workshop participants often ask me: "but I can move through all of these – how can I determine my preference?" They are right; usually, we access all or most effort movement qualities throughout our day. As all the BESS Effort Qualities lie on a spectrum, you will be able to determine your breadth and your preference. You have already started to do this in earlier chapters.

Some questions here for reflection: What was the Drive that felt most like 'you'? Which one did you struggle with? Which ones did you enjoy the most? We will reflect further on these in the next sections and there are additional questions for you.

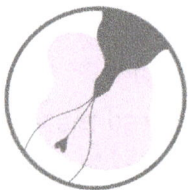

Reflexive Exercise: Action Drives Preferences

Reflect on the Action Drives through your preferred mode (drawing/words/sound/movement). Example: Here is an example of a note I might make with some key observations while engaging with Glide. I will try to keep it brief, but you can reflect on all of them, or pick some key ones, and leave the others for future reference.

Glide

Movement descriptor: Steady and stretching, long diagonal

- Emotion: felt engaged, focused, determined
- Sensations: Energising of upper body, negotiation of balance, felt grounded in lower half of the body
- Image: Kayaking through a calm river, ice skating
- Thoughts: This feels quite enjoyable! Felt so goal-oriented and clear!

Body Question I asked myself: Why does my body feel really calm while gliding?

How can I integrate Glide more in my life?

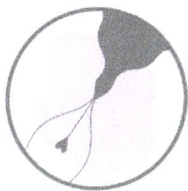

Reflexive Exercise: Action Drive Fill-in-the-Blank

If you are curious about Action Drives and want to take this reflection further, you can fill in the Drive(s) that suit the statements in Worksheet 6.3. You might not feel ready to do this just yet and might need more practice with the Drives, but here are some guiding questions you might want to fill out as we go along.

WORKSHEET 6.3 Action Drive Preferences; Fill in the Blanks

My 'default' personality Drive(s) are (usually):

and/or (optional):

My resting Drive(s) is/are:

I feel powerful using:

When I feel uncomfortable I use this/these Drive(s):

I need to work on/practice the following Drive(s) more:

I feel great when moving in the following Drive(s):

I would work/get along well with people who use this/these Drive(s):

and/or (optional):

If you discovered some Drives or Effort Qualities that might need more exploration, Table 6.2 offers a quick 'cheat' sheet of the Drives listed by their protagonist Effort category. You can use the music tracks related to each Action Drive to support your exploration.

TABLE 6.2 Action Drives Sorted by Effort Category

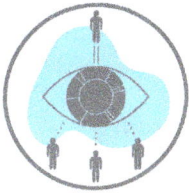

SPACE

Direct	Suggested Music		Indirect	Suggested Music	
	Track Title: Efforts: Directness **Duration:** 7:58 Music Composer: Ross Whyte			**Track Title:** Efforts: Indirectness **Duration:** 8:01 Music Composer: Ross Whyte	
Link for QR code: https://youtu.be/-4MKcLih_QU?si=m04W4dZyjrcNZpqS			**Link for QR code: https://youtu.be/l2hLxDxpK9g?si=LRUphboclgstN5gO>**		
Dab	Press	Float	Wring
Glide	Punch	Flick	Slash

WEIGHT/FORCE

Weight: Strong	Suggested Music		Weight: Light	Suggested Music	
	Track Title: Weight Efforts: Strong Force **Duration:** 7:49 Music Composer: Ross Whyte			**Track Title:** Weight Efforts: Lightness **Duration:** 7:44 Music Composer: Ross Whyte	
Link for QR code: https://youtu.be/grT4rxZa5V0?si=EuKtr26MdZvBneZH>			**Link for QR Code: https://youtu.be/MA9dt62tcnw?si=JAYf1sjaX8eS6BX2>**		
Press	Wring	Float	Dab
Punch	Slash	Flick	Glide

TIME

Time: Quick	Suggested Music		Time: Sustained	Suggested Music	
	Track Title: Time Efforts: Quickness **Duration:** 7:54 Music Composer: Ross Whyte			**Track Title:** Time Efforts: Sustained **Duration:** 7:47 Music Composer: Ross Whyte	
Link for QR Code: https://youtu.be/Hwx-tKeSsMc?si=LDupSdl7Hb7rklqZ>			**Link for QR code: https://youtu.be/9ZsTf9S8zng?si=rOabmWtlejXYsGvx>**		
Dab	Punch	Float	Press
Flick	Slash	Glide	Wring

Action Drives in Daily Life

Action Drives have equivalents to our ways of coping and managing everyday life, and decisions of course. Finding your movement styles is no easy feat. Each Action Drive serves an important purpose, and there is no right or wrong way of moving. These are all Body Questions to investigate.

There are Action Drives associated with the tasks we engage with as part of our daily routine. We might execute almost all the Action Drives in one day (or in one morning!) For example, you might wake up and feel quite Floaty, Glide by dragging your feet slowly to brush your teeth, then begin to accelerate, grabbing keys, Dabbing on face products, Flicking away some dust from your clothes, Dabbing away at the phone to set up the events for the day, and then once you realise you are running late you might slam some doors (Punch), fling your very heavy duvet onto your bed (Slash) and leave your place quickly.

In reflexivity practices, we can use some of the information gathered from the Drives we prefer (or use often) and see their compatibility with any given situation. Understanding Action Drives can help gain some needed aesthetic distance[13], which is when using a symbolic approach such as drama, music, visual art, and dance/movement can help us separate from the issue at hand. Aesthetic distance helps us gain perspective on whether the approach we are employing is useful, appropriate and/or sustainable for the situation[14]. Sometimes different types of artistic media can help us zoom in or out to understand life occurrences[15].

A bit of a caveat here: there has been a rise in online profiles that address personality traits, attachment styles, often used as personality profiles (like the Myers-Briggs Personality Test[16]) which this chapter doesn't aim to do. Your movement style might evolve through time, be affected by life events, and/or remain steady through time. As this is a complex system, it might take a while to see which movement style appeals to you the most. There might also be a discrepancy between the Drive we think we operate in, and which Drives are perceived by others. The idea here is to capture where you are at this moment in time, although you can use this system to analyse past events as well. For example, if your movement style is more of a Punch (preferring Quickness, more Force/Pressure, and Directness), you might find this useful in your workplace, but this would be difficult to engage in when having a holiday. If you approached relaxation with the Punch Drive, it would make it very hard to relax. This might then offer some insight into which movement preferences you might need to compromise/negotiate to be able to rest.

The opposite might be true if you have movement preferences aligned with the Float Action Drive (preferring to take your time, take in many perspectives, and apply a gentler pressure to things). There might come a time when you would need to access more Directness to accomplish a particular goal or clarify an intention. If you lead teams, you could have your teammates reflect on their own movement styles. You can then have conversations about the makeup of the team, and the strengths/ challenges of the team makeup. The card format of pros and cons of the Action Drives on Figures 6.3 and 6.4 can help guide those conversations. These cards offer the beginning points to many discussions about constructive and challenging aspects of the Drives. An important factor to consider is that each person should determine their own preferences rather than ascribing a movement style to someone without having their own full context. We view other people through our own filter, and we risk making assumptions based on our baseline preferences and sociocultural lens. I have used the Action Drives in my own interviews now by asking Body Questions to potential employees about their movement preferences. I wonder about the positive implications of including movement in Human Resources!

Action Drives in Professional Practice

As I mentioned before, BESS collaborators spent much of the first half of the 20th century grouping observations on people's movement preferences, which they called profiles. This book has explained principles of Movement Pattern Analysis, Bartenieff Fundamentals, and Kestenberg Movement Profile, extracting key elements to examine decisions.

An interesting research fact: Warren Lamb and his colleagues observed job interviewees in a business behind a one-way mirror without sound and recorded their movement preferences throughout the interview. Movement analysts grouped interviewees according to their profiles and made suggestions to management as to what types of occupations the person would excel in[17].

However, the challenge of observing people during a high-pressure situation is that stress and vulnerability have a massive impact on our body and how we move. There is also the role of bias in observation, which is important to consider[18]. Nowadays cultural nuance in movement observation might need further research and fine-tuning to make more culturally congruent observations[19].

FIGURE 6.3 Action Drives Deck Part 1 (Press-Float-Punch-Flick)

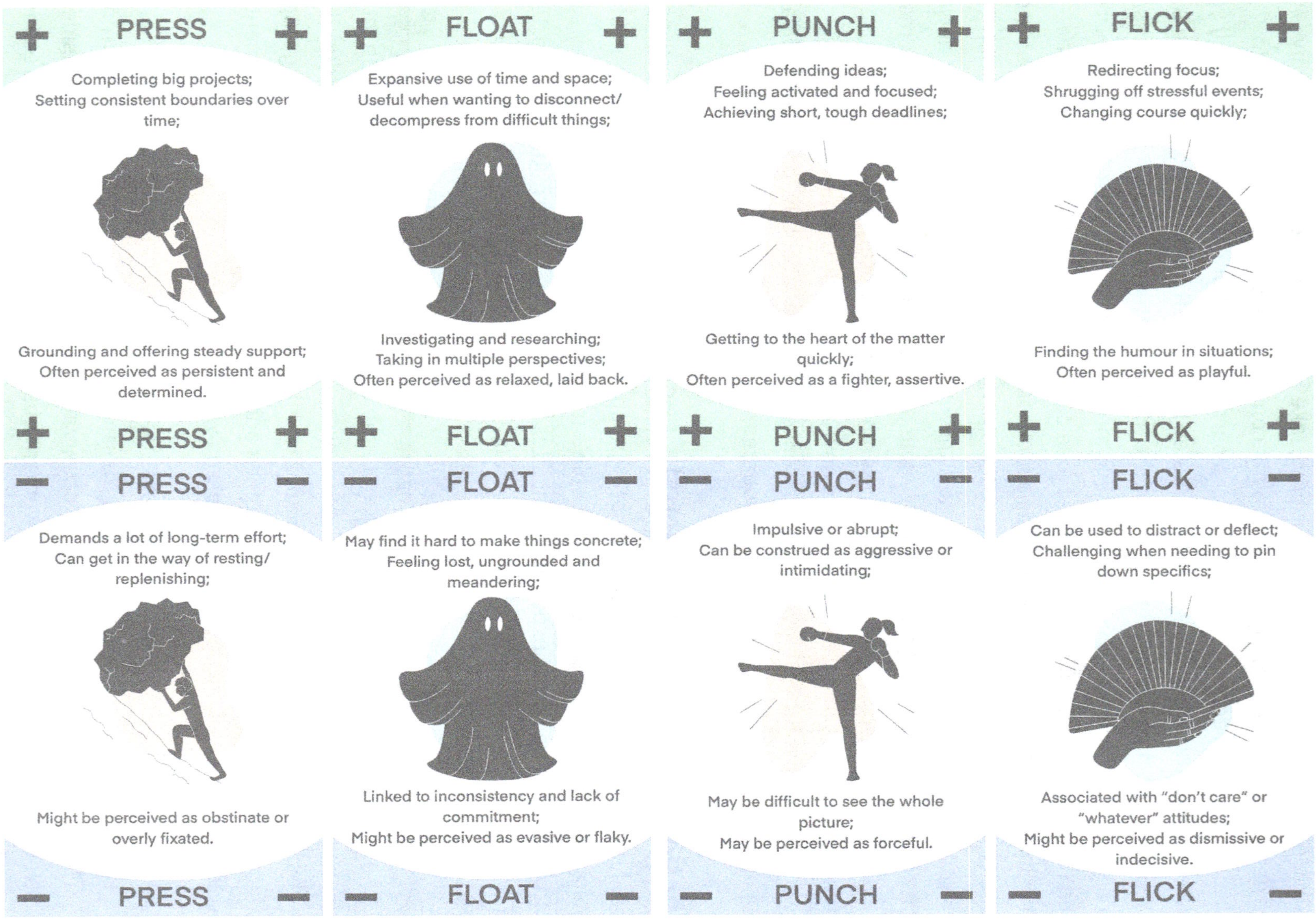
+ PRESS +
Completing big projects;
Setting consistent boundaries over time;
Grounding and offering steady support;
Often perceived as persistent and determined.
+ PRESS +
+ FLOAT +
Expansive use of time and space;
Useful when wanting to disconnect/ decompress from difficult things;
Investigating and researching;
Taking in multiple perspectives;
Often perceived as relaxed, laid back.
+ FLOAT +
+ PUNCH +
Defending ideas;
Feeling activated and focused;
Achieving short, tough deadlines;
Getting to the heart of the matter quickly;
Often perceived as a fighter, assertive.
+ PUNCH +
+ FLICK +
Redirecting focus;
Shrugging off stressful events;
Changing course quickly;
Finding the humour in situations;
Often perceived as playful.
+ FLICK +
– PRESS –
Demands a lot of long-term effort;
Can get in the way of resting/ replenishing;
Might be perceived as obstinate or overly fixated.
– PRESS –
– FLOAT –
May find it hard to make things concrete;
Feeling lost, ungrounded and meandering;
Linked to inconsistency and lack of commitment;
Might be perceived as evasive or flaky.
– FLOAT –
– PUNCH –
Impulsive or abrupt;
Can be construed as aggressive or intimidating;
May be difficult to see the whole picture;
May be perceived as forceful.
– PUNCH –
– FLICK –
Can be used to distract or deflect;
Challenging when needing to pin down specifics;
Associated with "don't care" or "whatever" attitudes;
Might be perceived as dismissive or indecisive.
– FLICK –

FIGURE 6.4 Action Drives Deck Part 2 (Dab-Wring-Glide-Slash)

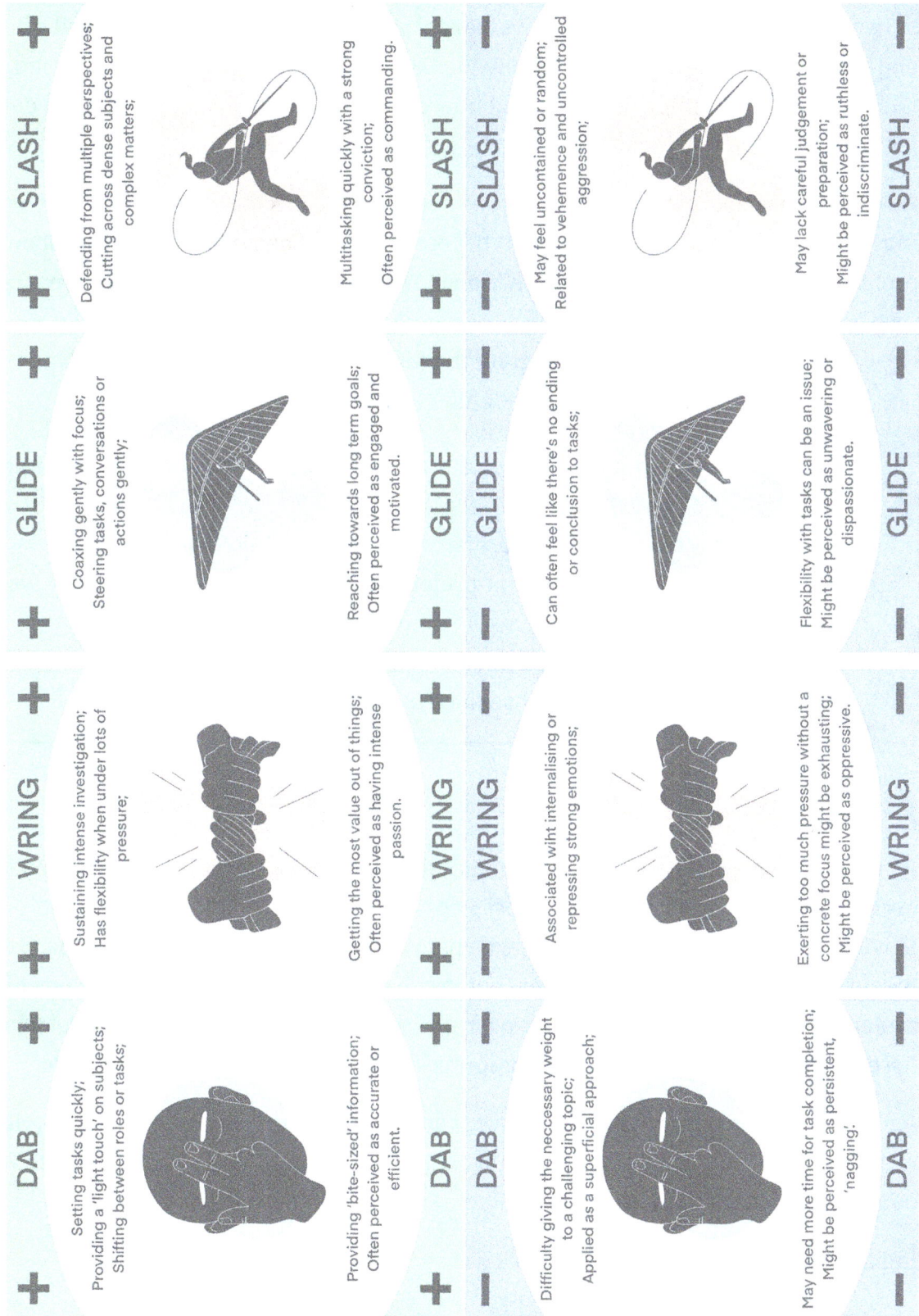

DAB +
- Setting tasks quickly;
- Providing a 'light touch' on subjects;
- Shifting between roles or tasks;
- Providing 'bite-sized' information;
- Often perceived as accurate or efficient.

WRING +
- Sustaining intense investigation;
- Has flexibility when under lots of pressure;
- Getting the most value out of things;
- Often perceived as having intense passion.

GLIDE +
- Coaxing gently with focus;
- Steering tasks, conversations or actions gently;
- Reaching towards long term goals;
- Often perceived as engaged and motivated.

SLASH +
- Defending from multiple perspectives;
- Cutting across dense subjects and complex matters;
- Multitasking quickly with a strong conviction;
- Often perceived as commanding.

DAB −
- Difficulty giving the necessary weight to a challenging topic;
- Applied as a superficial approach;
- May need more time for task completion;
- Might be perceived as persistent, 'nagging'.

WRING −
- Associated wiht internalising or repressing strong emotions;
- Exerting too much pressure without a concrete focus might be exhausting;
- Might be perceived as oppressive.

GLIDE −
- Can often feel like there's no ending or conclusion to tasks;
- Flexibility with tasks can be an issue;
- Might be perceived as unwavering or dispassionate.

SLASH −
- May feel uncontained or random;
- Related to vehemence and uncontrolled aggression;
- May lack careful judgement or preparation;
- Might be perceived as ruthless or indiscriminate.

According to philosopher Merleau-Ponty, we should perceive the world based on our senses, our preferences, and our lived experience[20]. This means that we will often engage with situations through our own lens. This occurs in both body and mind, and it is important to remain critical about how our own demographic, social, and cultural factors influence this lens.

However, the role of movement analysts as consultants begs the reflection: What would a movement analyst pick up about you? What recommendations might they make about your preferences to your employer/partner/friend? What would we do with that information?

We further reflect on the following Body Questions within our own professional identity:

- Do the core skills related to our job match our movement preferences?
- Do we modify our movement preferences to 'fit' within our workplace?
- What happens if our movement preferences don't match the ones our workplace prioritises?
- If you are engaging with this book on a personal level, we can reframe these questions around family and social dynamics as well.

Pros and Cons

As a result of my facilitation practice and research into decision-making, as I mentioned earlier, I have compiled examples of pros and cons in terms of each of the Action Drives that have come up amongst participant discussions in workshops. These are not meant to encompass all experiences, but they help demonstrate the applications of this system. Please remember there are no 'right' and 'wrong' Drives, as the useful analysis here is how they are applied and are appropriate and sustainable in our daily life.

As the workshops progressed, we have transformed these into a card-deck style worksheet you can use as you move through the system. A plain text table with fuller descriptions of the pros and cons is also available in the Appendices.

Laban grouped the Fighting Drives as Press, Wring, Punch, and Slash[21].

Fighting Drives, for example, can help us activate, defend, encourage, and discard. They usually demand a lot of energy and potentially could be difficult to sustain over periods of time if not balanced with the Indulging Drives (Float, Dab, Flick, and Glide).

Indulging Drives help us restore, specify, laugh, deflect, and orientate. They can demand less energy and can be done for longer periods of time. The following graph alternates between the Drives in the order from our Movement Break.

Illustrators Note: Eve has labelled these with the light orange blobs so you can distinguish between them from the Indulging Drives in light blue blobs. The Pros will be in Green and the Cons in Purple.

Case Example: Applications in Business Negotiation

Each situation will have an optimal proportion and ratio of Action Drives that we employ often unconsciously but could also be used consciously and with intent in our practice. For example: In my work at the University of South Wales, I was asked to coach business management students for the Negotiation Challenge Competition with the University of Trento. I designed a workshop for them based on the voice and body aspects of the Action Drives and used real-life scenarios to support them in exploring how nonverbal skills could be integrated into live debate situations. I had an incredible cohort of international students who had never engaged in movement before to explore how to apply movement styles to negotiation. They picked up the Action Drives quickly and started making connections. In the workshop we looked at strategies we could use when engaging with others and had lengthy discussions about how our movement styles helped us with negotiating differences with colleagues. One of them said, "AHA! I might use this with my partner at home". From these discussions I devised a compilation of strategies which I will detail next in Table 6.3.

Please note, these will vary in other cultural contexts, and they are worth a try to see if they still hold true in other places.

Hopefully these strategies come in handy as you start to apply this system in your own life. Make sure you keep journalling your observations of how your perception of your own movement and body awareness might be changing.

Culture and Caveats

Each culture and subculture will assign a value (consciously and unconsciously) to each of these Drives. If we view the workplace as a subculture, you will be able to reflect on what Drives are being rewarded in certain cases. Sometimes these 'rewards' are explicit, but often they exist between the lines. These might be also overtly expressed in the mission of the company or procedures, or these might also be implicit or unconscious.

As part of this process, I recommend an ongoing challenge of your own assumptions. Movement styles can play a role in our own biases. As we see life through our own body lens, understanding other viewpoints can help play a role in critically analysing privilege/disadvantage, prejudice, oppression, and power structures. Biased interpretations of this movement system can be problematic if there is no awareness of our own cultural bias when analysing movement qualities. For example: We need to be very wary of assigning a particular Action Drive to stereotype a culture or any of the protected characteristics of humans (age/disability/race/ethnic origin/gender identity/sexual orientation/pregnancy).

DMT Rachele Preda makes important points in terms of the power dynamics involved not only in the field, but applicable to movement practices in general, agreeing with philosopher Sheets-Johnstone on how privilege, power, and oppression have repercussions on the body. They agree that "by gaining insight into the corporeal foundations of power, we realise our power to rework pervasive culture spawned corporeal archetypes that thrive on oppression"[23]. Therefore, power dynamics remain present (and thriving) in the process of embodied interactions. While there are always assumptions made which are based on archetypes[24] and stereotypes, it is important to understand why you move the way you do and how cultural norms may/may not have contributed to this.

Reflexivity involves being challenged and allowing this to open new Body Questions. These exercises are not meant to provide a 'right' answer – but to model how this can be applied within a variety of contexts. There is no way to future-proof this system, as we continue to construct and deconstruct cultural norms which in turn inform how we move to manifest them.

In my workshops, exploring the role of movement styles and differences has opened up spaces for dialogue within workplace groups to begin exploring acceptance, conflict, compromise, and building/repairing relationships through movement. As part of my diversity training workshops, I have worked with the idea of moving our stereotypes in sessions when I know the participants well or have done an initial assessment of group safety. I have often worked to 'decentralise' dominant discourses and challenge existing structures, which is never an easy discussion, but necessary, in order to achieve social change. I often

TABLE 6.3 Movement Negotiation Strategies

Effort Qualities	Space: Attention (+ Direct and – Indirect) Strategy: Decreasing Directness Increasing Indirectness	Space: Attention (– Direct and + Indirect) Strategy: Decreasing indirectness Increasing directness
Themes: **Environment/** **Alternatives** **Focus** **Question: Where?**	Asking people to expand on a point, considering alternatives, describing the context or environment, considering other perspectives, widening the focus/scope of a project, perspective making	Honing-in or being specific about a subject, delineating tasks or asking about a specific point, narrowing down focus, making things more concrete, perspective taking
Body Tasks:	Looking around, activating senses, widening focus, becoming aware of one's environment/context	Finding a fixed point to focus on in the room, becoming aware of one's body, encouraging eye contact[22] (if comfortable/when appropriate)
Effort Qualities:	Weight – Intention (– Strong and + Light) Strategy: Decreasing Force/Strong Weight Increasing Gentleness/Light Weight	Weight – Intention (+ Strong and – Light) Strategy: Decreasing Gentleness/Light Weight Increasing Force/Strong Weight
Themes: **Identity** **Priorities** **Question: Why?**	Engaging with more diplomacy, releasing some of the pressure of tasks (might relate to urgency/importance), reassessing what's important, letting go and moving on	Increasing pressure, engaging with more passion, making more demands, using more emphasis or intensity
Body Tasks:	Releasing parts of the body, experimenting with gentleness, light touch/tapping	Engaging with resistance in the body, full-bodied use of Force, exploring increases with intensity in the body/voice
Effort Qualities:	Time – Action (– Quick and + Sustained) Strategy: Decelerating – Slowing Down	Time – Action (+ Quick and – Sustained) Strategy: Accelerating – Speeding Up
Themes: **Identity** **Priorities** **Question: Why?**	Relaxing the time pressure, asking for longer increments of time in-between tasks, extending the duration of a project, delaying the subject/task	Shortening time increments in a task, break down a task into smaller steps with quicker turnaround, rushing
Body Tasks:	Experimenting with slow motion, exploring decelerating a rhythm, walking/moving slower	Playing with moving at higher speeds, quickening a pulse, achieving faster rhythms

ask participants about what movement preferences they think are important to their home culture. It opens up some exciting discussions about what systems and procedures are in place in each culture to support or challenge these movement preferences.

This type of debate, when grounded in creativity and safe group norms, opened the door to explore many values and systems we are often unaware of. However, a caveat here is that this often feels very risky in terms of also perpetuating oppressive structures and there is an ongoing need to set clear boundaries with the group members about the negative and constructive ways stereotypes can be used for cultural conversations.

Chapter Conclusion

In this chapter, we looked at Action Drives to determine our movement preferences and reflect on our signature movement style. We explored these Drives in movement. If there are Action Drives you feel you need more practice with, I invite you to check our individual music tracks for each of the Drives and explore each of them more in-depth. I suggest you revisit these in challenging times or in situations where we might need more insight. I have included some written worksheets to keep checking back and invite you to keep reflecting on how the Action Drives are manifested in your daily life. After exploring the Drives and once we have explored all four stages in the decision-making process, we can then look at integrating all this body knowledge in the next chapter.

REVIEW POINTS ON MOVEMENT STYLES

- A Drive involves a combination of three Effort Qualities pertaining to the following categories: Space, Weight, and Time.
- Movement styles help us reflect on our own preferences and how we operate within our cultures and microenvironments.
- We each have a breadth and preference within our Drives, and reflecting on this can help us negotiate relationships with ourselves and others.
- Action Drives are dynamic and change in milliseconds, and we all have our strengths and areas to develop.
- Action Drives also help us reflect on cultural contexts and how these are unconsciously and consciously employed.

Notes

1 Davis, Martha, Dianne Dulicai, and Ildiko Viczian. 'Hitler's Movement Signature'. *TDR (1988–)* 36, no. 2 (1992): 152–172. https://doi.org/10.2307/1146204; Davis, Martha, Stan B. Walters, Neal Vorus, and Brenda Connors. 'Defensive Demeanor Profiles'. *American Journal of Dance Therapy* 22, no. 2 (June 2000): 103–121. https://doi.org/10.1023/A:1026582324633.

2 Connors, Brenda L., and Richard Rende. 'Embodied Decision-Making Style: Below and Beyond Cognition'. *Frontiers in Psychology* 9 (2018). https://doi.org/10.3389/fpsyg.2018.01123; Connors, Brenda L., Carol-Lynne Moore, Richard Rende, and Timothy J. Colton. 'Movement Pattern Analysis (MPA): Decoding Individual Differences in Embodied Decision-Making'. In *The Sage Handbook of Personality and Individual Differences: The Science of Personality and Individual Differences* (Sage Reference, 2018), 257–277. https://doi.org/10.4135/9781526451163.n11; Connors, Brenda L., Richard Rende, and Timothy J. Colton. 'Decision-Making Style in Leaders: Uncovering Cognitive Motivation Using Signature Movement Patterns'. *International Journal of Psychological Studies* 7, no. 2 (2015): 105; Connors, Brenda L., Richard Rende, and Timothy J. Colton. 'Beyond Self-Report: Emerging Methods for Capturing Individual Differences in Decision-Making Process'. *Frontiers in Psychology* 7 (2016). https://doi.org/10.3389/fpsyg.2016.00312.

3 Ramsden, Pamela. 'The Action Profile® System of Movement Assessment for Self Development'. *Dance Movement Therapy: Theory and Practice. London*, no. 1992 (2003): 218–241; Ramsden, Pamela J. 'The Power of Individual Motivation in Management'. *Journal of General Management* 3, no. 2 (December 1975): 52–66. https://doi.org/10.1177/030630707500300206.

4 Longstaff, Jeffrey Scott. 'Laban Analysis Reviews'. Website (Consultation, Research, Publication, 2004). www.laban-analyses.org/laban_analysis_reviews/laban_analysis_notation/effort_dynamics_eukinetics/element_factor_state_drive.htm.

5 Laban, Rudolf, and Frederick Charles Lawrence. *Effort: Economy of Human Movement* (Macdonald and Evans, 1974).

6 Longstaff, 2004.

7 Moore, Carol-Lynne, and Kaoru Yamamoto. *Beyond Words: Movement Observation and Analysis* (Routledge, 2012).

8 You will have notice that we have done a smaller/shorter version of these in our warmups leading up to this chapter. If you chose to start with this chapter, you will revisit these movement in other sections.

9 Bloom et al., 2017.

10 McCaw, Dick. *An Eye for Movement* (London: Brechin Books Ltd., 2006), 109.

11 North, 1975, 244.

12 North, Marion. *Personality Assessment Through Movement* (Boston: Plays, Inc., 1975).

13 Landy, 1983.

14 Bullough, 1912, 87–118.

15 Acarón, 'Traversing Distance and Proximity', 2015, 1–15.

16 Quenk, Naomi L. *Essentials of Myers-Briggs Type Indicator Assessment* (John Wiley & Sons, 2009).

17 Connors and Rende, 2018.

18 Kawano, Tomoyo, and Meg Chang. 'Applying Critical Consciousness to Dance/Movement Therapy Pedagogy and the Politics of the Body'. In *Social Justice in Dance/Movement Therapy: Practice, Research and Education*, edited by Laura Downey and Susan Kierr (Cham: Springer Nature, 2022), 97–118. https://doi.org/10.1007/978-3-031-19451-1_7.

19 Imus, 2022, 168–185.

20 Merleau-Ponty, Maurice. *Phenomenology of Perception* (Humanities Press, 1962).

21 McCaw, Dick. 'Understanding the Meaning of Movement'. *Theatre, Dance and Performance Training* (July 2015). www.tandfonline.com/doi/pdf/10.108 0/19443927.2015.1027453?casa_token=ZzM1Gjkt9iwAAAAA:3KEIJNshuM LPa92-yKvJjUuxY0IFwEo2iZxBFf5lEWLsWeLd_gcJ3iKi3dDDWElveX6t2egk-qg.

22 Please understand that eye contact is not a universally appropriate concept. Although encouraged in many Western cultures, other cultures might find this disrespectful. Additionally some people who are neurodivergent or extremely anxious may find this extremely uncomfortable. Please be mindful of difference.

23 Sheets-Johnstone, Maxine. *The Roots of Power: Animate Form and Gendered Bodies* (Open Court Publishing, 1994), 7–8; cited in: Preda, 2022, 71–80.

24 An archetype is a term that has roots in ancient history but was popularised in Jungian psychotherapy (branch of psychology developed by Carl Jung). Jung discussed the aspect of the collective unconscious, drawing upon commonalities across world cultures which, he claimed are all interconnected in our human experience. Archetypes are characteristics/personality and overarching types that humanity draws upon to code human behaviour and interactions. Jung applied archetypes to his work with clients in ways which shaped much of contemporary psychotherapy to this day. Reference: Jung, C. G. *The Archetypes and the Collective Unconscious*, 2nd ed. Collected Works of C. G. Jung, vol. 9 (London: Routledge, 2014).

7

MICRO-PROCESSES
Combining the Stages

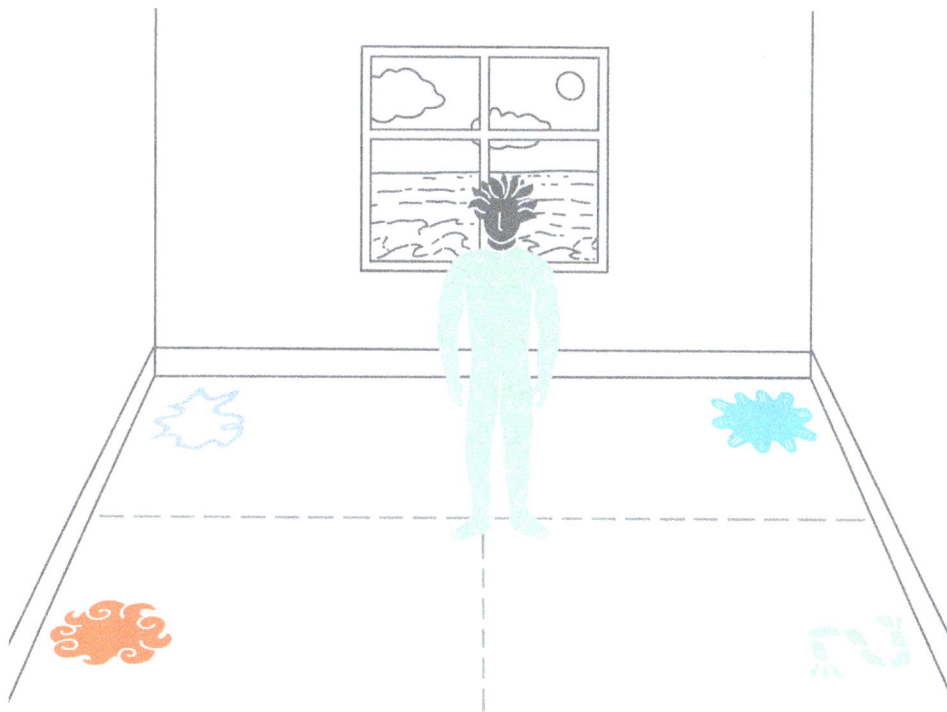

DOI: 10.4324/9781003360957-9

> ## Body Questions to Consider in This Chapter
> - What movement patterns have I discovered in myself?
> - How can I understand which stage I am in during a life transition?
> - How can these movement concepts support my decision-making?

In early chapters, we explored all the stages of decision-making. Now it is time to put all the stages together and see how the framework operates. One of the trickiest aspects of working with this model is that although it is illustrated as being linear, it is dynamic. It can start at any stage and go through any order. You can stay in stages, revisit them, or loop between them. Throughout your life, these stages have been enacted so many times; this book just highlights that you can be consciously aware of how your body can serve as a conduit for more information to help you understand how you arrive at decisions. Most decision-making systems explored in research have been mostly cognitive and rely on the 'rational' approaches to making decisions[1]. Research has also explored the role affect (which includes mood and emotions) can play in both the before and after of decisions (e.g. when you feel regret about a decision)[2]. Brain research has also concluded that decision-making is also regulated not only in your brain, but throughout your whole body, for example, through your sensory and nervous systems[3]. Intuition, about a potential pathway, interaction or a situation, usually associated with a "feeling in your gut" might also play a role in how your body informs you of decisions and relationships[4]. Decision-making is indeed a promising area for further research and I will share more research highlights later in this chapter.

As we explored in Chapter 4, for complicated decisions, you might need to take considerable time to weigh out options or alternatives that might carry heavier consequences. For instance, you might be contemplating a change in career, which might also involve a geographical move, or going through a life transition – retirement, new/break up of a relationship, having health concerns, or needing more quality of life, among so many transitional changes. For day-to-day decisions, you might go through this system thousands of times (consciously or unconsciously) and move through the decision-making system in milliseconds. You can use this system to guide you and now that you have all the movement qualities of each stage, we can start combining and exploring our Body Questions more in depth to progress through Attention, Intention, Action/Non-Action, while constantly reflecting on our Flow/Tension. This is what I will describe here as a *Micro-Process*.

In this chapter, you will continue to explore how to pay attention to the body and with the body (using bodily information to understand others and your environment/context)[5]. However, you might also notice that many events in your life are creating some themes and patterns that suggest one of the decision-making stages is taking priority. This is what I will term as a *Macro-process* and will cover this in Chapter 8.

Micro-Processes

Micro-Processes (internal process of decision-making) and *Macro-processes* (overarching themes and patterns) are two types of approaches to decision-making through movement. These were originally presented in your life as developmental tasks which you practised from an early age. You learned to regulate your concentration/focus, made your intentions and needs heard as you negotiated verticality, and practised regulating your timing when learning how to walk/locomote.

Through ongoing movement practice, we can tackle both mundane and challenging decisions with body awareness and continue developing our embodied skills. Think about how you decided what to buy at a grocery store or what to wear in the morning. In the grocery store situation, you might have additional limits/pressures such as time or budget, meaning you evaluate the priority items you need to buy. Or you might be in a hurry and decide to get only essential items. You will have also created some internal rules/norms (consciously or unconsciously) to buy certain things so that you make these decision-making processes even more efficient.

As another example, what you decided to wear this morning might have been a conglomeration of gender expression, mood, context you will need clothes for (work, home), social pressures, cultural norms, individual personality traits, and many other factors. Or you just picked up the first thing you saw! If fashion is something that is very important to you, this might have been a more complex decision. Therefore, the only person who can give weight/importance to a decision is ultimately: YOU.

Many movement analysts have focused mostly on what I term here as Micro-Processes. For example, Martha Eddy[6] described the development of effort dynamics in decision-making as follows:

1. Control of one's flow or tension
2. Awareness of space through the regulation of focus
3. Sensing and engaging one's weight for the regulation of Force
4. Deciding that this is the moment for action by sensitising to time

Or, as I suggested in the Action/Non-Action (Chapter 4), there could be an outcome where you decide to revisit the stages rather than take action on a decision. As with any decision – there will be additional context factors which will influence your process: access needs, exposure/prior experiences, relationships (decisions made on behalf of yourself or other individuals), mental and physical health, financial pressures, time, commitments, stress factors – the list is endless and quite unique to everyone. It is important to reflect on all environmental factors to ascertain some of the key variables that will offer insight into a specific situation, which we discussed in the Variables of Insight section in Chapter 1.

Worksheet 7.1 will support you to reflect as you engage with all of the stages. Additional Appendices (1–12) have printed worksheets in case you want more space to explore individual components in each stage. There are worksheets that have only the Body Questions we explored in each chapter introduction, or the movement qualities. To revisit the whole system and its movement qualities, please refer back to Worksheet 1.3 on page 47.

Decision-Making Styles

In the previous chapter about Movement Styles, we began to reflect on our preferences or 'default settings' in movement. Now we add the layer of understanding your *Decision-Making Style* by connecting all the stages together and seeing what emerges from pairing movement qualities with Body Questions about a specific decision. People trained in movement analysis observation in all systems (LBMA, MPA, KMP, etc.) are certified to notate and create profiles of other people's movements. Laban and Lawrence (who helped developed LBMA) initially observed factory workers during the Industrial Revolution to help optimise their movements to minimise repetitive movement injuries[7]. MPA practitioners, such as Brenda L Connors, Richard Rende, Timothy Colton, and Carol Lynne Moore, apply these Action Profiles from Warren Lamb's contributions for business management, by undertaking detailed observations and allocating scores to Attention, Intention, and Action[8]. They were interested in understanding how individuals vary in terms of their decision-making, stating previous research had only looked at standardised decision-making models. These profiles were used to make recommendations in terms of management and employer relations. For example, Connors, Rende, and their team included observational reports for the US Department of Defense and, in a very interesting study, analysed military officers' movement to suggest individual differences/approaches to decision-making styles and their relationship to leadership[9].

Connors, Rende, and their team agree that the system has less to do with the decision itself, but how we are engaging with it through our own embodied lens[10]. They refer to the Effort and Shape elements from BESS into the wider system, which they term *Assertion* (which is related to making the Effort to make things happen) and *Perspective* ("giving Shape to a task")[11]. The MPA system is quite complex, and therefore I streamline the system for self-reflexive practice in a more user-friendly way by highlighting the Planes of Movement (Horizontal, Vertical, and Sagittal) related to each stage and pairing them with Effort and Shaping Elements. You can always refer to the MPA and Action Profile literature cited throughout this book for more nuanced observational approaches to Lamb's work in managerial settings.

Movement Components: Combining Effort, Shape, and Space

We will now engage with movement to reconnect with Flow/Tension, and then with the Decision-making Planes (Horizontal, Vertical, and Sagittal). Practising the different layers involved with each decision-making stage at a movement level will help us reconnect and integrate these principles through movement. Treat this first warm-up as a movement practice. Don't worry about bringing in your decision just yet. Delving into the two layers of the work at the same time might prove too complex if trying out the system for the first time. Worksheet 7.2 is a 'cheat sheet' of decision-making through movement stages, which will guide you with some of the Body Questions themes that have emerged from my research and practice. Of course, there might be more themes that emerge as you make this practice your own.

WORKSHEET 7.1 Decision-Making Stages (Blank)

(FLOW) TENSION

ACTION/NON-ACTION (TIME)

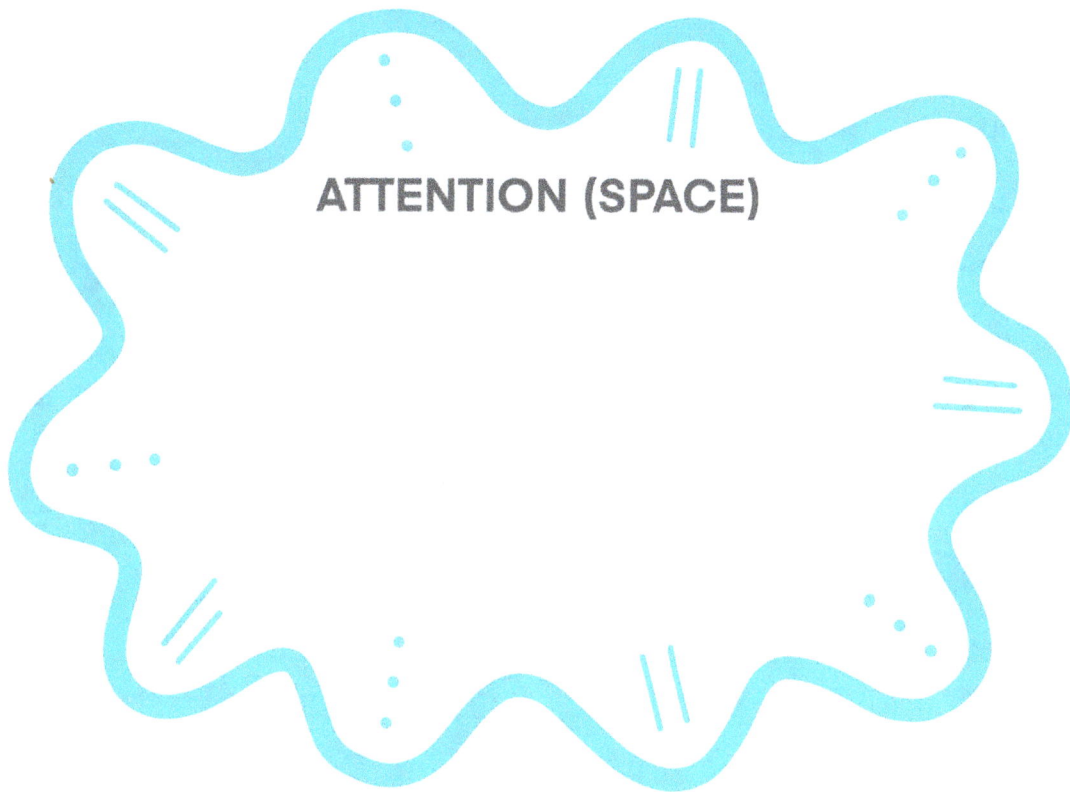

ATTENTION (SPACE)

INTENTION (WEIGHT)

WORKSHEET 7.2 Decision-Making Through Movement Themes

ATTENTION

ISSUE: Where?

THEMES:

-Environment & Alternatives

-Communication

-Protective factors/support network

INTENTION

ISSUE: So what?

THEMES:

-Confidence building

-Autonomy/Dependence

-Identity

-Prioritisation

-Assertiveness

(FLOW) TENSION

ISSUE: How?

THEMES:

-Self-regulation

-Breath & relaxation

-Body-based triggers (survival responses)

ACTION / NON-ACTION

ISSUE: When?

THEMES:

-Timing

-Commitment

-Impulsivity/Procrastination

Movement Break: Developmental Patterns Warm-Up

Suggested Music

Track Title: Contemplative

Duration: 05:52

Music Composer: Ross Whyte

Link for QR code: https://youtu.be/hlfecLU5T30?si=dlW2bTTFCgoRpny_

🎧 Link for Audio Description playlist (Movement Break is separated into four parts): www.youtube.com/playlist?list=PLtGm4qYm5yBQZqgY5_PFpJHa4jgs2R6Cw

In this warm-up I will include some elements of movements that we encountered in early stages in our human development. It is important to re-trace these patterns across our life, as they positively affect our brain pathways and support our wellbeing[12]. We will divide this warm-up into four parts to prepare for the four stages of decision-making.

For the readers who are coming from a background in movement, you will notice I also include some elements from a developmental movement system called Bartenieff Fundamentals, which was founded by BESS collaborator and movement innovator Irmgard Bartenieff and incorporated into an incredibly body of practice by somatic movement therapist Peggy Hackney[13]. I find developmental movement very meaningful in my practice as it helps people feel more connected and revitalised.

Flow/Tension Warm-Up (Part 1)

Start by lying down on a comfortable surface on the floor or sitting down. Begin by curling into a ball (foetal position) by bringing your limbs close to your core as far as it feels comfortable (Figure 7.1).

Take a couple of deep breaths in, just to centre yourself, when you are ready, breathe in deeply and as you exhale, **reach out your limbs in all directions**. Repeat this several times.

This is called a ***core-distal* connection** exercise (Figure 7.1 – top and middle images), which helps connect your body's centre to your limbs to support all other movement[14]. **Repeat this a few times and vary the directions of the stretch**. Then

FIGURE 7.1 Developmental Exercises

Core-distal Exercise: Foetal Position

Core-distal Extension

Contralateral Stretch

start bringing in more tension while remaining mindful of your breath. Increase Bound Flow as you come into yourself and then release using more Free Flow as you stretch out. Try this for a while and then change the Flow Effort qualities – releasing Tension as you move inwards and increasing Tension as you extend. Feel how Tension is negotiated as you move closer or further from your core. **Try moving each half independently using any combination of Tension (Bound/Free Flow).**

Come to stillness and lie back down on the ground (facing up). You are now going to place your arms and legs to make a star shape with your body on the floor, which will help support the next segment of the warm-up. You can do this by putting your hands on your head, and then extending your elbows, making two diagonals going outward while you are on the floor and place your legs wide in a V-shape (Figure 7.1 – bottom image). Notice the weight of your head on the floor and try some small movements to get your spine engaged. Become aware of the back of your pelvis (the triangle at the base of your spine which is called the sacrum). This is called the *head-tail connection*[15].

Feel the pull between one leg and the opposite arm (see bottom image in Figure 7.1). Try mobilising that diagonal (*contralateral* movement[16]), for example, moving the left arm and right leg. Explore as many movements as you can without activating the other diagonal. Switch to the other diagonal (opposite arm and opposite leg) when you are ready. **Try just moving the top half of the body and then just the bottom half** (Upper-Lower Connectivity[17]).

The next segment will explore *extension* and *flexion*. **Bend/stretch the elbow and knee joints.** Expand to other stretches and flexes, **moving in a way which feels good**. Remember to be mindful of the breath as to not hold any excess tension.

If you are lying down, take your time to roll to one side, and then slowly use your hands pressing on the ground to push your torso up and make your way to sitting. Close your eyes and do a brief body scan as we have done before from head to feet to notice how tense/relaxed different sections of the body are.

Which body parts feel present? Do you feel more activated?

Attention Stage Warm-Up (Part 2)

Next, you will revisit the Horizontal (Table) Plane from Chapter 2, characteristic of the Attention stage. You will engage with *Spreading* (growing wide with your body) and *Enclosing* (coming in towards yourself). Explore this with your arms and then with

FIGURE 7.2 Revisiting Horizontal (Table) Plane

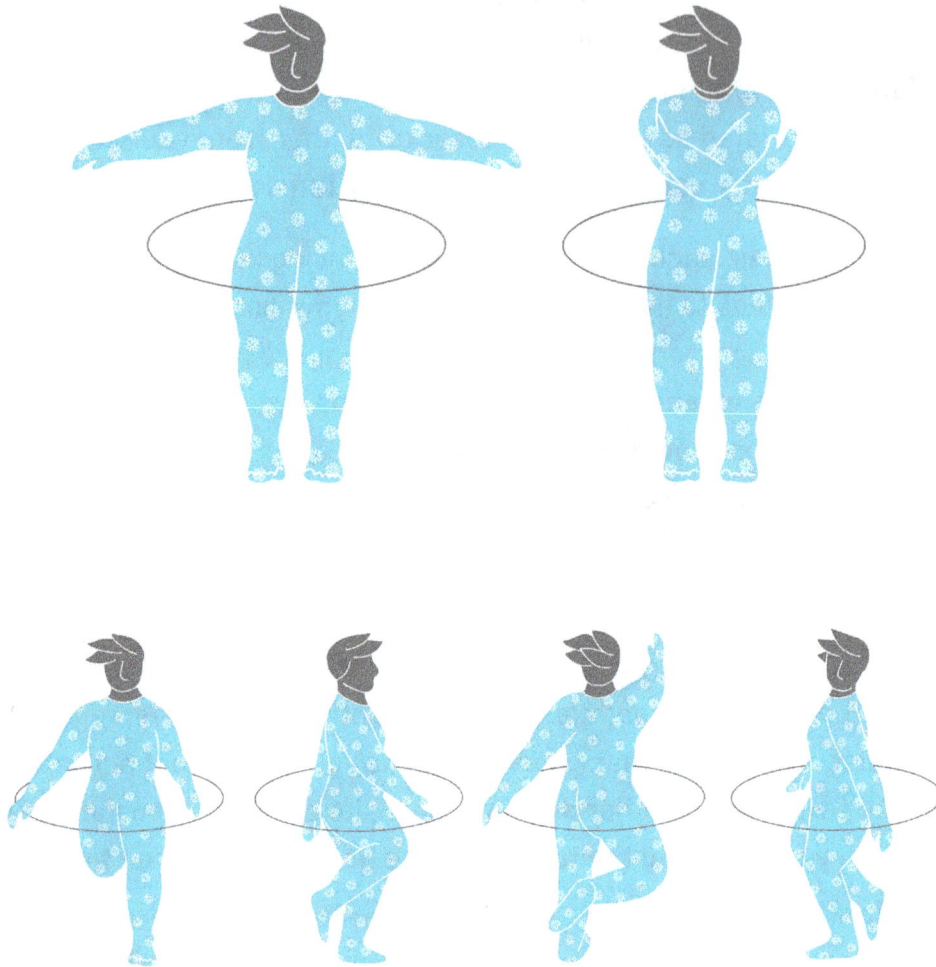

your whole body. You can move with eyes open or closed, but if you choose to move with your eyes closed just open them a tiny bit if you start moving fast.

Imagine yourself sitting/standing inside the centre of a round table. Take a moment to trace a circle with your hands in front of you and then twist your upper body to the side to continue to trace it towards the back as far as you can (Figure 7.2). Switch sides. Move your arms (or legs) forwards and backwards and to your sides with varying modes of attention to the space around you as if tracing the edges of the round table (Figure 7.2 – bottom image).

Play with different types of movements which would occur on this Plane, for instance: swimming (breaststroke), spreading seeds on a field, opening your arms wide for a hug, or encompassing a person or a pillow.

Let's add on the Attention stage Efforts here. Experiment with Directness and Indirectness (originally explored in Chapter 2). **Focus your movement with a specific intention in space.** Try this for a while, and then transition to open the movement to explore multiple points of focus. **Remember that Attention can be experienced with the whole body and not just visually. Then move with a specific intention.** You can focus on one point in the room and move towards or away from the point, or have specific task in mind.

Keep moving for a while, reviewing all the elements of this stage and then engage with some Body Questions related to Attention (pick the ones which resonate the most). The full sheet with the questions is on page 28 (Worksheet 1.1).

You can stop after each stage to reflect on the framework using the following themes: Sensations, Images, Thoughts and/or Emotions, or continue moving to the next stage.

After exploring the Attention stage for as long as you need, return to a neutral stance either sitting or standing. We are going to transition into the Intention stage and all its movement elements.

Intention Stage Warm-Up (Part 3)

Suggested Music

Track Title: Intention

Duration: 05:11

Music Composer: Ross Whyte

Link for QR Code: https://youtu.be/2GKq5MWCrHE?si=TZGCuYxASBauYffv

---

We will now revisit the Vertical Plane, otherwise called the Door Plane. Once you are in a comfortable position sitting or standing, **start drawing a figure eight shape with the top of your head**, noticing what other body parts might become involved. Take a moment to explore that connection between your head and your spine at your own pace and speed. Make it as big or small as possible. Return to a neutral stance when you're ready and be mindful of your breath. Notice whether your breath is even, deep, or shallow. **Always keep checking in with your breath as you move.** If you feel out of breath, offer yourself permission to pause.

Rolling Down Your Spine

While sitting or standing, **start dropping your head, chin to chest, and rolling your upper torso down towards the floor** as far as you feel comfortable, curl your spine forward and exhale as you drop down (*head-tail connectivity*)[18]. **Slowly roll your spine upwards up to vertical**, leaving your head to come up last (Figure 7.3). Be mindful of not holding tension in

FIGURE 7.3 Rolling down your spine

the back of your neck and letting the head completely drop, leaving the chin as close to the chest in both rolling down and rolling up. Repeat at different speeds a couple of times.

Bring both arms up and trace a rainbow above you with your fingertips, sweeping the arms and torso from side to side (Figure 7.4). This is also a great stretch for your upper body.

Imagine a rectangular doorway, but a bit wider than the regular kind. If you are standing, widen your stance and keep your knees bent slightly. We will experiment with bending your elbows in and reaching towards the top corner edges of the imaginary doorway. Next, you will bring the arms in and reach (or bend) to the bottom corners. Bring the arms in one last time, and then stretch to reach the sides of the doorway. Alternate several times between each direction, mixing the directions with different limbs if you want a challenge. Reconnect to your breath and notice how these movements feel in your body.

Engage with curiosity about the edges of your reach in this doorway. If you are standing, you can incorporate bending and extending your knees with stretching beyond your reach towards the sides more to create different levels (low, middle, high) towards the corners (Figure 7.4). If you are sitting, you can concentrate on mobilising the rib cage and the side core muscles to see how far you can stretch. An image that I like to apply here is drawing out an asterisk [*] with your whole body by coming into the centre and then out to the corners. Then revisit the archway image from the beginning, and if you are able, engage both the lower and higher extremities here (*upper-lower half connectivity*[19]).

Next, we incorporate the Shaping Qualities of Rising and Sinking, which you might be already doing. We will remain intentional of the shaping qualities to register these

FIGURE 7.4 Revisiting Vertical (Door) Plane

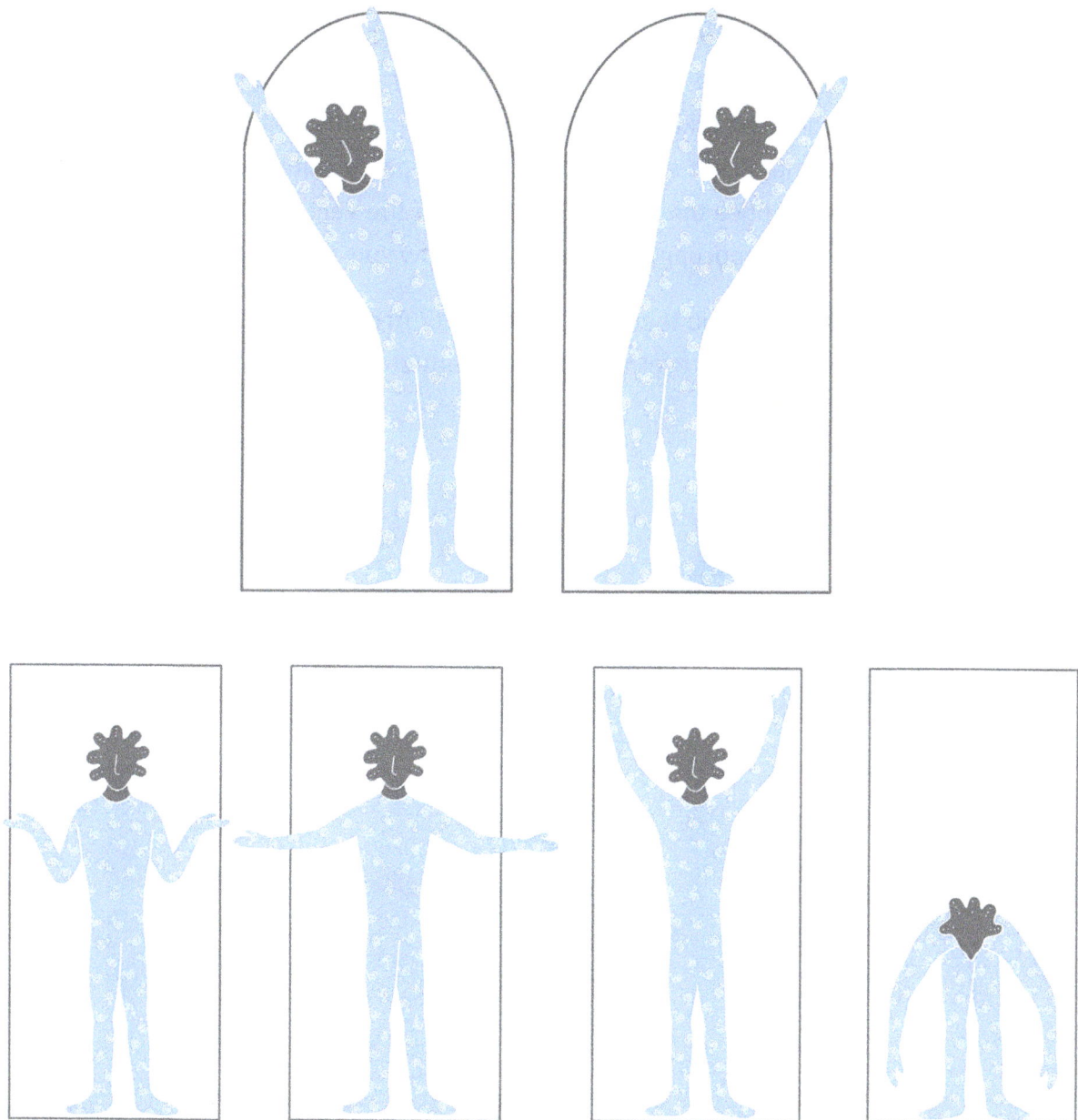

within our movement repertoire. Let the arms float up and down, and if you are standing, then engage your lower half to also rise and sink by bending and stretching your knees and extending that movement to the entire body (see Figure 7.5). Try to minimise the forward/backward motion at first to trial out the Vertical Plane in its essence. Engage your knees to hips to elbows to hands. **Try moving opposite hands with legs; can you sink with some body parts and rise with others?**

Add the Effort Qualities of Lightness and Strength using more Force with the Rising and Sinking. Then gradually decrease pressure to become lighter while doing both Rising and Sinking movements. You can also play with Time here, accelerating or decelerating with Strength or Lightness. Start light first for a while and then increase the pressure to use stronger Force (Strong Weight). For fun, if you are standing, try stomping or jumping (with full body or just arms). If you are sitting, try stomping with your fists in a sinking motion. You can even take it a step further and try different images that come up for you with this plane. Some suggestions from my participants: a sumo wrestler or Peter Pan's Tinkerbell! Notice the body negotiations of the Vertical Plane. Add the layer of meaning here if it feels appropriate – connect to how you are feeling now.

What level of confidence do you feel at this moment? Are you feeling lighter or heavier in your mood? Energy level? How is this reflected in our body? What Body Questions emerge?

FIGURE 7.5 Rising and Sinking

Once you have explored the Vertical (Door Plane), we will engage with the Sagittal Plane (Wheel). The best image offered by one of my workshop participants was imagining oneself inside a hamster wheel (but one which moves with us rather than is fixed at a point). **Reach out with one arm in front of your nose, then trace an arc which goes up towards your head** (keeping the front-ness of the movement), and then trace back down towards your knees (see Figure 7.6). **Now try drawing out the full**

range towards the back into a big arm circle. If you are a swimmer, this is close to a backstroke and then a front crawl (UK)/freestyle stroke (US).

Action/Non-Action: Sagittal Stage Warm-Up (Part 4)

Now let's engage the torso and/full body. **We will start by reaching towards the low diagonal in front of you.** That can be a point in-between both feet, but a footprint forward (more or less 30 cm). Practice doing some brushes (almost like an elephant's trunk) at a low level, and then back to neutral. Then reach at arm's length to a high diagonal in front of you. If you are standing, try taking a step forward and then coming back to neutral, alternating between moving from a low diagonal front – neutral to high diagonal front – neutral and alternate the arms. Give this a go for a bit and we will build up to our back reach. **Go from the low front diagonal and then reach the high diagonal behind you** (this might be easiest on a chair). Come back to neutral. Try now doing high front diagonal to low back diagonal (as if reaching towards something behind you that is on the floor). The ideal is to minimise the side-to-side action as much as possible. **You can now try using your fingertips to trace out the full Wheel Plane.** If you are standing, try travelling forwards and backwards by taking some steps. If you are in a wheelchair, roll the chair forwards/ backwards and then extend your arm/arms in the different directions (see Figure 7.6).

Next, play with the Time aspects of this plane. You can accelerate as you move forward and decelerate Time as you move backwards. Then explore moving quicker as you move backwards (be careful to be moving in an open space without obstacles) and moving slower as you take some steps forward. Repeat that a few times. **Envision now some 'attitude' states related to the Action/Non-Action stage –** try moving forwards or backwards with hesitation, curiosity, impulsivity, reluctance, excitement – what movement patterns occur?

FIGURE 7.6 Sagittal Plane (Advancing and Retreating)

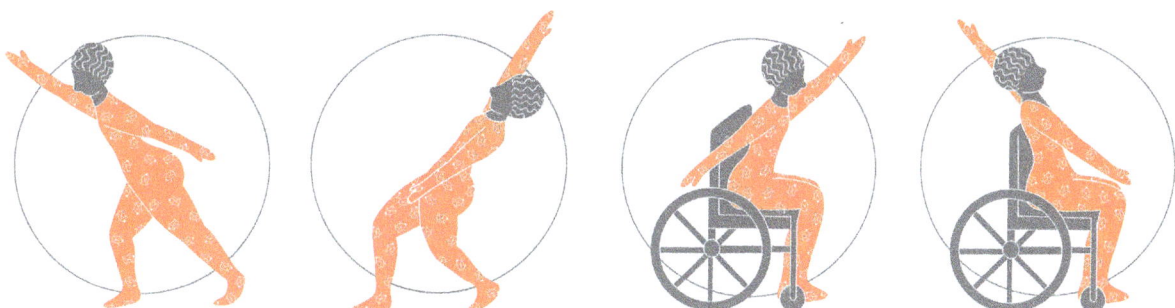

Have a play with the three planes (Table, Door, Wheel) for a while and take some time to reflect using the journal guidelines or the way you reflect best. See if you had any preferred ways of moving and whether they belonged to a particular plane. We will use this format very soon to explore with your own decision.

Reflecting on Our Stage Preferences

The connections to decision-making might be already becoming apparent while you were moving. We will add some meaning to the movement and hold the intention of the decision-making question present while we move. You will start practising how the system works all together in the next section.

Movement Break: Micro-Processes in Decision-Making: Practising the Full System

Suggested Music

Track Title: Micro Process (Introspective)

Duration: 19:12

Music Composer: Ross Whyte

Link for QR Code: https://youtu.be/OGekdjhTook?si=G7idpWYJCzgzaFT9

Suggested Music

Track Title: Micro Process (Scoping)

Duration: 19:11

Music Composer: Ross Whyte

Link for QR Code: https://youtu.be/1HhNrpVEuHQ?si=t4CkNe0wAYGU4L42>

Suggested Music

Track Title: Micro Process (Developmental)

Duration: 19:20

Music Composer: Ross Whyte

Link for QR Code: https://youtu.be/Vmaj0tq_4-8?si=zXe6oJb3vpgE7uNx>

This will be a 15–20 minute exploration to get you moving with a particular intention and representing a situation through movement. I will reiterate the main guidance I use with workshop participants: focus on a decision that is significant to you, but not transcendental. If you pick something like – 'What should I eat for dinner?', you will engage with the micro-decision-making process, of course, but perhaps at a more superficial level. You might want to start out a bit light, and then dig deeper in later exercises to understand the process in terms of their themes more. Conversely, if you pick a huge decision or transition that you are very emotionally involved with now, you might not be able to practise some of the embodied processes with enough emotional distance from the subject. Although I do see the applicability of decision-making through movement to huge, transcendental issues we might face, it is important to honour that these might need additional support than a book or an activity might offer. Practising with something manageable will support deeper processes down the line. Examples of a 'significant-but-not-transcendental' event might be one of the following: whether to stay or leave a job, deciding on an extracurricular activity you need for your wellbeing, preparing for a period of holiday/leave, getting ready to meet a client for the first time, deciding how to celebrate a major milestone in your life, deliberating on a research topic of an assignment, deciding whether to take a new responsibility at the job, among so many others. (These are my suggestions, but these might hold different meanings for you.) I'll use the celebration of a milestone event as a Micro-Process example here to help illustrate. However, if you are not ready yet and want to pick a day-to-day decision, that is fine as well – gauge how you feel.

Once you have your 'significant-but-not-transcendental' decision in mind – you will formulate a Body Question regarding this decision. A Body Question can act sometimes like a research question, something you want to explore or want you to know more about your decision. You can also refer to the Appendices for worksheets to guide your process.

Here are Some Examples of Body Questions for Micro-Processes

- How is this decision impacting my body? (Flow/Tension)
- What alternative pathways in this environment can I explore with my body? (Attention)
- Where is my body in the context of this decision? (Attention)
- What feels important in my body about this decision right now? (Intention)
- What timing and type of commitment do I need to apply here? (Action/Non-Action)
- What happens in my body as I traverse each stage? (All)

You can also go through the developmental patterns warm-up exercise again but lay out each stage on the floor and reflect on key aspects that might have been activated in each stage while moving. This might help with reconnecting to the key Body Question you want to explore. Browse through the options of worksheets and select the one you think will suit best. Use the individual sheets for each corner (provided in Appendices 1–12) or take four pieces of paper and write out the name of the stage (and maybe some descriptive factors which might help you remember) or copy some of the worksheets for each stage provided. You can use the movement descriptors and images/reflections you have generated in each chapter to guide you.

Once you have written out labels for each of the stages or retrieved the ones I have provided, if you have an open space to move in, you can lay them down on the floor. You can also tape the sheets to the walls or specific spaces you want to move in. I usually divide the space up into quadrants (Worksheet 7.1) to allow people to move easily across them, but this set-up usually requires a bigger space. If you are moving in a smaller space, don't worry, you can put them in front of you and shuffle them as you need, placing the stage that you want to explore at that time. Worksheet 7.1 is an example of our four corners blank sheet you can use or create your own.

You can use the reflexive music provided, work in silence, or choose your own music. Just be mindful that the music you choose doesn't overpower your experience but supports it – I always like to start in silence to see what happens, but music sometimes helps!

In this exploration I would like you to 'visit' each of the stages and explore them in movement in relation to your decision or question. There are often two ways I approach these: Either I think about the issue and hold it in mind as I move (a term called representation which I explain in Chapter 1), or I move first and let the body speak in relation to the issue (Activation). It is a process of not holding on too tightly to the issue so that you are able to be surprised and discover what emerges, while retaining clarity of intention while moving. Some people might need more structure while delving into each stage. Others might need more space to explore without any specific tasks in mind. At this stage in the practice of decision-making through movement, remain open to options. The most important aspect of this is that you find a way that works for you.

For this initial practice, give yourself about 3–5 minutes in each stage, and 12–15 minutes for the whole exploration with some time at the end where you can explore in general (like a movement summary time). You can take longer if needed. Set a timer (for each stage and/or for the whole exercise) if that is useful. I have found that some workshop participants prefer to have less structure and determine which stages need more time. If this is the case, then I would recommend setting a timer for the whole exercise rather than time each stage. Others prefer to give equal time to each stage to allow full exploration. You can trial out different versions as you come back to this process in the future. Take the opportunity to travel to different parts of the space and use each stage as a prompt for moving. After you explore in movement, take a moment to draw it out, write it out, or just keep it close as an image or an embodied sensation. You may want to reflect in between the stages or move through all of them and do a summative reflection. I will provide an example of a participant exploration and their decision-making process.

Case Example: One-to-One Decision-Making Sessions

Martin (pseudonym) is a White, cisgender[20], British male in his 50s, exploring a work transition into freelance/consultancy after working full time in steady, long-term jobs for all his career. He had some prior experience with movement, but he was engaging with the decision-making through movement framework for the first time. Martin had no preconceived understanding of any of the BESS concepts prior to engaging with the work. We decided to work together to see how the decision-making framework could be applied to one-to-one sessions in a more individualised way. We had two sessions, one held online for 1.5 hours to introduce some of the key concepts and one face-to-face for 2 hours to explore the full range of movement in a larger space. The two sessions were two months apart, which was helpful to see if the framework had a longer term impact on more transcendental career decisions.

Our approach was to have the decision-making stages exploration guided by Martin, where I engaged as a witness of the process. As we detailed in Chapter 3, witnessing is a practice from dance movement therapy where you observe and experience someone moving without any judgement or interpretation. There are many types of embodied witness practices, where the witness can be completely silent, offer verbal or nonverbal feedback (within a particular structure which is practised in Authentic Movement), and other forms of reflection and somatic feedback (when you communicate how what you witness was reflected/present in your body).

In each session, we did a warm-up of the three planes and enacted the movements associated with each stage (as we have done earlier in this chapter). Martin initially talked through some of the key issues of his decision, and as he spoke, I wrote down some of the key themes that were evolving (more on this later). Martin wanted to explore two types of work roles: freelance/consultant vs. permanent/contract-work.

Note: As a facilitator I often use the four quadrants in Worksheet 7.1 to make notes and observations while a participant speaks/moves, and notice where these aspects might be categorised using the decision-making framework. I then check these out with the participant to make sure the meaning is co-created. It is my aim to focus on the process through which he identifies the stages, rather than my interpretation of his experience, in keeping with the reflexive ethos of this book.

I also checked in with Martin's understanding of the movement language in terms of decision-making to see what connections he was making and what Body Questions emerged. I asked Martin to represent an issue in movement – either through a still shape or a short movement sequence as he talked through the situation to keep the connection between moving and talking. As sometimes decisions have many layers and additional factors, I kept reverting to some of the Body Questions to get clarity on which issue was the most salient.

Online Session

In the online session we had more limited space to move, and it was Martin's first time engaging with the planes. We followed a similar prompt of a verbal check-in (with me taking notes on the stages), a warm-up and Body Question-based suggestions which combined movement and talking. I asked Martin a Body Question that emerged: What are your embodied reactions to this transition between freelance/consultant and permanent/contract-work? Martin's movement mostly occurred in the Horizontal Plane. He opened his arms wide while remaining with his eyes closed and uses his head to trace figure eights in the Horizontal Plane. He connected this to his strengths in evaluation, research, working with difference, and his strength in including multiple perspectives within his work. After exploring how the work types of freelancer vs. permanent staff were represented in movement, the overall theme that emerged was Control vs. Freedom.

We shifted more into movement by representing more questions for each stage. In the Flow/Tension stage in our online session, Martin explored the question: What is my somatic reaction to these types of jobs? We looked closely at the movement qualities that came up for him when asked to represent the two work types. The freelance work type inspired very free and flowy movements. Martin engaged in expansive movements, looking outward, and used his whole body to spin. When exploring the permanent type of work, he instinctively brought his arms into himself, what he expressed was a 'blocked' or 'closed' body shape, and his knees dropped to the floor. Martin said that the notion of longer term contracted work provoked this very blocked, almost protective stance, which for him at this time felt quite oppressive and limiting. We were both struck with the sharp contrast in movement at the mention of this type of work. This was reflected in the Intention stage, which we identified as the area that needed more support – both in movement, by developing more practice in engaging upper-lower halves in his body and having more opportunities to play with Weight factors. He identified that he needed to work more on highlighting his strengths and developing his self-worth by embracing this big change. His Body Question regarding the Intention stage was: How do I challenge my own perspective?

In the online session, we didn't delve very much into the Action stage, as we identified that there needed to be more space and time for him to explore this transition between roles, as this decision had been forced by an abrupt change of circumstances. This felt important, and we ended the session with some goals to work on in terms of the Intention stage. At the end of the online session, we discussed what the next steps would look like and what outcomes he expected. Martin identified the need to explore his sense of verticality more. We connected the topic of verticality explorations to Martin looking deeper into his unique selling point. These themes connected to accepting, discovering, and highlighting his strengths (to himself and others), which Martin accepted was an ongoing challenge he was currently working on.

In-Person Session

In our face-to-face session a few months later, Martin brought in (as the main decision-making issue) another crossroads between taking an interim short-term position and continuing on exploring consultancies that had arisen since we last did our initial exploration. I witnessed Martin's movement for the 12-minute Micro-Process exploration we did in the beginning of this chapter and reflected some of his movement in key moments. We used the worksheets with stages with some key movement aspects (Appendices 9-12) and laid them out in quadrants. My responsibilities were to witness his process and keep time for him. Martin chose to time each stage to 3 minutes and chose to have me give verbal prompts for him to transition after time ran out. Martin chose the order of the stages, which ended up being: (1) Attention, (2) Intention, (3) Flow/Tension, and (4) Action/Non-Action. We had a bit of time after the 12 minutes for Martin to explore in movement without a particular structure. We used Ross' composition for the full system which is available in the Suggested Music track title "Micro Process (Developmental)".

Developmental Micro Process

Suggested Music

Track Title: Micro Process (Developmental)

Duration: 19:20

Music Composer: Ross Whyte

Link for QR code: https://youtu.be/Vmaj0tq_4-8?si=587h1e8_-tdJfSYV

In the first stage of exploration (Attention), Martin initiated movement using both arms and traced the middle level space around his kinesphere. Most of his movements across the exploration were symmetrical. As he enclosed his arms, he held himself in an embrace for a short amount of time, rocking from side to side. He then had moments of slowly spinning around. Movements kept to a medium to slow speed. He later responded that there was nothing innovative he felt occurred in this stage, as he had spent a lot of time in the past months exploring his options and assessing the current work environment.

In the Intention stage, he had fleeting moments of bending and stretching his knees, finding his ground, which liberated his upper torso as he rose up into the high level. Additional context relevant for this stage which was brought up in both sessions in the initial check-ins: Martin had come from a contracted employment experience where he hadn't felt valued and had been constantly undermined by management. He stated he was constantly being treated as if he was interviewing for his role even though he had been in the post for several years. This ultimately had a negative effect on him, and after leaving the former job, there was a sense of regaining his confidence and reconnecting to his strengths as he considered new possibilities. In these initial assessments during both sessions, Martin identified this situation to be more Intention stage related during our first post-movement debrief in this session, which connected to his online session. He did this setting a clear goal and determining his baseline before addressing the other stages.

Movement Exploration Key Moments

Back to the in-person session: Martin repeated the movements of Rising and Sinking a couple of times but remained quite still within this stage. The main aim of emphasising the Intention stage in this more in-depth movement exploration was to be able to look at what he could offer, which tied into his true work interests. The aim was then to be able to find work 'anchors' which he could draw upon in his search for new freelance projects, solid aspects that help him feel confident.

Martin identified that the career choice between an interim position (short-term contract) or to keep developing his portfolio of new consultancies came up most during his 'visit' to the Flow/Tension stage. Most of Martin's movements up to this point had included swaying and sweeping motions around the periphery of all the planes. He had not done any gestural movements in any of the sessions. As he entered the Flow/Tension stage, Martin brought his hands wide in the Door Plane to the high diagonals, and then slowly brought the hands in front of his chest and clasped his hands together. He then formed two small circles by bringing the thumb and fingers together with both hands and interlaced them – forming a figure eight between both hands as show in the image of two hands. This gesture became very significant when he discussed his experience, as he connected this gesture to his ongoing worry about the uncertainty of his work situation. As a witness, I was not trying to figure out what Martin was doing and what the gesture symbolised – that was not my role. I kept connecting to my own body while supporting his process and being present for him as he moved.

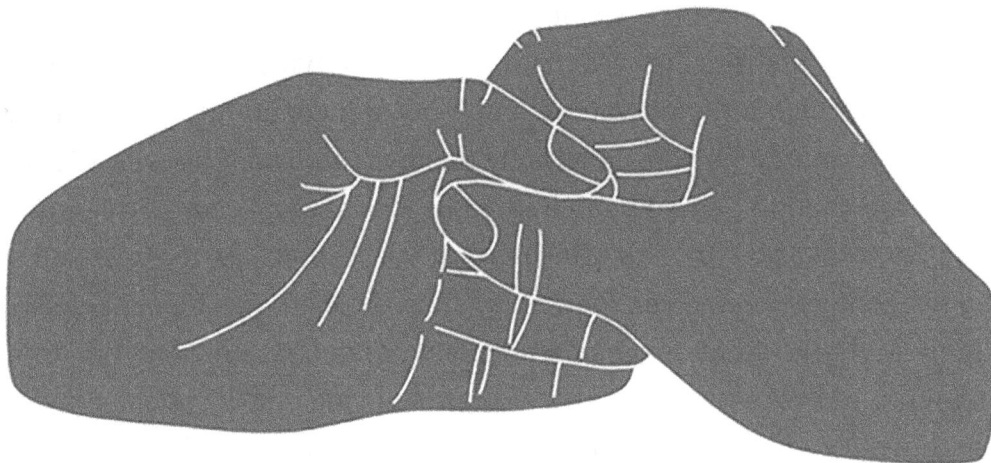

Martin widened his arms above his head with hands in two fists and built-up tension in his fingers. He held this shape for a while, with Bound Flow in his arms as he held them to each side. When we discussed this stage, he identified Flow/Tension as one of the most surprising ones. He described himself growing with tension upon the possibility of taking this short-term contracted position, which he said, "felt right" as it was an upwards development career-wise. Before the movement exploration, he had expressed concern about stepping outside his comfort zone with the new consultancies, while also taking on a new bigger position in the short term. He said he expected the pressure of being part of a larger institution in this short-term role as a "shrinking with tension" – but that this was not the case when he embodied it. He described the new opportunity as 'bound' by time, but that there was a possibility to grow within it. This was an insightful moment where the movement activated a different perspective.

As Martin's witness, I shared with him (after the whole decision-making stages exploration) how I felt some tension in my upper chest when he did that specific figure eight gesture. As he transitioned then into the Action/Non-Action stage, Martin took a big sudden step forward reaching towards the low diagonal in front of him, he maintained some of the swaying from side to side as he explored. He repeated a rocking forward to back, shifting weight between his front and back legs, moving in the Sagittal Plane with what seemed like a hesitation when accelerating (I asked about this later). He then turned 180 degrees into a different direction and held a high diagonal back lean of his upper torso with his hands clasped behind his head. In this Action/Non-Action stage, the pattern of wavering in time during the forwardness and returning to centre seemed prevalent. Towards the end of the exploration, Martin took bigger steps, but each of them with a rock backwards. He later connected these movements to the potential of a new short-term role. Martin explained that although it was a big step forward in terms of his career, the rock backwards connected to him to what he was used to doing, and back to his 'comfort zone' of permanent, steady roles. The difference of this opportunity being short term, however, was that it offers him some security to be able to be in steadier footing to continue his consultancies. He expressed some hesitation about the suddenness of this opportunity, but then identified this as an advantage – the quick timing meant less anxiety about the upcoming change. It is always interesting to see the correlation between the movements and the participants' content, and how participants connect the content between the two modes. It is fascinating when the words exactly mirror what the movements were as it occurred here.

After visiting all the stages, I encouraged him to do his own short exploration in movement of all the key moments or things he might need to revisit from the whole experience. Then we held a discussion where Martin described his experience and shared some insights, which I have interwoven with the movement aspects throughout.

A month later, Martin got in touch and told me he had accepted the interim role. He felt excited about the prospect and was glad he had been able to explore this transition in movement. He remarked on the surprises and discoveries that movement offered him, in a stressful situation that he had held 'in his head'. The interim role later led him to new consultancies, and he is now at the central management for a small company, doing what he loves.

This is an example of one application of the process – but there are many variants of this activity which can develop out of your movement practice.

Self-Witnessing: Video as a Tool for Our Own Reflexivity

A valuable tool I have found which helps develop our inner witness (and tame the inner critic) is to videotape my own decision-making process and witness my own process privately. It takes some time to get used to seeing oneself on video and not be critical about the way we move. However, if we use the same principles of non-judgement, we can start looking beyond the aesthetics of movement and other expectations we might have about our body and our movement, and look for connections between movement and experience, gain insight and note discoveries. You can also use the worksheets provided to note down some of the key moments in each stage as you witness yourself and notice patterns as they emerge.

Culture and Caveats

There are several caveats to doing more introspective movement work. The first is that we exercise a duty of care. This kind of work, where we deeply reflect on a significant aspect of our lives, begs a vulnerability that needs some protective factors to scaffold it. If you are a therapist/facilitator, you should be mindful of any mental health conditions that could be detrimental to your client. Sometimes, introspective movement work has been contraindicated for people with a history of schizophrenia, hallucinations, extreme chronic pain, and states in which we might be volatile or requiring a higher level of mental health care. It is hard to make a steadfast rule here, as everyone has a different Window of Tolerance. Window of Tolerance is a model of working which has been developed within trauma education, which

> proposes that individuals have an optimal zone of arousal within the window of tolerance where they can manage daily stress and challenges. . . . As an individual's reactions to stressors intensify, it becomes more difficult to access strategies and resources to manage distress. This often shows up as overwhelming emotions, unwanted thoughts, uncomfortable sensations, or unhealthy behavioral impulses. This model can be used to help clients mindfully track these states, build resources to tolerate daily stressors, and proactively implement resources to widen their window of tolerance[21].

In the reflection we did on our spectrum of movement qualities in Worksheet 6.1 in Chapter 6, often the ones that fall beyond our range and preference also could be theorised to lay outside our Window of Tolerance. People who are in more delicate physical, psychological, or emotional states might benefit more from focusing on the exercises here that could support them to connect with others, identify strengths, and build resilience. Another caveat here is noticing the socio-cultural associations with the wordings of these stages. In your own culture there might be different meanings associated with the titles of each stage. You will also notice your experience of the four stages of decision-making is strongly linked to your own cultural context, and it might be a good point of reflection to unpack this context as part of your own reflective practice.

There are many cultural considerations as well for working with others and interpreting movement symbols. When this process is done with a client/participant the process should be participant-led and the meanings that they ascribe to their movement are always valid. The cultural context and identity of the person needs to be honoured and our biases as facilitators acknowledged and worked through with our own clinical/process supervision, and support network (e.g. personal therapy) where applicable. Please do not try to do this with other people if you have not facilitated before or this system is completely new to you. There is further training out there to continue this as part of your professional development down the line.

In these sessions, my training as a dance movement therapist was crucial in gathering information, attuning to the movement, and drawing upon experience to keep content focused on professional identity. It was always made clear that there was not a therapeutic relationship or contract between Martin and me and all the participants from professional development workshops cited in this book. I also kept my own notes of my own embodied experiences and took these to my own clinical supervision for support. I illustrate here the example of bringing my DMT experience into a professional development context and frame how my training can contribute to other models of arts, health and wellbeing sessions, or business coaching.

Chapter Conclusion

In this chapter, I recommended exercises that combine all decision-making stages, described here as a Micro-Process. I suggested explorations to visit each decision stage from a movement perspective, and then added another exploration which adds the layer of meaning. We explored an application through the case example of Martin and his decision of a career change.

> **REVIEW POINTS ON THE MICRO-PROCESSES OF DECISION-MAKING THROUGH MOVEMENT AND THE ARTS**
>
> - In summary, the Micro-Processes of decision-making consists of:
>
>   - Exploring the stages (Flow/Tension, Attention, Intention, and Action/Non-Action) by combining their movement components: Planes, Shaping Qualities, and Effort Qualities
>   - Embodying the movement qualities and noticing our own preferences
>   - Adding the layer of the decision we want to explore (if needed)
>   - Reflecting on Images, Sensations, Thoughts, and Emotions that arise
>   - Analysing its applicability to personal and professional realms.
>
> - We can watch for connections and patterns between our movement and the situation we are exploring.
> - In Micro-Processes we can home in our skills in witnessing our own process.

The next chapter will explore Macro-Processes and look at the system in terms of ongoing themes, patterns, and life stages.

Notes

1 Connors and Rende, 2018.

2 Lerner, Jennifer S., Ye Li, Piercarlo Valdesolo, and Karim S. Kassam. 'Emotion and Decision-Making'. *Annual Review of Psychology* 66 (January 2015): 799–823. https://doi.org/10.1146/annurev-psych-010213-115043.

3 Bechara, Antoine, Hanna Damasio, and Antonio R. Damasio. 'Emotion, Decision-Making and the Orbitofrontal Cortex'. *Cerebral Cortex* 10, no. 3 (January 2000): 295–307. https://doi.org/10.1093/cercor/10.3.295.

4 Tantia, Jennifer Frank. 'Is Intuition Embodied? A Phenomenological Study of Clinical Intuition in Somatic Psychotherapy Practice'. *Body, Movement and Dance in Psychotherapy* 9, no. 4 (2014): 211–223.

5 Csordas, 1993; Tantia, 2012.

6 Eddy, 2009, 111.

7 Laban and Lawrence, 1974.

8 Connors, Brenda L., Richard Rende, and Timothy J. Colton. 'Predicting Individual Differences in Decision-Making Process from Signature Movement Styles: An Illustrative Study of Leaders'. *Frontiers in Psychology* 4 (2013). https://doi.org/10.3389/fpsyg.2013.00658; Connors, Brenda L., Carol-Lynne Moore, Richard Rende, and Timothy J. Colton. 'Movement Pattern Analysis (MPA): Decoding Individual Differences in Embodied Decision Making'. In *The SAGE Handbook of Personality and Individual Differences: The Science of Personality and Individual Differences* (Sage Reference, 2018), 257–277. https://doi.org/10.4135/9781526451163.n11.

9 Connors, Rende, and Colton, 2013.

10 Connors and Rende, 2018, 2.

11 Ramsden, Pamela, and Jody Zacharias. 'The Action Profile System of Movement Assessment for Self Development'. In *Action Profiling: Generating Competitive Edge Through Realizing Management Potential* (Ashgate Pub Co., 1993), 22.

12 Hackney, 2002.

13 Hackney, 2002.

14 Derived from the principal developmental movement concepts within the framework of Bartenieff Fundamentals, as covered in Hackney, 2002, 14, 21.

15 Hackney, 2002, 85–110.

16 Hackney, 2002, 259.

17 Hackney, 2002, 111–165.

18 Hackney, 2002, 85–110.

19 Hackney, 2002, 111–165.

20 Cisgender means someone whose gender identity (how they see themselves aligned within the gender spectrum) and the sex assigned at birth correlate. Please search for your local LGBTQ+ organisation to verify the language used, as they vary according to where you are based.

21 Hershler, Abby. 'Window of Tolerance'. In *Looking at Trauma: A Tool Kit for Clinicians*, edited by Abby Hershler, Lesley Hughes, Patricia Nguyen, and Shelley Wall (Penn State University Press, 2021), 25–28. https://doi.org/10.1515/9780271092287-008.

8
MACRO-PROCESSES
Threading Themes Through

DOI: 10.4324/9781003360957-10

Body Questions to Consider in This Chapter

- What themes emerge from movement that connect across different aspects of your life?
- How are they serving me? Are they sustainable?
- How does change impact my body?

In previous chapters, we experienced how each stage can be a step in the Micro-Process of a decision. Moreover, if we think of each of the stages (Flow/Tension, Attention, Intention, and Action/Non-Action) as broader categories within our life, the system can also help us make connections om a larger scale. For example, let's say you are starting to consider leaving your job as you are getting quite frustrated with the overwhelming time it is consuming in your life (Flow/Tension). You have gone through the Micro-Process, as discussed in earlier chapters, exploring ways in which you could improve/address the issues within your current job (Attention), identifying that you need to prioritise a better work-life ratio, have better working hours (Intention), and set up a plan to apply for several job postings you found online (Action). However, you also find that your body is having similar reactions and situations in other aspects of your life. You might be reconsidering whether to address some issues with a long-time friendship or relationship or finding it difficult to find time to access some activity you love, or perhaps you are feeling unappreciated and taken for granted both at work and in your personal life. These situations, as a collection of experiences, might be signalling to you that there is a wider issue here that is pervasive across many of your life dimensions: a Macro-Process.

This chapter will also make connections to DMT research to provide a larger scope for decision-making through movement. A review of the themes that have emerged from my research can be found on Worksheet 7.2 on page 202.

Attention   Let's review the thematic connections we have made so far.

The Attention stage connects to the 'typical' developmental stage of regulating focus. In DMT and movement analysis research, this stage has been linked to communication[1], and our ability to be able to encompass multiple perspectives (specific and general), assess our environment, and explore alternatives.

Intention The Intention stage connects to the 'typical' developmental stage of negotiating our verticality. In DMT research, it has been commonly referred to as the Plane of the Self and our Identity, linking some of the key challenges and opportunities to how we assert our needs, establish our relationship to autonomy/dependence, agency, and positions of authority. Confidence, dejection, assertion, 'giving in', 'stepping up', and 'finding our feet' are some examples of aspects of themes related to the Macro-Processes of this stage.

Action/Non-Action The Action/Non-Action stage connects to the 'typical' developmental stage of regulating timing and pacing, connected to advancing/ retreating regarding a goal. In DMT research, it is particularly related to violence prevention and peacebuilding; this is connected to our sense of commitment and activism[2]. This stage is also related to impulsivity and procrastination and to the implementation of our plans. In this book, we include the option of Non-Action, which involves revisiting the other stages without the emphasis on an outcome or product. Non-Action is still a decision!

(Flow) Tension Flow/Tension addresses our internal mechanisms which regulate stress, repression, release, and pleasure and are connected to our primal autonomic responses within our nervous system. Kestenberg Movement Profile research has focused on the understanding of Flow across the life span[3], and DMT research has made connections between how bodily states are affected during stressful situations or when people have experienced trauma[4]. The Macro-Processes of this stage have to do with the practice of embodied reflexivity, listening to our body for cues as to what might be going on for us. This stage is often our first indicator that something needs to change[5].

Like all the stages, there are both constructive and challenging sides to each of the Macro-Processes described here. I will aim to present various options, as there is no right way to engage with macro-themes. The idea here is not necessarily to polarise themes as "good" or "bad" or place them on a hierarchy, as they are often more complex. Our job here is to notice, try to understand (while being kind to ourselves), and reflect on whether change is needed and how to go about it.

We will begin by reflecting on the proportion of time and energy you might devote to each of these stages. For the time being, we will set Flow/Tension aside as we have discovered that Flow/Tension will be our constant stage of reconnecting to our body. We will make some embodied guesses to start us off. When we move through a decision in later activities, then we can compare back with the somatic information we have gathered.

First, we will create a diagram of the proportion of time/energy you spend on the three decision-making stages using examples from your personal[6] life, which I will explain shortly. We will overgeneralise at first to demonstrate a way to get perspective on decisions using viewpoints. (Remember you can always come back and change these.)

Reflexive Exercise: Proportions Between the Stages

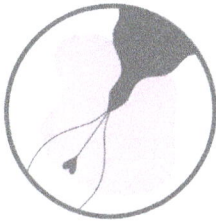

Suggested Music

Track Title: Journalling

Duration: 04:00

Music Composer: Ross Whyte

Link for QR Code: https://youtu.be/Lw9tNU-DkUg?si=N8hB5YuksrUuKblU>

Here, we will draw a diagram to represent this proportion of stages. Remember that there is no right and wrong way of doing this, and keep in mind that these proportions may change during different periods in your life. In theory there are no hierarchies to the stages – they all might need equal consideration. In practise, however, the stages vary according to the situation, environment, your own preferences, and how they clash/complement/align with other people's movement preferences.

You have a few options, and there will be diagrams with examples provided.

All diagrams will answer the following Body Questions:

1. In my personal life, in general (usually), what is the proportion of time and energy I spend across the stages?

Another option might be related to your decision:

2. What proportion might this specific situation require?

Figure 8.1 Top Image (Spectrum):

If someone drew this proportion, this person prefers Intention and Action more and spends more time/energy on these two stages.

Figure 8.1 Middle Image (Percentages):

If numbers tend to help you more, you can estimate, in general cases, what the proportion of the three stages would be in percentages. For example, this person spends most of the time actioning things, dedicating less time to delineating priorities, and even less time researching alternatives or assessing the environment.

Figure 8.1 Bottom Image (Geometrical Figures):

You can also draw the stages as geometrical figures if you want to access a more visual language. This person has more of a balanced proportion between researching alternatives and determining what is important, but still tends to spend more time actioning decisions.

All diagrams will answer the following Body Questions:

Option 1. In my personal life, in general (usually), what is the proportion of time and energy I spend across the stages?

Another option might be related to your decision:

Option 2. What proportion might this specific situation require?

Figure 8.1 Top Image (Spectrum):

If someone drew this proportion, this person prefers Intention and Action more and spends more time/energy on these two stages.

Figure 8.1 Middle Image (Percentages):

Option 3. If numbers tend to help you more, you can estimate, in general cases, what the proportion of the three stages would be in percentages. For example, this person spends most of the time actioning things, dedicating less time to delineating priorities, and even less time researching alternatives or assessing the environment.

Option 4: Getting Creative

Our illustrator Eve has come up with some fun variations on Carol-Lynne Moore's proportion diagrams[7] for decision-making, where Moore used pyramids and

FIGURE 8.1 Proportion Diagrams

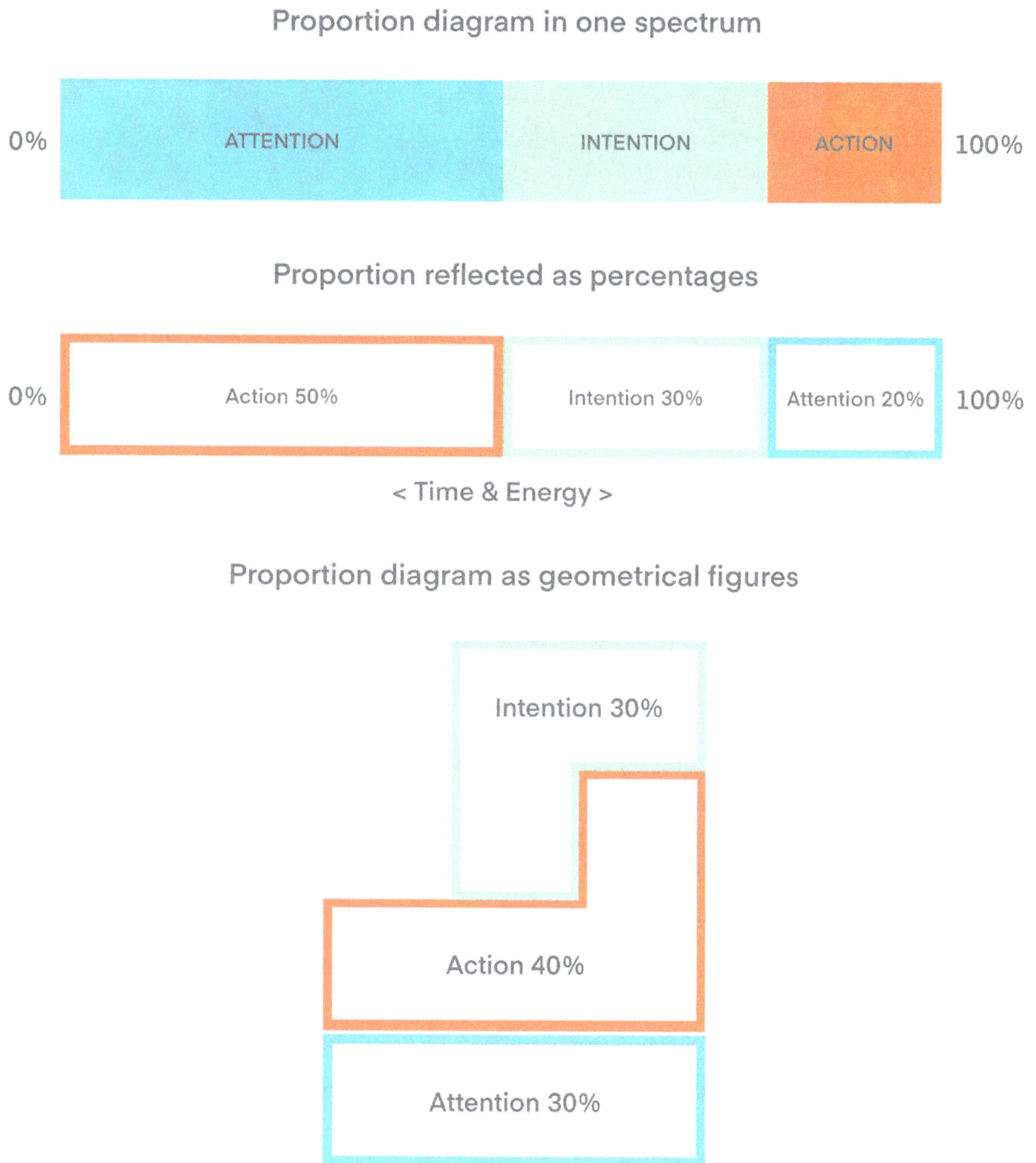

Proportion diagram in one spectrum

0% | ATTENTION | INTENTION | ACTION | 100%

Proportion reflected as percentages

0% | Action 50% | Intention 30% | Attention 20% | 100%

< Time & Energy >

Proportion diagram as geometrical figures

Intention 30%

Action 40%

Attention 30%

diamond shapes for each stage. In Figure 8.2, we devised our own version of how we can illustrate proportion of time and energy we tend to use. Remember, these proportions can capture moments in time, or a specific situation and might change depending on your context.

FIGURE 8.2 Geometric Diagrams

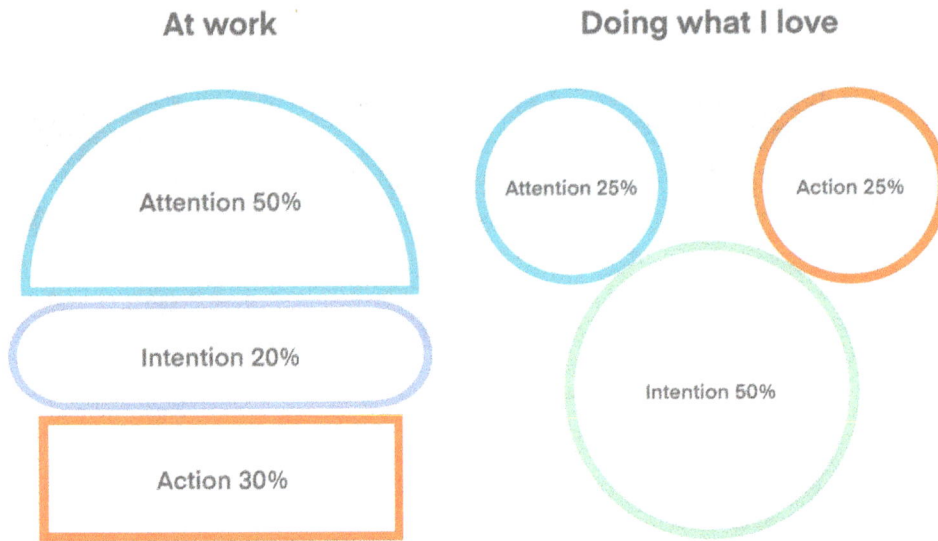

For example, in the right of Figure 8.2, the person at their work prioritises Intention – it could be by enforcing rules, regulations, or looking at policies – and spends less time assessing the issue or committing to actioning or to specific timeframe. Because of the equal proportion of time/energy in Attention/Action, it seems that this person might be stuck/be confident/proficient in the Vertical Plane. In the left of Figure 8.2, the person prioritises Attention, more than Intention, and spends less time/energy assessing things. This person might prefer activities which involve more taking in the environment. They might spend less energy deciding on priorities within this activity, and potentially could prefer activities that go from taking in the environment to action. This might be the proportion for someone who enjoys hiking alongside a beautiful cliff, for instance. The possibilities for this reflection are endless. These are other scenarios you might want to add to your initial observations noticing the proportion between work and personal life. Here we have gotten more creative with the drawings:

- Which one appeals to you the most?
- Are the proportions in your personal and professional life different? The same?
- Do you feel there might be a difference between how you perceive yourself and how others perceive you?

Worksheet 8.1 is provided for you to draw your proportion.

Macro-Processes: Stage Proportion Worksheet

Create your own proportion diagram
using the examples provided here

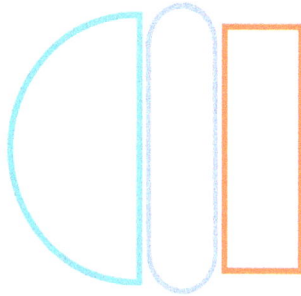

Your movement preferences might naturally align with what you love to do, with your romantic or friendship choices, or with your job, if you are employed. If they do not align, understanding your Macro-Process theme, together with your movement style (Action Drives reflection from Chapter 6) can offer some insight into some of the misalignments and the Body Questions they provoke.

The Macro-Processes portrayed here are examinations of themes in which we might find both challenge and support. My clinical supervisor, dramatherapist[8] Melanie Beer, refers to a continuum of challenge vs. support. She explained that we can look at attitudes, behaviours, needs, thoughts, and movements that challenge and/or support our world view. Challenging this world view can potentially support us and others, and at the same time, supporting our world view can be challenging to ourselves and others. Support to challenge, challenge to support, and support is challenge!

Attention Macro-Process Themes: Communication and Pursuit of Knowledge

If you are in a life stage in which you are seeking possibilities, craving more knowledge, gathering options, or intensely focusing on one specific issue, your macro-stage theme related to Attention. Davies called this profile in MPA the "Communicators"[9]. I find the term "Seekers" also fitting for people who prefer this stage. As we covered in Chapter 2, those who are dominant in or have a preference to the Attention stage are usually big-picture thinkers, researchers, and information seekers in their families/communities. They could be the strategists, philosophers, assessors, or surveyors. In their personal lives they may be the connectors, the gatherers and disseminators of information or resources. If this feels like your style, you might have naturally gravitated towards these kinds of jobs and/or took on those roles within your family and/or friendship circle.

There is an ongoing craving for more knowledge about possibilities that is characteristic of Attention Macro-Processes. However, persistence in the Attention stage might make you feel disconnected and lost without engaging with the Intention stage. Plans might not have any timing and may be constantly up in the air, or there might be a loss of a sense of purpose. There might be decision paralysis – where it is all too overwhelming. Conversely, this might be a time of opening to possibilities, relaxing, and letting go of expectations and plans.

Culture and Caveats on the Attention Stage Macro-Process

Body language experts, movement coaches, or nonverbal communication specialists have whole careers dedicated to train others in public speaking. They aim to teach people nonverbal 'tips and tricks' to engage audiences and build confidence in talking to wider audiences. The objective behind these techniques is to draw from culturally accepted notions of (dare I say – probably Western) portrayals of nonverbal confidence. While this might be effective in some environments, and there are some notions of communication that might be cross-cultural, I feel it is important to insert a 'cultural caveat' here and say that these might not necessarily fit all forms of communication and all contexts. Additional research in this aspect is direly needed to understand how communication styles are reinforced in other cultures. There is an element of human nature and developmental building blocks in nonverbal behaviour which might cut across cultures, but this is why it is important to analyse the dominating movement preferences in your context to see if these apply.

Intention Macro-Process Themes: Self and Identity

Macro-themes pertaining to the Intention stage often are linked to the exploration of how we are and who we are. People might be in a stage in their life where the situations that they are in are reflecting important questions on voice, agency, and what is important. Often, circumstances knock us off our feet or require us to assert boundaries. In my violence prevention research, the theme of 'voicing our needs' came up, which was later highlighted in many workshops on the topic of exploring our intersectional identity[10]. Participants often refer to the fact that they feel they have 'lost their voice' and have difficulty having their say in the things that matter most to them. Others mentioned that their self-confidence had taken a blow and that they need to rebuild themselves back up again. It is not a coincidence that I am using body metaphors here that relate to verticality. There is an important movement characteristic of this stage: first to find our own feet in terms of the present. Finding our own sense of Weight will help us evaluate what is at hand and perhaps take some steps forward or backward (Action/Non-Action).

According to Davies, people who prefer this stage are Confronters, or I'd prefer to say Prioritisers[11]. Some cultures place lot of negative cultural value to confronting issues, and therefore I thought it best to reframe some of the language to help it remain open. People who prefer the Intention stage might thrive in clarifying their needs and priorities; decisions might be values driven. Preferences in the Intention stage might support people to assert and defend their core values and stand up to injustices when needed without question. In corporate places, people might be attracted to roles in which they thrive in making (or reinforcing) policies and procedures. Other roles in corporate workplaces that (generally) prioritise the Intention stage are people in human resources, quality assurance, health and safety, and similar job types that prioritise norms and standards. Some of the pros of this preference might be that norms and procedures might keep people safe, and this keen eye may prevent accidents or injury, or maintain and defend the core values of a community, organisation, or group of people. There is also a confidence and self-efficacy that emerges from standing on your own two feet and voicing what you need. However, it can also be exhausting to bear all the weight of this responsibility. Some challenges with this theme are that there could be a rigid adherence to rules which might make systems inflexible and cause interpersonal conflict. It can also block progress, challenges, or change. Also, in the effort of defending an organisation's core values, it might alienate the possibility of nuance and diversity, which requires more of an Attention stage approach. These themes are hypotheses based on the movement qualities of this stage. There might be variances across cultures and contexts.

Developmental psychologist Erik Erickson correlated the negotiation of verticality between 9–24 months where infants negotiate standing up with the psychosocial stage relating to autonomy vs. shame/self-doubt[12]. Erickson's theory of psychosocial development describes that in this stage of identity formation, young children learn about negotiating their independence, and developing confidence in separating from caregivers. Erikson states,

> The conviction that emerges during this stage is "I am what I will be," reflecting the child's new sense of autonomy. The syntonic attributes that are commonly gained during this stage are pride, control, self-assurance, autonomy, self-certainty, and the will to be oneself[13].

This is why people often refer to the toddler stages as the 'terrible twos' or terrible 3s, 4s . . . the process of obtaining autonomy, building confidence, and feeling our own Weight is often a tumultuous one, but gratifying at the same time.

Erickson's psychosocial stages have been applied to self-management in older adults[14], sustaining that adults reintegrate earlier stages later in life, which helps them "reapply wisdom learned in other contexts and maintain autonomy in decision-making". This further evidences Hackney's and Bartenieff's work on integrating developmental movement in wellbeing/therapeutic practice. Although Erickson's stages have been criticised due to its difficulty in capturing gender role nuances and multicultural and multidimensional understandings of identity[15], the idea of challenges and polarities in each developmental stage is a useful launching point for our understanding of themes in decision-making.

The Intention stage also connects to another early pattern called *Yield and Push* (Figure 8.3). Hackney[16] links yield and push patterning with the negotiation of verticality and thus of the self as we have been exploring in the Intention stage.

The individual yields and pushes and gets feedback in the ground of [their] own being. This Yield and Push patterning underlies the development of strength and relationship to gravity. Yield and Push patterns also provide the power to "get away," to separate Self from Other, to establish personal kinesphere, to become an individual.

The Intention stage is indeed the grounding stage – where we can discover where we are placed, who we are, and engage with examining the core essential aspects of our Self. I revisit here the example with Martin from Chapter 7, when he made a connection between his goal of expanding range of movement in the Vertical Plane to explore the current stage in his career where he needed to connect with and build confidence in his strengths.

Other themes related to this stage which emerged during my workshops are

self-doubt	insecurity
confidence	self-defence

FIGURE 8.3 The Yield and Push Pattern

centring	assertiveness
reconnection with oneself	finding our voice
boundary-setting	presenting oneself to others

What other themes do you connect with this stage?

In the professional realm, the Intention stage helps with establishing and clarifying one's role within the workplace. Setting boundaries on the demands asked of us requires strength, confidence, and assertion. Oftentimes, we hold multiple roles at work, and these can often get confusing and demanding. We might be overloaded with responsibilities from many directions which might get to be too much. In contrast, much like the myth of Icarus[17], we might become too overconfident and potentially end up getting overextended, which many times underlies burnout. We might be holding on rigidly to the Intention stage, digging in our heels and becoming obstinate in our view.

Another example for Macro-Processes in the Intention stage happened to me during the process of developing my company (The Body Hotel). My team and I examined and scrutinised our core values so that they were interlinked from logos all the way to policies and choosing the partner organisations we engage with. We asked ourselves many questions about what was important and what was a priority. It was a stimulating process – since, for example, we wanted our core values to be LGBTQ+ affirmative, explicitly trans inclusive, and always keep pushing our knowledge to be inclusive for people of all abilities while prioritising dance and movement as a tool for wellbeing. At times, this meant some tough choices about who we ended up working with and where, but the Intention stage helped us keep facing the tough questions of who we wanted to be as a company. The themes that emerged out of these decisions then became our core values.

Self-Defence

In my peacebuilding research, I found that anger management and self-defence are other themes related to the Intention stage[18]. This is because often in this stage there is a struggle for self-determination, a connection to parts of us which might not have been seen and heard. Self-defence is often socially misconstrued as something negative, but this aspect of decision-making is quite crucial. Self-defence is of course necessary in the face of violence, but it is also important in terms of setting your own boundaries and space in nonviolent contexts. It might become important to assess whether the situation is indeed one that requires defending – which is often uncomfortable, disturbing, and extremely energy consuming. Working with our Weight Efforts, activating our core and grounding is an important part of self-defence, be it through words, mind, body, or all the above.

Insecurity/Self-Doubt

Whether it was due to upbringing or our current or previous experiences, there are times in which we might be doubting our abilities. Potentially, we might feel like we have 'lost ourselves'. We might be focusing more on others and prioritising their needs. Body metaphors often used (in US/UK) are 'dragging our feet', 'down on the dumps', 'feeling deflated', 'untethered'. Oftentimes, in terms of Macro-Process themes, one blow to your confidence in one arena can have a knock-on effect on other realms of your life.

As many of these stages involve many dualities, we might have come into a space in our lives where we know what we want, have mustered up some confidence to voice it, and desire to explore this deeper. Then it might be time to see if there are other stages that need equal attention.

Where are you located in terms of this stage? You may use the worksheets provided in the Appendices to reflect more on this stage.

Case Example: Supervision Practice

Another example of the Intention Macro-Process emerged during my supervision practice. I have supervised recent graduates from dance movement therapy courses for a long time, and often find that the Macro-Process themes are often very present as the students leave the cosy 'bubble' of their cohort and begin to find their own voice in the professional world (usually towards the last term of their final year). Despite the arduous work involved and multiple placements DMT trainees need to undergo, I was often surprised at this massive blow to their confidence and the disconnection to how far they have come in their progress. Often, there will be an overall questioning of everything they encountered during their degree. Phrases I would hear often were: "I don't think I am ready", "I feel like I haven't done much", "I don't know where I stand", "I have forgotten everything I learned", "I didn't learn anything". We were able to process these themes as a group and I saw movement equivalents in the sessions that signalled a direct co-relation with the themes that were emerging. As with any process, it was not about me having to remind them or make these connections for them, but it became clear to me that they needed to reconnect with their own strengths and start believing in their own unique voice as practitioners as they stepped into new career paths and job opportunities, which we were able to explore in movement. The relationship between decision-making themes and supervisory practice group process is a future direction for research.

One of the activities I often did with soon-to-be-graduates or recent graduates was a self-reflexive drawing of their full body in large pieces of paper. These activities supported the macro-themes related to their professional identity post-graduation or in preparation for their internships. Then I had them draw a strength they felt they had as a soon-to-be therapist. They were then to draw a visual representation of this strength and locate it inside their body drawing. They taped the full drawing to a wall or vertical surface, and we engaged in movement where they reflected on their connection to this strength and the potential blocks that they found in this process (Figure 8.4). Oftentimes, the hardest process for them was to identify that strength

FIGURE 8.4 Embodied Reflection Drawing

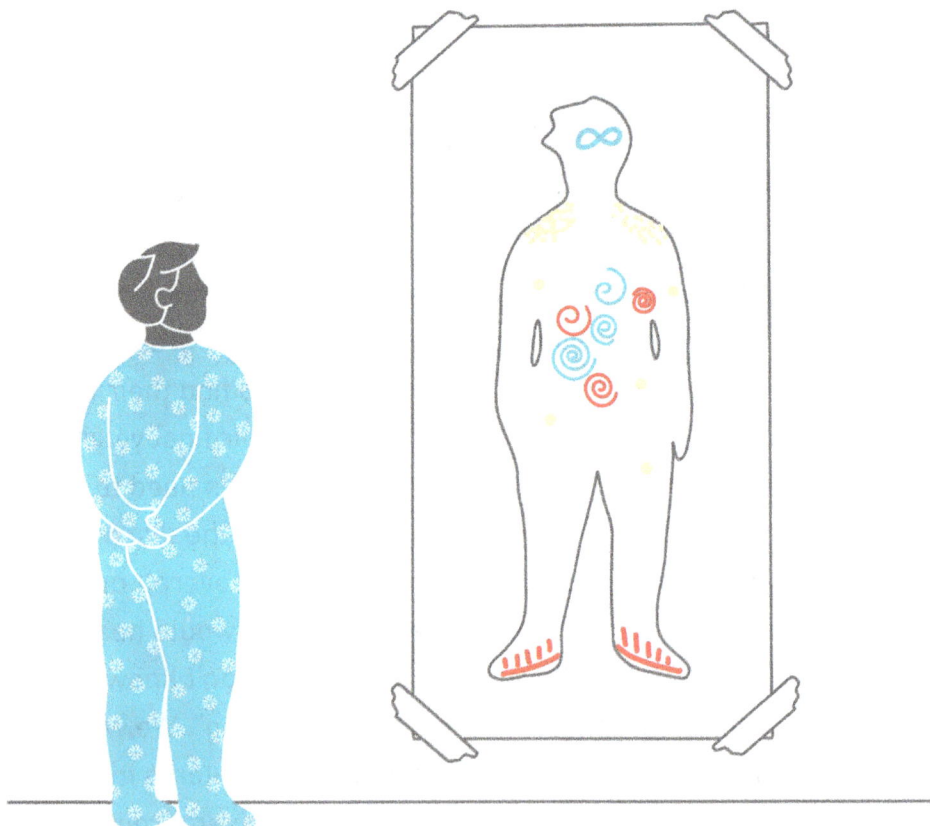

and embody it. We often discussed why this was, and peers offered feedback on each other. In other events, I introduced an activity where they enacted or did a role play on what was blocking their access to the strength. We embodied the strengths, and we embodied the blocks. This helped students reflect, challenge some of the negative thinking, and propose ways in which access can be granted and strengths celebrated.

The embodied reflection on what they felt was blocking this strength proved meaningful and paved the way to keep building up the professional identity to prepare for the outside world. By identifying strengths, and what can support these strengths, we begin to develop 'anchors' which help us feel grounded and connected.

This method has similarly been used in a DMT Context by Zeynep Çatay and Marcia Plevin[19]. Çatay and Plevin discuss the methodology of the technique they call Transformational Body Tracings (TBT) and how they have applied this practice in their DMT training workshops. The authors compared 54 photographs of 13 body tracings to explain different processes that demonstrate the encounter with our body image. It was very interesting for me to read about this practice because even though I had been using body tracings for a long time in my own work, their visual art-movement integration brings lots of therapeutic possibilities for clients to connect with their own bodies, with mediators of experiences in motion such as colour, shape, symbolic content, and art materials used as tools for self-discovery while mirroring on paper and resonating in our bodies.

Çatay and Plevin explore how the manifestation of TBT illustrates processes of integration in the bodies of the participants/clients. They explain how choosing certain colours or tracing certain shapes represent our experiences, reflections, and change. They analyse the relationship between the centre of the body and the periphery or distal extremities, which made me think about the Bartenieff Fundamentals and the developmental implications of this method.

It is wonderful to find synergies with other practitioners. There are then many connections we can make between self and identity, which can be explored by multiple arts mediums to support participants in movement, particularly as they explore Macro-Processes in decision-making and life transitions.

World Context: COVID-19

I wanted to take a moment to acknowledge this very defining time in our life during COVID-19. Survival and self-care became one of the central themes since the lockdown forced core issues to come to the surface. A claim can therefore be made that we were forced into the Intention stage. Most people were compelled into an extended period of the Attention stage when deprived of being able to leave our homes, and as such, we were inescapably faced with what was difficult and essential. Inequality and access to basic needs (housing, safety, health, food, work) were highlighted. Internet access emerged as a vehicle for access to information, support, and connection to others, and the media and research demonstrated that internet access was often a privilege worldwide that not everyone was able to obtain.

One of my coping mechanisms during the pandemic was to do the Micro-Process movement sequence detailed in Chapter 7. I set a timer for the activity and then made drawing reflections after I moved. I videotaped the process and posted 'Self-Isolation' dance clips on social media, which helped me express the difficulties of that time through dance. Although there isn't space here to delve too deeply into this subject, I want to reiterate how important this framework became for me in times of crisis, as it kept me anchored and connected to my practice.

During this very impactful time in our life, we might have come face-to-face with a difficult question: What resources do we have and lack? How can we resource ourselves when our current way of engaging with the world is impacted? If we are no longer able to socialise or connect with others outside our immediate bubble in person, what else feeds us? We can take those lessons into everyday life. This section explored several activities that connected the Intention Macro-Process themes, with examples from professional and personal life contexts, to suggest wider applications of decision-making through movement.

Culture and Caveats on the Intention Stage Macro-Process
Privilege

I realise the privilege and resources involved to be in a place in which we feel capable of voicing our needs. I had a 'privileged' pandemic experience, where I was able to work online in a safe place with internet access. In writing these examples I am very aware that in some cases the lockdown restrictions deeply affected and traumatised many people, and that the recovery from this period will take a lot of time. I also don't want to wash over anyone's individual journey or minimise painful and difficult experiences that arose. Here, I mainly want to draw a parallel between the macro-movement theme equivalents to lived experience. The Intention stage is often quite tricky as it forces us to look at ourselves to crystallise our purpose. It is our ongoing responsibility to do the work to continue to reflect on privilege if this is our life circumstance.

One of my favourite theories around this is the Coin Model of Privilege and Critical Allyship[20] that uses the metaphor that social currency is gained by an accumulation of different coins that make up our identity (e.g. protected characteristics and dominant characteristics, like age, gender identity, sexual orientation, etc.) We might be on top or bottom of that coin in many different facets depending on the dominant characteristics in our society, which will provoke different types of access to services, perks, resources, and advantage/disadvantage. These systems may also block access to many people living with disabilities, as ableist views tend to dominate many societal norms, services, and even the design of spaces and transport. These introduce an element of precariousness to the Intention stage since despite our determination, there might be larger processes at play that might make enacting decisions much more difficult. We might gain earned or unearned access, and these decisions might be easy for you due to privilege, but tough for others. This is way too big of a topic to give it full justice, but I wanted to acknowledge that this is an element of inequality, equity, access, and inclusion within Intention Macro-Processes that would need much more depth in future research.

Available Resources

Throughout my PhD research, I learned that safety is first and foremost when deciding to be assertive, raising our voice in dissent, or stating what we need. Some structures and contexts might want to completely discourage and even oppress this behaviour. For example, domestic violence researchers speak about being engaging with survivors to support their own self-efficacy[21]. The healing work might be centred around supporting people to access and cultivate their personal resources (emotional, physical, cultural, social) to make sure they are safe to be able to leave an abusive relationship and working with them to support their sense of agency to make a decision that will help them rebuild their lives safely[22]. It is not as simple as saying, "Leave this person now", as the Action of a decision. Availability of resources, a person's protective factors and current support network (and many other variables) become crucial for someone traversing a life-threatening transition. There is a massive caveat here in terms of how resourced we will need to be/become to engage in decision-making.

These are just a few of the considerations around privilege, availability of resources, and cultural influences that I hope future research will continue to address. It is often a constant learning curve to keep understanding the nuance of lived experience.

Summarising this Intention macro-theme – people who are finding general patterns related to the Intention stage might be confronted with issues/situations which relate to their Identity and Sense of Self. As I demonstrated in Chapter 3, frustration with the Intention stage macro-themes can lead to many tantrums (expressed and unexpressed) which channel our uneasiness with not knowing or not feeling able to express (or identify) our needs or even violence towards ourselves or others (more on this later). Additionally, we might not be in a place where we have enough emotional, physical, social, economic, and/or cultural capacity or resources to be able to enact our choices.

This will be tied into many of the factors that determine our identity: culture, ethnicity, race, gender identity, disability, sexual orientation, age, groups which we associate with, and even personal/community interests which play a role in building our identity. Body Questions will then emerge regarding these macro-themes, which will motivate focusing on practising on our verticality, our connection to the ground, and what our 'anchors' are at this moment.

Point of reflection: How much self-efficacy and agency do we have over our decisions? How assertive can we be about what we want? What is the potential impact or consequence (positive/neutral/negative) of expressing our needs?

Action/Non-Action Macro-Themes: Impulsivity vs. Procrastination

Decisions are often portrayed as performance- or product-oriented, requiring a particular outcome. However, if we understand decisions as dynamic, non-linear processes, an outcome is not necessarily the goal. In the Micro-Processes chapter (Chapter 7), we understood that decisions can occur in milliseconds and that Non-Action is an option. Here we explore the preference towards Action (common to many cultures and professions) and how it may impact many facets of our life.

People who prefer or spend the most time and energy in the Action stage usually tend to make things happen: plan and execute. As I mentioned in Chapter 6, in a corporate workplace, roles that primarily engage in this stage are administrative assistants, technicians, and salespeople. These are often described as the 'go-getters', 'active' people, 'results-oriented', or the people who 'get it done'. These might also be the activators, and people who are out there doing activism work (which also entails a strong preference for the Attention Stage). Although in some work cultures, actioning might be the preferred or most rewarded posture, every stage has its pros and cons.

As you might have noticed from the proportion diagram in Figure 8.1, in MPA, Commitment is the term associated with the Action/Non-Action stage[23]. This is no coincidence, as once we have connected to our options, and aligned these with our intentions, we can offer events a structure by applying the Time Effort. Our relationship to the word commitment might be a tricky one. We can engage with, follow-through, and incorporate as many strategies as possible to determine the adequate timing needed for this decision/transition.

Competitiveness will immediately generate a tendency in movement towards Advancing or Retreating (Shaping Qualities). Some workplace settings will have preferences for advancing quickly. They will reward diligence, effectiveness, and quick results. Other places of work might engage in cautious approaches – think through things, do your market research, risk-taking might be moderate. Perhaps here, the Intention stage shows up, where places/people might exert more pressure to provoke people to act.

Similarly, this can be a decision-making style of your family or friendship circle.

Do you experience a pressure to act? To retreat? Does it provoke hesitation?

What is your embodied experience of Commitment?

Movement Break: Time Dial: Situational Assessment Tool

Suggested Music

Track Title: Dreamy / Wintery

Duration: 1:30

Music Composer: Ross Whyte

Link for QR Code: https://youtu.be/7Quy4s4x4jQ?si=Lt_lxm_ceuzZwTEI>

We are going use the Variable of Insight of *representation* to explore current through the traditional terms for Time: Past, Present, and Future. For this, you can use your hand (or an object like a water bottle if hand mobility is limited). Extend your arm forward with your palm facing down. Then bend your elbow. The palm of the hand will end up facing away from you. Your thumb will be pointing in the direction of your opposite shoulder (see Figure 8.5). Think of the fingers of our hand as a 'dial', and you have up to 180 degrees of motion from one side to the other.

FIGURE 8.5 The Time Dial Exercise

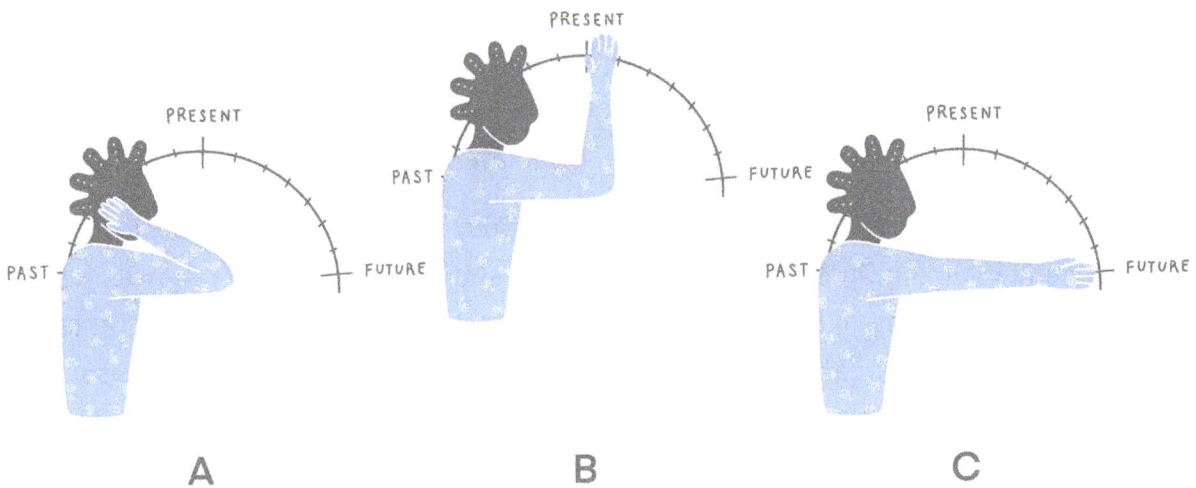

Body Questions

If you picture your current situation in terms of this decision, what is your attitude or tendency in relationship to Past, Present, Future?

- Are you leaning more forwards (thinking too much about the future?)
- Are you planted in the present?
- Are you stuck thinking about the past?
- Where are you in this movement dial at this moment?
- How is it serving you?

The three reference points for this question are in Figure 8.5.

A. Fingers pointing backwards at an angle (elbow is bent with fingers towards the should on the same side). Reclining on the PAST. You are leaning more towards previous experiences and what has happened to you or others. You might be reminiscing about what has worked in the past and what usually tends to happen. You might be focusing more on prior behaviours, repeating previous patterns, or dwelling on what used to be (Figure 8.5).

B. Fingers are pointing up (forearm is parallel). Remaining in the PRESENT. You are working with the variables at hand. You feel planted on your own two feet. You are dealing with the situation in the present moment. You may be very aware of your senses and feel grounded in the situation. Conversely, you might feel stuck where you are – there might be some Intention stage macro-processes happening here that might need some exploration.

C. Fingers pointing forward (forearm at a 45 degree angle in the Sagittal Plane) Leaning towards the FUTURE: a tendency to be preoccupied about the future, looking at all the possibilities, acting constantly, with a 'forward' attitude. You are concerned with potential consequences, outcomes, or solutions.

This exercise helps assess the current situation in terms of your positioning within the Sagittal Plane. Exploring what is sustainable and ideal for the situation will help clarify whether the tendency is helpful for yourself at this moment or not.

I used this situational assessment tool during the session with Martin (described in page 215). After we had moved through the four stages, he mentioned his worry about change and the potential instability of freelance work vs. contracted work. I asked him to choose a gesture within this 'Time Dial' that symbolised his attitude or preoccupation toward the issue he was exploring. Martin put his hand leaning more towards the past, as his thoughts about his past work experience were influencing this decision quite significantly.

I often do this to clarify a particular situation that a participant is going through. It offers a chance to reflect on whether the preoccupation with either Past, Present, or Future is either interfering or supporting their process. It also invites more questions about how the participant is feeling in relation to their decisions – offering more nuance to potential worry, anticipation, or anxiety regarding a transition. Someone might be clinging on to past experiences, or only considering what is happening now, or is too worried about future consequences to have enough clarity to make a decision.

The flip side of the Action macro-theme is the delaying or retreating from making decisions across different realms in our life. This involves looping movements between Action/Non-Action and Attention. Someone might advance towards a decision but then quickly retreat and go into the Attention stage by deflecting responsibility, expanding out, redirecting, thus creating an exploration 'loop'. The dance of indecision. There might also be a macro-theme here related to procrastination. With workshop participants who identified with this stage, they often referred to the pressure to act, often complained about not having (or making) time to digest or process things. On the other hand, participants who preferred, or experienced persistent macro-themes related to the Attention stage often expressed they had trouble committing to action plans or concrete timings in many aspects of their lives.

Commitment is difficult for some people, as it will often need a full-bodied response, and a sustained engagement over time. You might be constantly retreating from any kind of obligation: plans, relationships, career, long-term purchases, family and loved ones. At the root of noncommittal behaviour will be fear, feeling unsafe, not trusting the outcome (or other people), or negative past experiences. If this is all resonating with you, this is an area in your life which might need more in-depth reflection and additional support.

Another example of retreating movement would be to cede the spotlight or responsibility to someone else. We will step away, deflect, or steer things in another direction. This might happen only in some instances or with particular people, but if you find yourself doing this regularly, it might be worth reflecting on why this is. In situations of hesitation, or stagnation, this might feel like a salsa dance – one step forward, one step back – we spin, but still step back – and it starts again. Hesitation about most decisions will have movement equivalents: it might look like short, quick advancing and retreating rhythms, or starting/stopping rhythms in which we dart and stop, dart, and stop. Conversely, impulsivity (shifting forward) would perhaps motivate someone to take the spotlight, assume responsibility for planning/doing, taking action without considering others, and/or not allowing others to execute tasks themselves. Impulsivity will often engage a sudden, at times abrupt, acceleration in time with a particular directionality. If this behaviour crosses over several realms, it begs slowing down to consider why this is. In summary: Impulsivity will foster forward constant positioning in terms of the Action Plane, while hesitation will entail backwards positioning.

Action Stage Macro-Process Theme: Violence

In my doctoral research, I interviewed practitioners who believed that intervening at the Attention stage and helping people offer ample time to go through the decision-making process through dance/movement and connect to the body could help with violence prevention and with reflecting on violent actions and/or healing from violence and trauma[24]. An impulsive violent act usually undergoes the Micro-Process of decision-making. It might traverse the Attention and Intention stages very quickly and go from Flow/Tension (GRRR feeling/trigger) to Action in seconds. A premeditated violent act or a violent pattern might have both Micro-Process and engage with Macro-Process themes and behavioural patterns. One of the conclusions of the peacebuilding practitioners who participated in my research was that embodied practices across the decision-making stages can help resource someone to prevent them from acting impulsively, thus preventing a violent action from taking place or healing relationships whenever this is possible.

It feels relevant to highlight that decisions can be made that negatively impact others or hurt others regardless of whether it is done with intention. Martha Eddy's research claims that every peaceable and violent action involves conscious or unconscious movement-based decisions[25]. Rena Kornblum also claimed that violence has a spatial component, as most violent encounters entail an invasion of mental, physical and/or psychological space:

> Spatial intrusion is a key ingredient in violence. People who are violent have a lack of respect (if the intent is malicious) or a lack of awareness (if the intent is accidental or careless) for personal boundaries. . . All people need to develop an awareness of and respect for the different spatial preferences and needs of others and a sense of the cultural norms.[26]

Although in this book we mostly focus on decisions related to transitions and choosing between different paths, we need to be aware that some of these movement decisions might impact others.

Furthermore, I analysed the links of the Action stage to activism and social engagement which were initially explored by somatic specialist Martha Eddy in my thesis[27]. Her research found a strong correlation between the Intention to Action stages – where strong beliefs are linked with calls to action and changemaking.

Social justice involves the connection between something we feel passionate about and want to change (Intention), and eliciting Action from policymakers, leaders, and the wider community[28].

Culture and Caveats on the Action/ Non-Action Stage Macro-Process

Each culture and subculture will have constructed ways in which it deals with Action and Non-Action. At times there is high cultural value placed on acting quickly vs. in other cultures where there might be more pressure to slow down and consider things thoroughly. The context will often ascribe positive descriptors to this position, stating someone is 'strong' or 'wise' when they . . . (for example: act swiftly/consider things thoroughly/take their time with decisions/defend priorities) and on the other hand, be considered 'weak' or 'inexperienced' when [place your effort/situation here]. You might not have noticed this messaging, as it can be very implicit or woven in very tightly within our social fabric. Social/political/moral/ethical priorities are located within each culture's and subculture's own values, which are highly specific to each context and most, if not all, have movement equivalents. They also may change or remain the same over time. These norms might be overt or very encrypted, but nevertheless, they suggest human behaviour. The claim here is that there is always a movement equivalent to these norms, and it can be useful to understand the preferences at play in each of the stages, here focusing on Action/Non-Action.

One of the applications of movement analysis here is to start asking Body Questions of the context you are surrounded by. The cultural nuances here would be too many to properly do them justice in this book. I am aware that there are some assumptions of jobs, postures, and attitudes I have included in order to illustrate these macro-themes, and they will always be up for debate. I see them as a starting point for new discussions and challenges. Additionally, we will have biases that might have been influenced by the context in which we grew up and developed in. This is why developing a self-reflexive practice becomes important. It might be difficult at times to distinguish between our own lenses, as we will experience life through our movement preferences. How we move and how we move within our environment continue to offer challenging questions about how we operate within our world. As these movement preferences fluctuate and our context is constantly informing and being informed by our experience, it continues to be an ongoing discussion and negotiation. Some guiding questions are here:

- What is prioritised?
- What is rewarded?
- What is admonished?
- What is excluded/included?
- What is oppressed or considered as 'other'?
- How do you fit in/concede/compromise? Is it a challenge? Or does it feel comfortable?

Remember that this will be an ongoing practice which might fluctuate. This is why it is important to keep coming back to Body Questions when new questions emerge or old questions return.

Flow/Tension Macro-Process Stage: Connecting and Listening to Our Body

Body Question: How do we moderate Flow/Tension in our body to cope, negotiate, modulate, and de-escalate?

Jennifer Frank Tantia's[29] dance movement therapy and somatic work is based on the theory by anthropologist Thomas Csordas, who claims that we pay attention with the body and to the body. With the body because our senses give us the story of what we are doing, and to the body when we listen internally to what the body has to say[30]. DMT Christine Caldwell[31], in her book *Bodyfulness*, describes in a parallel way that the body undergoes many processes of oscillation "going back and forth between two positions or states"[32], which Caldwell links to states of consciousness, attention, body identity, and in relationships. She discusses that bodily systems rely on oscillation to function. Many of the shifts we have investigated in movement in this book have involved the aspects of oscillation or attention shifts as these movement specialists have claimed. It is in this shifting that the impetus for change can occur.

Connecting to activities which induce feelings of satisfaction, challenge, and constructive tension can instigate the understanding of movement qualities. Variables of Insight in movement incite reflexive processes that may trigger transitions or change. There is a plethora of activities related to modulating Flow/Tension. Breathing exercises, meditation, yoga, swimming, dancing, Tai Chi, kayaking, and working with clay are some examples. All have these Flow/Tension components which help the body integrate and assimilate techniques to regulate the tension in our body. They have a proportion of Free and Bound Flow and their aim is to instil more techniques for regulation, which is essential for stress management. Of course, this will depend on your own needs and what protective factors can support you to cope with stress in your life.

A final addition to this process is the fact that by being intrinsically connected to our autonomic responses. Our nervous system might be overactivated during stressful events, threatening situations and/or traumatic experiences. Somatic practitioners can therefore support people in working through trauma and challenging life experiences. One of the participants of my PhD research offered an example of how he worked with clients who had experienced highly traumatic experiences through these responses. Paul Linden is a somatic practitioner and Aikido master, and he explains one of his exercises:

> I'd start by throwing [face tissues] to . . . a willing guinea pig. Show people what the process is . . . I'd get him or her into being able to speak body-based language. I hear that you're surprised. Where in your body are you doing the action of surprisedness. Okay, when you do it there, what are you doing? Now if you loosen your tongue, loosen your belly, etcetera. . . . The sequence is: start with core relaxation, then smiling heart, then reaching out your awareness into space all around you and put it all together. So you have an expansive, kind-hearted, stable, relaxed, body and body awareness. . . . That is what I'm building towards[33].

Linden describes this exercise of throwing a tissue at an unsuspecting trainee and working with the trainee's autonomic body reactions and language. Here Linden makes an important connection between an awareness of the space and surroundings (Attention) and being able to work through instinctive defensive actions (fight, flight, freeze). He integrates bodily states and emotional states with body awareness. In the earlier exercise excerpt, although Linden doesn't necessarily term it as decision-making through movement, his description of the process is congruent with Micro-Processes of the whole system and can be categorised alongside the macro-themes related to the Flow/Tension Stage and Action/Non-Action Stage[34]. The themes connect to our reactions to tension how we hold tension in our bodies and what proportion of Flow/Tension you ascribe to a decision.

Although the Flow/Tension stage is one that underlies all the other stages, the overarching theme here is somatic responses: the information that is provided via our bodies which offers us a way to understand what is going on for us internally and the outside world. The Flow/Tension stage, as I mentioned in Chapter 5, is usually associated with the build of stress in the body and extreme duress. But as discussed there, another catalyst for change, which is not usually given the attention it deserves – is joy and pleasure. The search for what is pleasurable and enjoyable is equally as important and offers a 'buffer zone' for burnout, as it counteracts stress and offers some nurturing to build more resilience. Exercise, eating, playing, exploring, and physical/mental/emotional stimulation bring about this intrinsic feeling. The patterns here might offer some insight into how change may happen (connecting with our protective factors), or how to reduce/counteract tension in the body (and in life).

Expanding our coping mechanisms becomes very important to address the macro-themes of this stage as well as developing positive bodily practices that keep us connected to what our body has to say. The build-up of tension or needing to sustain Bound Flow for long periods of time can be very harmful to our physical, mental, social, and spiritual health.

An interesting exploration is looking at what our optimal Flow rhythm could be within these decisions.

Case Example

I was commissioned to do a decision-making workshop at the University of South-Eastern Norway for the Norway Dance Therapy Association (NODAK), where I offer an introduction to the whole system. The workshop culminates with the whole group engaging in our Micro-Process exploration detailed in Chapter 7. The space is usually laid out in quadrants, like this:

Flow/Tension	Attention
Action/Non-Action	Intention

I have been doing this workshop annually since 2016, but there was a particular year that stood out. That year, we were in a smaller space with a long corridor facing the beautiful Drammen River. I therefore had to provide a different layout, with the sections for each stage being next to each other:

Flow/Tension	Attention	Intention	Action/ Non-Action

The participants engaged in our earlier exercise on Micro-Processes when we explored all the stages together. As the participants embody the decision-making stages (in any order), they move, draw, and reflect in the stages they choose within a timeframe we determine. I often witness their process following the Authentic Movement guiding principles I described in Chapter 3, which has provided me insight into the nature of each of the stages and the variety of explorations participants can engage with. I witness participants spend different proportions of time on each stage, staying in one stage for the duration of the period or experience many oscillating paths between the stages. Often, we hold feedback sessions after the Micro-Process exploration, and the participants may share their experiences and potentially make connections to their own Macro-Process.

One participant provided a key insight into the model by beginning their movement on the 'Action/Non-Action' quadrant all the way down the corridor, which stood out to me due to the different layout. They crossed all the way through the three other spaces with clear determination and spatial intent. While other participants meandered through the room in no specific order, she moved through every stage in 'reverse' order (Action/Non-Action> Intention > Attention > Flow Tension. Even though I reiterate this process is dynamic, the linear layout in this workshop made it seem this way. During the debriefing stage, they commented that they began with a decision they had already made, and then visited the other aspects that had led to that decision. In the process, she explored other alternative paths she could have taken during the Attention stage. In the end, she was able to get insight into why she had chosen this path. As I had facilitated so many workshops and never seen this done quite in this way, this confirmed the reflexive nature of the model and the infinite possibilities it offers for exploring decision-making processes at any stage, including post-decision!

Review Points on Macro-Processes in Decision-Making Through Movement and the Arts

- Every decision goes through stages across varying lengths of time. Understanding ongoing themes can also give us information about the environment in which we operate.
- Macro-processes provoke reflection on bigger questions across different realms of our life.
- Macro-processes suggest overarching themes and signal towards life questions that might need to be explored.
- Macro-themes arise within our life transitions and the process helps us understand if there is a particular decision-making stage that is needing more space and time.
- We explored how we can engage with communication in the Attention stage; questions around self and identity in the Intention stage; commitment, impulsivity, and procrastination on the Action/Non-Action stage; and finally how Flow/Tension is intrinsically connected to our autonomic nervous system and muscular system.

I hope to hear from you what new themes emerge as you continue your exploration of the Macro-Processes of the system.

One Last Movement Break Before We End: A Dance Break!!

Suggested Music

Track Title: Celebration Dance Break

Duration: 2:49

Music Composer: Ross Whyte

Link for QR Code: https://youtu.be/8dOaJr85VUA?si=FeDSB6AzehzE1FZr>

During the pandemic, I started this ritual with a colleague. We would call each other online, one of us would pick a song, and without speaking, we would dance virtually.

After the song was over, we would say goodbye and go on with our day. It made such a difference. Here is an invitation for you to pick your favourite song and have a dance. Celebrate everything you have discovered about yourself by engaging with movement in this book. Dance your indecision or decision and celebrate that you can move, activate, and breathe. Celebrate the difficulties and challenges that lie ahead and have a boogie for the strength you continue to show to meet these challenges head on!

Notes

1 White, Elissa Queyquep. 'Laban's Movement Theories: A Dance/Movement Therapist's Perspective'. In *The Art and Science of Dance/Movement Therapy* (Routledge, 2015), 235–253.
2 Acarón, 2018; Eddy, 2009; Eddy, 2002.
3 Kestenberg et al., 1999.
4 Rivera, Furcron, and Beardall, 2022, 24–39.
5 Yilmazer, Yagmur Çolak, Kadriye Buldukoglu, Tuğçe Tuna, and Sevin Seda Güney. 'Dance and Movement Therapy Methods for Compassion Satisfaction, Burnout, and Compassion Fatigue in Nurses: A Pilot Study'. *Journal of Psychosocial Nursing and Mental Health Services* 58, no. 4 (April 2020): 43–51. https://doi.org/10.3928/02793695-20200211-01.
6 You can also choose to start with your professional life if that feels better at this time.
7 Moore, 2005, 83.
8 Dramatherapy is the protected title in the United Kingdom. The profession.
9 Davies, 2006, 104–106.
10 Acarón, 'The Practitioner's Body of Knowledge', 2015, 169–172.
11 Davies, 2006, 106. I prefer the word Prioritiser since 'Confronter' might evoke negative connotations in some people.
12 Erikson, Erik. 'Theory of Identity Development'. In *Identity and the Life Cycle* (New York: International Universities Press, 1959), 42–57.
13 Erikson, 1959, 49.
14 Evans et al., 2019, 2.
15 Karkouti, Ibrahim Mohamad. 'Examining Psychosocial Identity Development Theories: A Guideline for Professional Practice'. *Education* 135, no. 2 (December 2014): 257–264. https://go.gale.com/ps/i.do?p=AONE&sw=w&issn=00131172&v=2.1&it=r&id=GALE%7CA3 98073165&sid=googleScholar&linkaccess=abs.
16 Hackney, 2002, 90.
17 The Icarus Greek myth involves him being held captive in a tower. His father, Daedalus, a great inventor, created some wax wings for him to escape, telling him to stay in the

middle and not fly too low or too high. Icarus got overzealous and flew too close to the sun, which melted his wings, and he fell into the sea and perished. It is often a myth used to look at the negotiation of extremes.

18 Acarón, 'The Practitioner's Body of Knowledge', 2015, 244–246; Eddy, 2009, 93–143; Linden, Paul. *Embodied Peacemaking: Body Awareness, Self-Regulation and Conflict Resolution* (Columbus, OH: CCMS Publications, 2007). www.being-in-movement.com.
19 Çatay, Zeynep, and Marcia Plevin, 'A Way to Embodiment Through Aesthetic Relationship: Transformational Body Tracings'. In *Dance and Creativity Within Dance Movement Therapy*, edited by Hilda Wengrower and Sharon Chaiklin (Routledge, 2021), 84–95.
20 Nixon, Stephanie A. 'The Coin Model of Privilege and Critical Allyship: Implications for Health'. *BMC Public Health* 19, no. 1 (December 2019): 1637. https://doi.org/10.1186/s12889-019-7884-9.
21 Gray, Amber Elizabeth Lynn. 'Body as Voice: Restorative Dance/Movement Psychotherapy with Survivors of Relational Trauma'. In *The Routledge International Handbook of Embodied Perspectives in Psychotherapy* (Routledge, 2019).
22 Bernstein, 2019, 193–213.
23 Ramsden 1973; Ramsden, 2003, 218–241.
24 Acarón, 'The Practitioner's Body of Knowledge', 2015.
25 Eddy, 2009, in Acarón, 'The Practitioner's Body of Knowledge', 2015, 179.
26 Kornblum, 2002, 23–25; Acarón, 'Traversing Distance and Proximity', 2015, 1–15.
27 Eddy, 2009; Eddy, 2002.
28 Acarón, 'The Practitioner's Body of Knowledge', 2015; Eddy, 2009; Eddy 2002.
29 Tantia, 2012.
30 Csordas, 1994; Csordas, 1993, 135–156.
31 Caldwell, Christine. *Bodyfulness: Somatic Practices for Presence, Empowerment, and Waking Up in This Life* (Shambhala Publications, 2018).
32 Caldwell, 2018, 4.
33 Acarón, 'The Practitioner's Body of Knowledge', 2015, 167.
34 Linden, Paul. 'Aikido Roots and Branches: Body Awareness Training Methods and Their Applications in Daily Life' (2002): 1–26; Linden, 2007.

9

BOOK CONCLUSION

Decision-making through movement and the arts helps you reflexively analyse events occurring in your life and assess the stage they are in and what themes emerge. We have also explored your preference for certain movement patterns. You reflected on how these movement preferences affect and are affected by your environment, relationships, or social context. Cross-examining for common themes and identifying protective factors offer additional resources for breaking down a situation into manageable chunks.

Reflecting on what is occurring in our bodies, identifying our movement patterns and responses, and considering whether the pattern is constructive, appropriate to the situation, and sustainable is a way to activate our own self-efficacy and facilitate this embodied dialogue. The book demonstrated how the body plays a key role in decisions and how we operate in our daily life. You explored how movement operates as a lens through which you can understand, experience, and explore your patterns, preferences, and behaviours. In a previous article, I described how the arts can offer a 'zoom lens' into or away from our experience[1]. In the same manner, movement can offer a 'zoom lens' into our body. Movement can allow proximity to an issue, or enough distance to be able to get perspective. Other arts interventions (group shapes, role play) can help people 'zoom out' from the situation to investigate a situation from different angles. Drama and dance/movement, alongside other arts media, play with distance and proximity from our experience, as we have demonstrated throughout this book. Each situation we are in will need different moments of closeness and perspective to help us prevent being overwhelmed or completely numbed (or isolated?) from the issues and begin to cultivate resources to tackle life stress.

As we draw this book to a close, we can look back across all the activities we have experienced and review all our notes on our self-development and reflexivity, which

DOI: 10.4324/9781003360957-11

arose from our exploration into decision-making and crucial life transitions. We touched upon Variables of Insight (Representation and Activation) in the Macro-Process chapter, when we linked Attention to communication, Intention to the development of self and identity, and Action/Non-Action to commitment. An example of representation is the Time Dial exercise, where I invited you to represent your positioning on a situation by moving your arm as a dial facing forwards, upwards, or backwards. Then you engaged with movement to offer an embodied equivalent of the situation. Another example is the Journey Map exercise, where you *represented* a trajectory of your life, both by executing movements across the space, translating them into drawing, and then enacting them through movement.

In the Tantrum exercise, for example, we allowed the body to generate and engage with tension in varying intensities, which hopefully *activated* a prompt towards a cognitive process of identification (our need). We had an initial prompt of channelling frustration and connected to how that manifested in our body. Whenever we engaged with the movement concepts of each stage, if connections to our own life emerged out of the movement, that was an example of activation.

We reflected in this way throughout each exercise. Look back at your notes – Can you think of any of the exercises you have engaged with in this book and identify the elements of activation and/or representation in them?

The exercises in our Micro-Process chapter allowed both processes to happen either individually, simultaneously or as a process of one unfolding into the other. It is often not important to get into a chicken vs. egg situation of deciding which type of process is which, or which type of process comes first. Each of the stages can be understood as a world in themselves. This world can offer a collection of themes which are mobile and constantly shifting. Listening to an embodied source of information helps maintain, develop, and repair the relationship with our body. We can listen closely to our body for clues (Flow/Tension) as to what is going on in our lives and how to begin to contemplate a transition or change. Attention helps us to connect with both flexibility and focus within the environment, researching alternatives and cultivating our interpersonal network. Examining the value and priorities of what we need (Intention) and connecting to our strengths to cope with external and internal pressure. Through the Action/Non-Action stage, we can consider what we can commit to: Is there a plan or are we throwing away the plan? We can notice how we approach or retreat from situations and look at the pacing and timing that would suit best.

Both Micro- and Macro-Processes, accompanied by ongoing embodied practice can help you focus on the here-and-now, while also fostering relationships between decision-making and behaviour to help you manage issues in the future. A deeper analysis and evaluation of Micro- and Macro-Processes themes in decision-making through movement and the arts is a future research direction for this work.

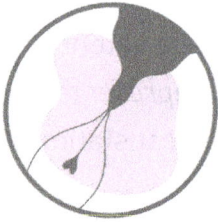

Can you reflect on the Flow Pattern or Journey Map (page 132) of the process you have gone through as you have read this book and engaged with its activities? How would you represent this and what does it activate? Trust that anything that emerges serves a purpose in showing you something you already knew, give you a glimmer of a shift or help you discover a new path altogether. Thank your body for all the information it has given you and continues to give. I hope we get to move and dance together again very soon.

Note

1 Acarón, 'Traversing Distance and Proximity', 2015, 1–15.

10

EPILOGUE

The Process Behind the Process
(With Ross Whyte and Eve Pyra)

In this epilogue, I team up with composer Ross Whyte and illustrator Eve Pyra to talk you through the process of creating the multimedia elements involved in this book. There were many conversations, versions, and translations between music, visual art, illustration, and movement 'languages' which we thought would be significant to share.

As is often said in performance, sometimes the audience is only privy to the finished product – the final show, an exhibition that has been polished numerous times, but we don't usually show the internal processes that go towards making something. We rarely see the rehearsals and the discussions 'behind the scenes'. It is important to look at how interdisciplinary work is undertaken and the many contributions it offers.

The Music: 'Translating' BESS into Composition (Ross Whyte)

Thania: Ross and I have been collaborating since 2012 in numerous dance projects. Our productions were inherently interdisciplinary, as we worked with circus artists, dancers, physical theatre performers, filmmakers, and designers

DOI: 10.4324/9781003360957-12

in five major productions as part of Orphaned Limbs Collective during my time in Scotland. Ross has worked successfully with dancers in his career as a composer and is always in high demand due to his sensibility to movement, incredible improvisational skills, and his ability to translate what he experiences in classes and rehearsals into powerful music. Within our music partnership, the biggest challenge was to find a selection of 'textures' – the beginnings of a musical-movement language. Ross and I had already come into this with a shared knowledge of what had worked with us in the past, but here we needed to add a musical texture to concepts within movement analysis which was our first creative task.

Postcards

The first part of the process was to get an initial sampler of how each of the Effort Qualities and categories would sound. This is often the hardest part when Ross and I come together: We need to come up with the palette of music – how we want each piece to sound and what elements make it cohesive when compiled together.

During one of our first workshop trials at University of South Wales, one of the participants asked about whether the music and movement were created separately and asked, "Which comes first?" We wondered what would happen if we had a music-movement exchange where music and movement were created separately or in responses without any order, rather than composed based solely on the movement. To get us started, we did some activities called music and movement 'postcards'. We would then send each other postcards either in movement or in music that would inspire the other person to respond to them in their own media. We started with Action Drives postcards since they were our most accessible tool, and from those, we were able to create a shared language we distilled into the Effort and Shape qualities.

We used the postcard format to include Eve in the process in the Journey Map activity page 132, where Eve did the movement exercise, drew her map, and sent it to Ross, who composed according to her journey, and then Eve sent revisions. This was a wonderful way to combine movement, visual representations, with original music composition.

Ross: The postcards proved to be a great launchpad for developing an overall musical palette (i.e. instrumentation, textures, timbres, and rhythms) from which to draw. Compositionally, it became clear very early on from the workshops, that the music had to function in a very immediate way. To explain, a musical composition's structure and form would usually be one of my first considerations – e.g. how does the music begin, progress, and conclude? What is the 'narrative' arc within this work's given duration? – but that compositional thinking was, for the most part, not appropriate here. The music needed to occupy a theme, mood, or rhythm from start to finish.

Thania: It was fun to trial out movement responses to music and music responses to movement – the postcards opened up a new way for us to collaborate. We got together in Glasgow, and we then experimented with translating from music to movement and movement to music live. Another creative process which we found interesting was working with themes, such as the Elements (wind, earth, water, fire) and whether they also had music equivalents to Space, Weight, Time and Flow. Ah, the discussions that ensued! Ross then used different types of instruments (wood, string) to complement the movement qualities in some of the tracks. Can you hear the specific elements in them?

After Ross composed the music, we then co-led some workshops in person and online with USW students from the Business Clinic and MA Drama and with the dance movement psychotherapy association (ADMP UK) Scotland group in person to gather feedback. Here, Ross discovered that each stage would be independent yet cohesive, and he has created a wonderful way to have the music resemble the interactive elements of the stages in the book. The music for the decision-making stages, like the chapters, can be played in any order. Same goes for the Action Drives! This speaks to how Ross has held a dynamic and engaging palette across this project that supports and uplifts the movement.

The Illustration: Diversity and Representation (Eve Pyra)

The illustrator, Eve also had a unique way to approach all the images created for this book:

Eve: We want every reader to feel represented, included and welcomed to the *Body Questions* book experience, and want the readers to feel safe and supported in their exploration of self. I was interested in the multi-cultural and multi-faceted representation of people and their complex inner lives. We wanted to represent humanity without judgment or rigid boundaries around gender, form or style. This can be seen in the varied body composition and hairstyle choices as well as "featureless" faces. Although the subject matter in this book could be highly emotional and profound to the readers, we tried to keep the tone of the book and the illustrations light, hopeful and empathetic, using multi-colour pastels and pattern embellished onesies to create an inviting and inclusive call to engage with the contents of this book.

Thania: That became apparent in conversations about what our 'figures' would wear. We transitioned between them wearing clothes (which would give a sense of place and time to the figures). We were fascinated by how quickly our initial intention wasn't working. I was flabbergasted by how much age and gender could be perceived through body outlines and we wanted to open discussions about body diversity and representation. We then transitioned them into wearing onesies, with a little addition of Taíno symbols, which are the native tribe of Puerto Rico to have a 'boricua' flavour!! (Boricua is the taíno/taína equivalent name for someone native of Puerto Rico, which was originally called Borikén). This was a great idea prompted by my good friend Gareth Pahl to honour a bit of my culture. We also made conscious choices to have many different body types and shapes represented, and decided to have some funky hairstyles, which Eve created to have the figures also have an otherworldly feel. We also placed an emphasis on making every movement exercise inclusive to people of all movement abilities by using seated figures when possible and offering multiple exercise variations.

The multimedia nature of this book, combining written word, illustration, and music allows the reader to be transported into another dimension of body experience and mirrors a workshop experience. We believe that this multisensory experience will create a deeper and more impactful experience and a better assimilation of the theory of Body Questions.

APPENDICES

Music Index

Movement Breaks Music Tracks

Reflexive Music

Action Drives Music

Decision-Making Stages: Micro-/Macro-Processes Music

Efforts Music

Shaping Qualities Music

Worksheets Index

Visit https://resourcecentre.routledge.com/books/9781032420448 for downloadable versions of the worksheets.

(In main book)

Worksheet 1.1 Decision-Making Stages and Their Body Questions

Worksheet 1.2 Body Check-in Chart

Worksheet 1.3 Decision-Making Stages and Their Movement Qualities

Worksheet 3.1 Embodied Journalling (Sensations, Images, Thoughts, Emotions)

Worksheet 6.1 Spectrum Worksheet (Combined)

Worksheet 6.2 Thania's Spectrum Worksheet Example

Worksheet 6.3 Action Drive Preferences; Fill in the Blanks

Worksheet 7.1 Decision Making Stages (Blank)

Worksheet 7.2 Decision-Making Through Movement Themes

Worksheet 8.1 Macro-Processes: Stage Proportion Worksheet

Additional Worksheets

Appendix 1. Full Page Flow/Tension Sheet

Appendix 2. Full Page Attention Sheet

Appendix 3. Full Page Intention Sheet

Appendix 4. Full Page Action/Non-Action Sheet

Appendix 5. Corner Flow/Tension With Body Questions

Appendix 6. Corner Attention With Body Questions

Appendices

Appendix 7. Corner Intention With Body Questions
Appendix 8. Corner Action/Non-Action With Body Questions
Appendix 9. Corner Flow/Tension With Movement Qualities
Appendix 10. Corner Attention With Movement Qualities
Appendix 11. Corner Intention With Movement Qualities
Appendix 12. Corner Action/Non-Action With Movement Qualities
Appendix 13. Decision-Making Combined Research Themes With Flow at Centre

Movement Breaks Music Tracks

Track Title	YouTube Link	QR Code / Duration
All Tracks	https://youtube.com/playlist?list=PLtGm4qYm5yBSl2Jl3Cs0scqQnk6Gv97Vv&si=hAPqzGJEEyUJzg4W	**Music Playlist: All Tracks** — Music Composer: Ross Whyte
Audio Description Playlist	https://youtube.com/playlist?list=PLtGm4qYm5yBQZqgY5_PFpJHa4jgs2R6Cw&si=yd3CJMGBAH9UKeJ3	**Body Questions** Book Audio Description Playlist — Narrated by: Dr Thania Acarón
Body Check-In	https://youtu.be/f62GawQJ34U?si=027faCP0V4e4Go1Z	**Suggested Music** — Track Title: Mysterious / Curious — Duration: 04:16 — Music Composer: Ross Whyte
Dance Break	https://youtu.be/8dOaJr85VUA?si=pC2fV5DizEzVK6Fc	**Suggested Music** — Track Title: Celebration Dance Break — Duration: 2:49 — Music Composer: Ross Whyte
Invisible Cord	https://youtu.be/IfaV-TYeX3A?si=jjut0d6vswHWud6a	**Suggested Music** — Track Title: Serious - Pensive — Duration: 01:51 — Music Composer: Ross Whyte

Appendices

Track Title	YouTube Link	QR Code / Duration
Journey Map	https://youtu.be/T7T6UKJ0ywQ?si=LeknV8Sfd8SHKo7v	**Suggested Music** Track Title: Journey Map (Eve) Duration: 2:36 Music Composer: Ross Whyte
Safety Backpack	https://youtu.be/2DdF7PG8d2Y?si=iuWnU1dlWQ7LxGwc	**Suggested Music** Track Title: Earthy Duration: 03:00 Music Composer: Ross Whyte
Tantrum Exercise	https://youtu.be/xw3DXVn2g0A?si=sIR1L8FFcZq_YyBS_	**Suggested Music** Track Title: Tantrum Exercise Duration: 2:20 Music Composer: Ross Whyte

Reflexive Music

Appendices

Track Title	YouTube Link	QR Code / Duration
Contemplative	https://youtu.be/hlfecLU5T30?si=4-D8xRaVlClKxmx5	Suggested Music Track Title: Contemplative Duration: 05:52 Music Composer: Ross Whyte
Discover – Explore	https://youtu.be/fgkKbOLWCPc?si=UFJqryTHkRLceeha	Suggested Music Track Title: Discover – Explore Duration: 02:56 Music Composer: Ross Whyte
Dreamy-Wintery	https://youtu.be/7Quy4s4x4jQ?si=aq2mZpXR5ub2JCW8	Suggested Music Track Title: Dreamy / Wintery Duration: 1:30 Music Composer: Ross Whyte
Earthy	https://youtu.be/2DdF7PG8d2Y?si=iuWnU1dlWQ7LxGwc	Suggested Music Track Title: Earthy Duration: 03:00 Music Composer: Ross Whyte
Floaty	https://youtu.be/EXpUKLvnB5Y?si=McsrW-rvHEGM9dYe	Suggested Music Reflexive Style: Floaty Duration: 2:16 Music Composer: Ross Whyte
Goofy	https://youtu.be/18H-vcxs2lo?si=32A64pbLxKFa0lnf	Suggested Music Track Title: Goofy Duration: 03:12 Music Composer: Ross Whyte

269

Track Title	YouTube Link	QR Code / Duration
Journalling	https://youtu.be/Lw9tNU-DkUg?si=paxWmsSa7mYB7YtS	Suggested Music **Track Title:** Journalling **Duration:** 04:00 Music Composer: Ross Whyte
Mysterious-Curious	https://youtu.be/f62GawQJ34U?si=027faCP0V4e4Go1Z	Suggested Music **Track Title:** Mysterious / Curious **Duration:** 04:16 Music Composer: Ross Whyte
Serious – Pensive	https://youtu.be/IfaV-TYeX3A?si=ijut0d6vswHWud6a	Suggested Music **Track Title:** Serious - Pensive **Duration:** 01:51 Music Composer: Ross Whyte

Action Drives Music

Title	YouTube Link	QR Code / Duration
Action Drives Compilation	https://youtu.be/t1USwhrH8lQ?si=qOPeKk-sJdtEmbth	**Suggested Music** — Track Title: Action Drives Combined — Duration: 17:04 — Music Composer: Ross Whyte
Press	https://youtu.be/7g3P39WWYGY?si=42_dY-Xcq-e9vEDW	**Suggested Music** — Track Title: Press — Duration: 02:21 — Music Composer: Ross Whyte
Float	https://youtu.be/LAB-R6TGobo?si=EP8-PE1TcYmIMP9i	**Suggested Music** — Track Title: Float — Duration: 02:15 — Music Composer: Ross Whyte
Punch	https://youtu.be/DSxK43Mu3t4?si=eKMMFrGYNhLZiDsT	**Suggested Music** — Track Title: Punch — Duration: 02:00 — Music Composer: Ross Whyte
Flick	https://youtu.be/JhypU-vhTnU?si=3Boabx09svaEXtPE	**Suggested Music** — Track Title: Flick — Duration: 02:08 — Music Composer: Ross Whyte
Dab	https://youtu.be/J46L1CEbaSc?si=iPMrt09TeilGBkIL	**Suggested Music** — Track Title: Dab — Duration: 02:04 — Music Composer: Ross Whyte

Appendices

Title	YouTube Link	QR Code	Duration
Wring	https://youtu.be/zB_zthWXZol?si=HX7JVmmHVYDTatKl		Suggested Music — Track Title: Wring — Duration: 02:08 — Music Composer: Ross Whyte
Glide	https://youtu.be/_JkGkPOHhbU?si=BbwnxFaylVsq2IT8		Suggested Music — Track Title: Glide — Duration: 02:00 — Music Composer: Ross Whyte
Slash	https://youtu.be/nNgCRwlTYoA?si=75xB61Lro6WMOBsy		Suggested Music — Track Title: Slash — Duration: 02:04 — Music Composer: Ross Whyte

Decision-Making Stages: Micro-/Macro-Processes Music

QR Code	Track Title	YouTube Link
Flow/Tension Stage	https://youtu.be/-LnCGS-dPh0?si=Z7NM39ssPXFFBSl9	Suggested Music **Track Title:** Flow/Tension **Duration:** 01:08 Music Composer: Ross Whyte
Attention Stage	https://youtu.be/pZJhAoMas3Q?si=D5D3KT37bRlmRxQx	Suggested Music **Track Title:** Attention **Duration:** 04:50 Music Composer: Ross Whyte
Intention Stage	https://youtu.be/2GKq5MWCrHE?si=IjAfiJSX-Ai1xDXP	Suggested Music **Track Title:** Intention **Duration:** 05:11 Music Composer: Ross Whyte
Action/Non-Action Stage	https://youtu.be/HjeKC6o8264?si=wvr2DfmL4ahVPX8N	Suggested Music **Track Title:** Action / Non-Action **Duration:** 04:22 Music Composer: Ross Whyte
Micro-Process Developmental (Flow-Attention-Intention-Action)	https://youtu.be/Vmaj0tq_4-8?si=587h1e8_-tdJfSYV	Suggested Music **Track Title:** Micro Process (Developmental) **Duration:** 19:20 Music Composer: Ross Whyte

QR Code	Track Title	YouTube Link
Micro-Process Introspective (Attention-Flow-Action-Intention)	https://youtu.be/OGekdjhTook?si=VF_BJuZcgdwg8Ibs	**Suggested Music** **Track Title:** Micro Process (Introspective) **Duration:** 19:12 Music Composer: Ross Whyte
Micro-Process Scoping (Intention-Attention-Action-Flow)	https://youtu.be/1HhNrpVEuHQ?si=evuOPf9OCnBFHrY8	**Suggested Music** **Track Title:** Micro Process (Scoping) **Duration:** 19:11 Music Composer: Ross Whyte

Efforts Music

Track Title	YouTube Link	QR Code	Suggested Music
Directness	https://youtu.be/-4MKcLih_QU?si=dDXG_29yP3JHDfPV		**Suggested Music** **Track Title:** Efforts: Directness **Duration:** 7:58 Music Composer: Ross Whyte
Indirectness	https://youtu.be/l2hLxDxpK9g?si=SeHWNLkMaPpFn8pG		**Suggested Music** **Track Title:** Efforts: Indirectness **Duration:** 8:01 Music Composer: Ross Whyte
Strong Weight	https://youtu.be/grT4rxZa5V0?feature=shared		**Suggested Music** **Track Title:** Weight Efforts: Strong Force **Duration:** 7:49 Music Composer: Ross Whyte
Light Weight	https://youtu.be/MA9dt62tcnw?si=wBMTMpA_4vNcJekH		**Suggested Music** **Track Title:** Weight Efforts: Lightness **Duration:** 7:44 Music Composer: Ross Whyte
Quick Time	https://youtu.be/Hwx-tKeSsMc?si=eBtcS0Ia7MnuMZG		**Suggested Music** **Track Title:** Time Efforts: Quickness **Duration:** 7:54 Music Composer: Ross Whyte
Sustained Time	https://youtu.be/9ZsTf9S8zng?si=AfjreY1znVdI__QM		**Suggested Music** **Track Title:** Time Efforts: Sustained **Duration:** 7:47 Music Composer: Ross Whyte

Shaping Qualities Music

		Suggested Music
Spreading/ Enclosing	https://youtu.be/pZJhAoMas3Q?si=D5D3KT37bRlmRxQx	**Suggested Music** **Track Title:** Spreading/ Enclosing **Duration:** 04:50 Music Composer: Ross Whyte
Risking/Sinking	https://youtu.be/2GKq5MWCrHE?si=IjAfiJSX-Ai1xDXP	**Suggested Music** **Track Title:** Rising/Sinking **Duration:** 05:11 Music Composer: Ross Whyte
Advancing/ Retreating	https://youtu.be/HjeKC6o8264?si=wvr2DfmL4ahVPX8N	**Suggested Music** **Track Title:** Advancing/ Retreating **Duration:** 04:22 Music Composer: Ross Whyte

ADDITIONAL
WORKSHEETS

(FLOW) TENSION

Appendix 1. Full Page Flow/Tension Sheet

Appendix 2. Full Page Attention Sheet

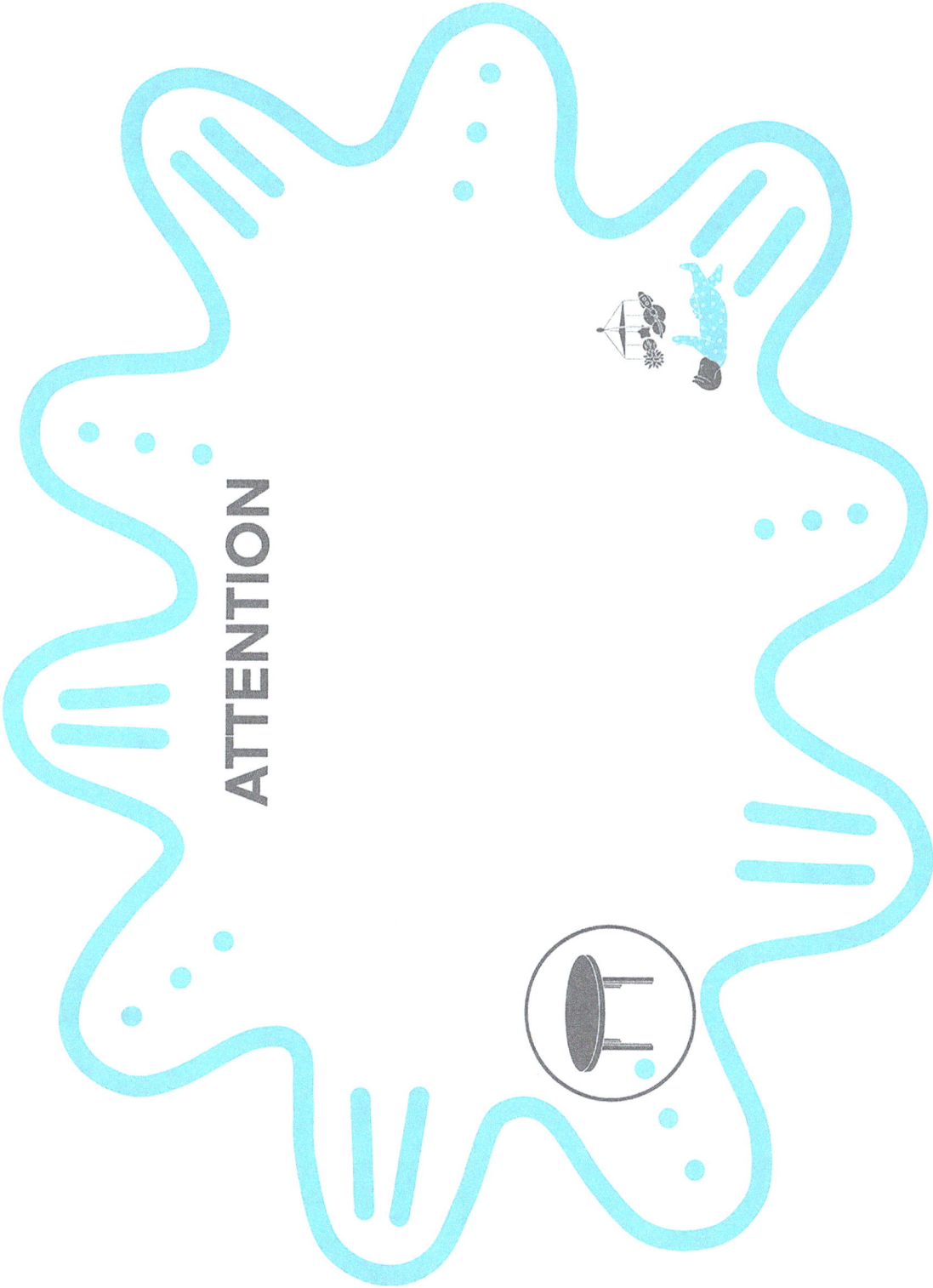

ATTENTION

Appendix 3. Full Page Intention Sheet

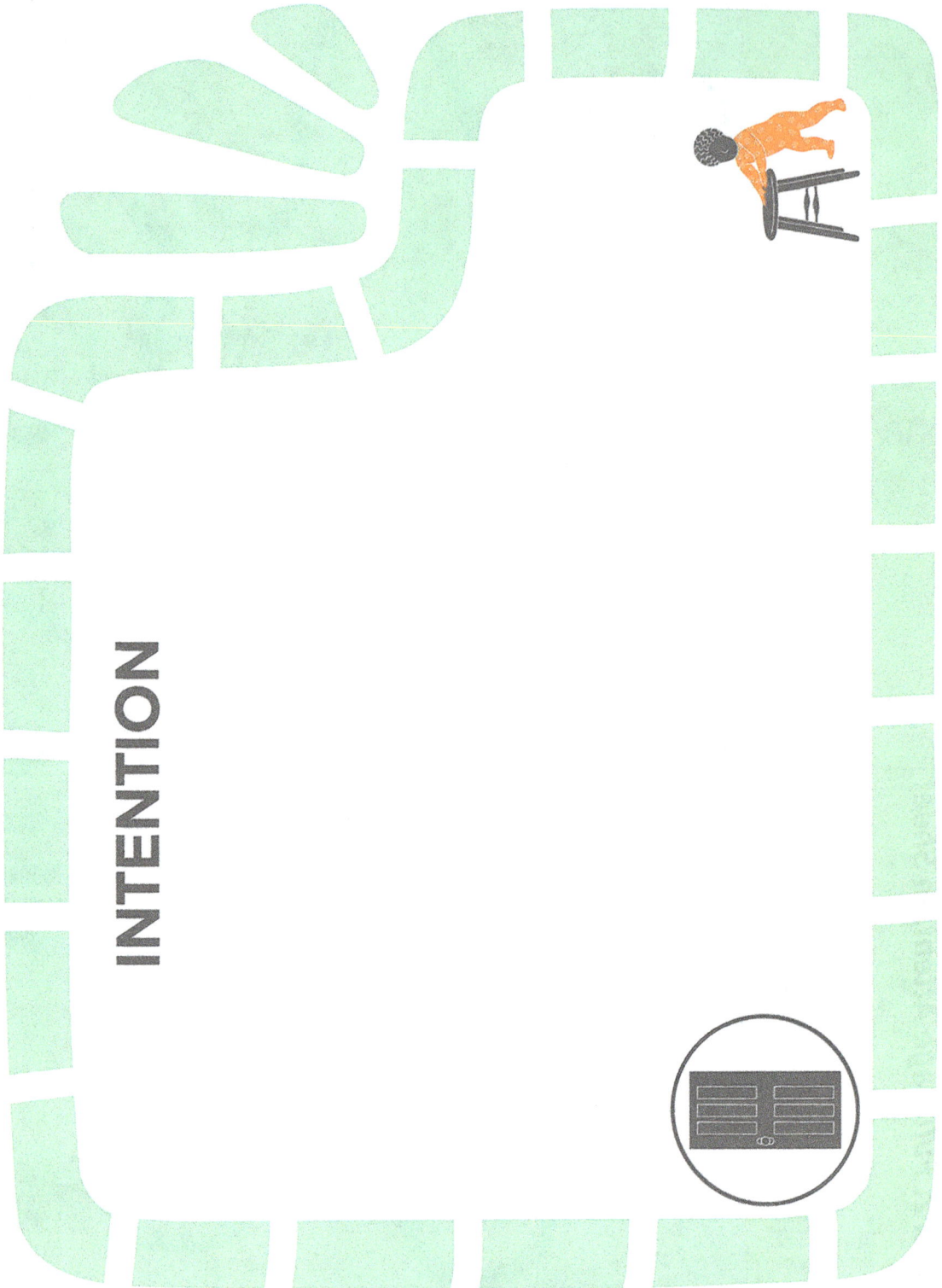

INTENTION

Appendix 4. Full Page Action/Non-Action Sheet

ACTION / NON-ACTION

Appendix 5. Corner Flow/Tension With Body Questions

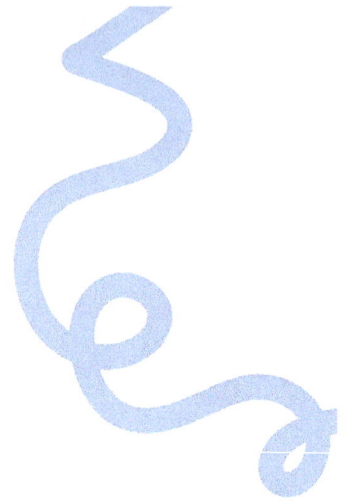

(FLOW) TENSION

What tension exists?

What sparks joy/pleasure?
(Constructive Tension)

What produces annoyance/discomfort and/or curiosity?

Where do I feel this is my body?

ATTENTION (SPACE)

What is my environment like?

What options/alternatives can I explore?

What do I need to research/know more about?

What information do I already have?

Appendix 6. Corner Attention With Body Questions

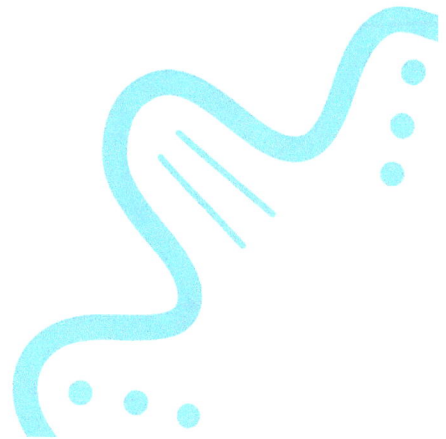

Appendix 7. Corner Intention With Body Questions

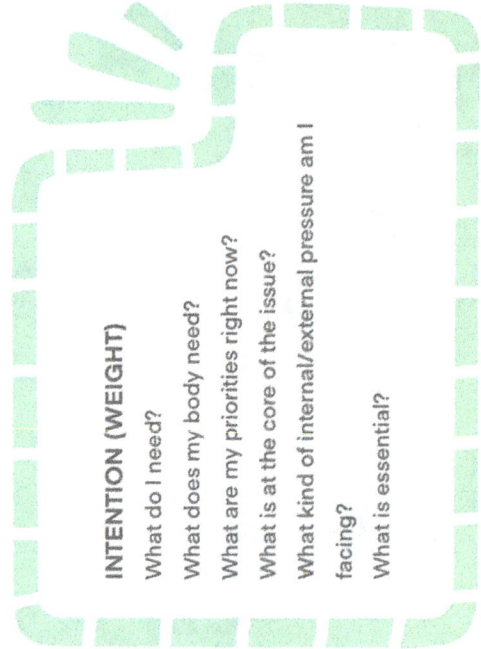

INTENTION (WEIGHT)

What do I need?

What does my body need?

What are my priorities right now?

What is at the core of the issue?

What kind of internal/external pressure am I facing?

What is essential?

Appendix 8. Corner Action/Non-Action With Body Questions

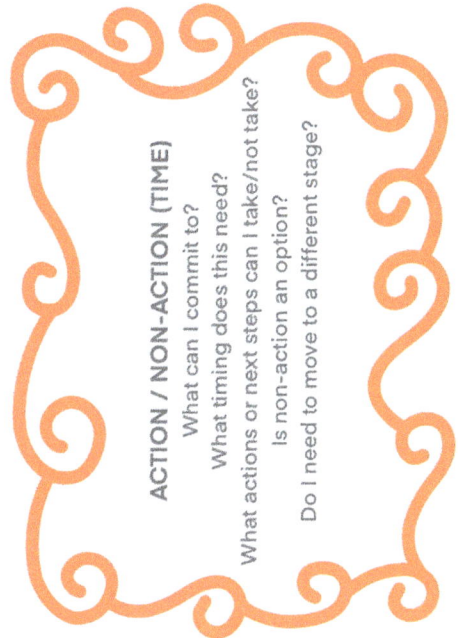

ACTION / NON-ACTION (TIME)

What can I commit to?

What timing does this need?

What actions or next steps can I take/not take?

Is non-action an option?

Do I need to move to a different stage?

Appendix 9. Corner Flow/Tension With Movement Qualities

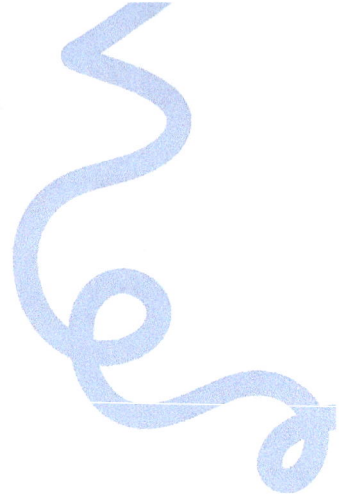

(FLOW) TENSION

EFFORTS: Bound / Free Flow

SHAPE FLOW QUALITITES: Growing / Shrinking

Appendix 10. Corner Attention With Movement Qualities

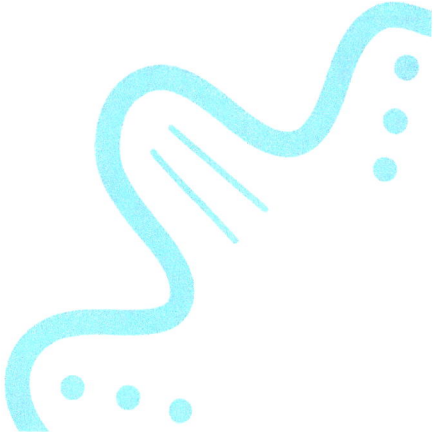

ATTENTION (SPACE)

PLANE: Horizontal

EFFORT CATEGORY: Space

EFFORTS: Direct / Indirect

SHAPING QUALITIES:
Spreading / Enclosing

Appendix 11. Corner Intention With Movement Qualities

INTENTION

PLANE: Vertical

EFFORT CATEGORY: Weight

EFFORTS: Light / Strong

SHAPING QUALITIES:
Rising / Shrinking

Appendix 12. Corner Action/Non-Action With Movement Qualities

ACTION / NON-ACTION (TIME)
PLANE: Saggital
EFFORT CATEGORY: Time
EFFORTS: Quick / Sustained
SHAPING QUALITIES:
Advancing / Retreating

Appendix 13. Decision-Making Combined Research Themes With Flow at Centre

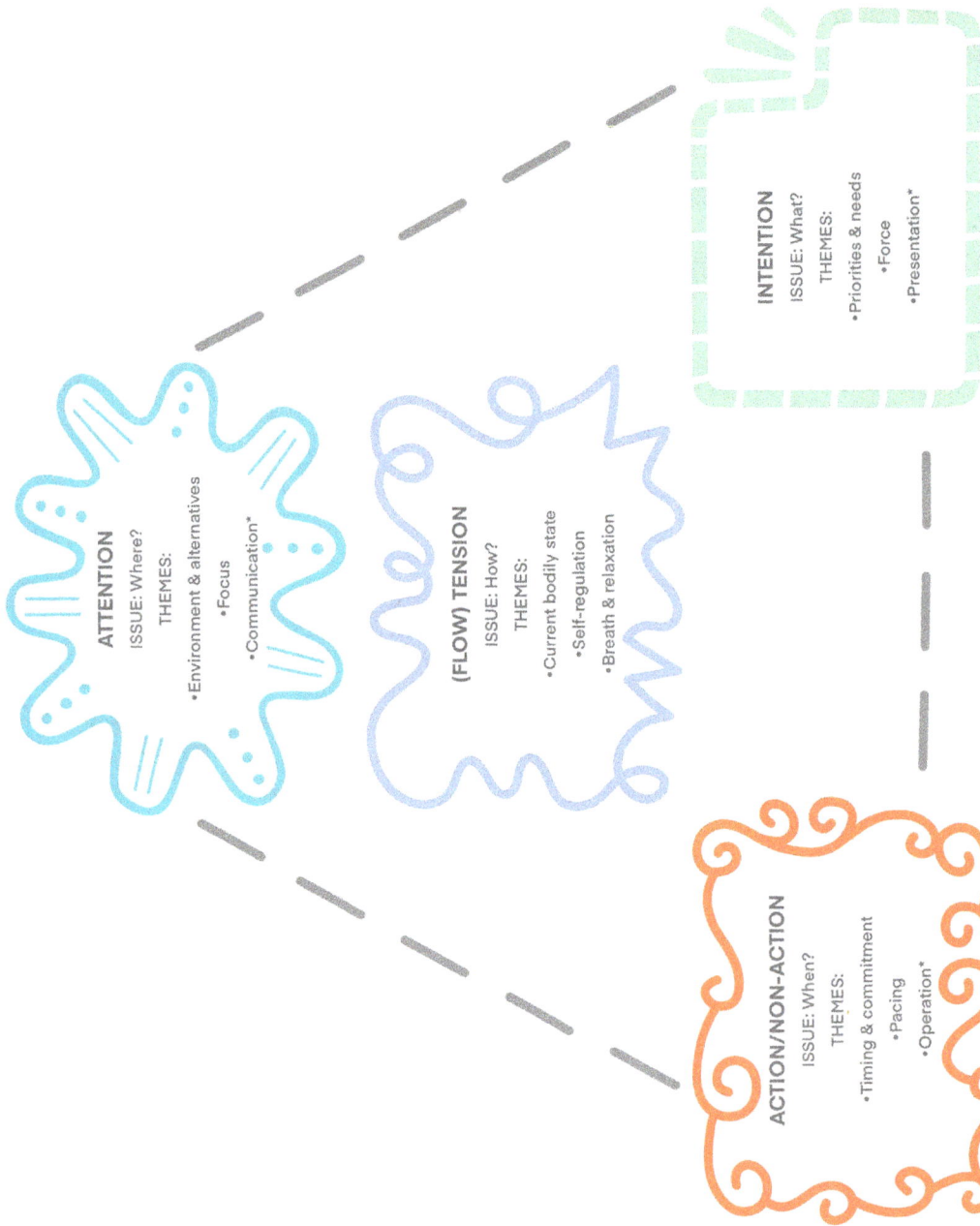

ATTENTION
ISSUE: Where?
THEMES:
•Environment & alternatives
•Focus
•Communication*

(FLOW) TENSION
ISSUE: How?
THEMES:
•Current bodily state
•Self-regulation
•Breath & relaxation

INTENTION
ISSUE: What?
THEMES:
•Priorities & needs
•Force
•Presentation*

ACTION/NON-ACTION
ISSUE: When?
THEMES:
•Timing & commitment
•Pacing
•Operation*

*Lamb, Warren. Posture and Gesture: An Introduction to the Study of Physical Behaviour (G. Duckworth, 1965) 115

REFERENCES

Acarón, Thania. 'The Practitioner's Body of Knowledge: Dance/Movement in Training Programmes That Address Violence, Conflict and Peace' (University of Aberdeen, 2015). http://ethos.bl.uk/OrderDetails.do?did=1&uin=uk.bl.ethos.683450.

Acarón, Thania. 'Traversing Distance and Proximity: The Integration of Psychodrama and Dance Movement Therapy Techniques in Supervision'. *Body, Movement and Dance in Psychotherapy* 11, no. 1 (November 2015): 1–15. https://doi.org/10.1080/17432979.2015.1109550.

Acarón, Thania. 'Shape-in(g) Space: Body, Boundaries, and Violence'. *Space and Culture* 19, no. 2 (2016): 139–149.

Acarón, Thania. 'Therapeutic Performance: When Private Moves into Public'. In *The Oxford Handbook for Dance and Wellbeing*, edited by Vassiliki Karkou, Sue Oliver, and Sophia Lycouris (New York: Oxford University Press, 2017), 219–238.

Acarón, Thania. 'Movement Decision-Making in Violence Prevention and Peace Practices'. *Journal of Peace Education* 15, no. 2 (May 2018): 191–215. https://doi.org/10.1080/17400201.2018.1463913.

Acarón, Thania, and Alison Wren. 'Under the Skin: Barriers and Opportunities for Dance Movement Therapy & Art Psychotherapy with LGBT+ Clients'. In *Gender and Difference in the Arts Therapies: Inscribed on the Body*, edited by Susan Hogan (London and New York: Routledge, 2019), 24–35.

Adler, Janet. *Offering from the Conscious Body: The Discipline of Authentic Movement* (Simon and Schuster, 2002).

Anderson, Cheryl, and Linda Rouse. 'Intervention in Cases of Woman Battering: An Application of Symbolic Interactionism and Critical Theory'. *Clinical Sociology Review* 6, no. 1 (January 1988). http://digitalcommons.wayne.edu/csr/vol6/iss1/17.

Appelt, Kirstin C., Kerry F. Milch, Michel J. J. Handgraaf, and Elke U. Weber. 'The Decision-Making Individual Differences Inventory and Guidelines for the Study of Individual Differences in Judgment and Decision-Making Research'. *Judgment and Decision-Making* 6, no. 3 (2011): 252–262.

Ashinoff, Brandon K., and Ahmad Abu-Akel. 'Hyperfocus: The Forgotten Frontier of Attention'. *Psychological Research* 85, no. 1 (February 2021): 1–19. https://doi.org/10.1007/s00426-019-01245-8.

Ayers, Susan. 'The Application of Chaos Theory to Psychology'. *Theory & Psychology* 7, no. 3 (June 1997): 373–398. https://doi.org/10.1177/0959354397073005.

Bandura, Albert. 'Self-Efficacy'. In *The Corsini Encyclopedia of Psychology* (American Cancer Society, 2010), 1–3. https://doi.org/10.1002/9780470479216.corpsy0836.

References

Barbour, Karen. 'Embodied Values and Ethical Principles in Somatic Dance Classes: Considering Implicit Motor Learning'. *Text* (December 2016). https://doi.org/info:doi/10.1386/jdsp.8.2.189_1.

Bartenieff, Irmgard, Peggy Hackney, Betty True Jones, Judy Van Zile, and Carl Wolz. 'The Potential of Movement Analysis as a Research Tool: A Preliminary Analysis'. *Dance Research Journal* 16, no. 1 (1984): 3–26.

Bartenieff, Irmgard, and Dori Lewis. *Body Movement: Coping with the Environment* (Routledge, 2013).

Beardall, Nancy, Valerie Blanc, Ebony Nichols, Yaya Cofield, Fernanda Greco Quentel, Sofia Lee, Marea Newroz, Sahita Pierre-Antoine, and Stephanie Sinclair. 'Creating Spaces for Discoveries in Movement Observation and Beyond'. *American Journal of Dance Therapy* (January 2024). https://doi.org/10.1007/s10465-023-09395-4.

Bechara, Antoine, Hanna Damasio, and Antonio R. Damasio. 'Emotion, Decision-Making and the Orbitofrontal Cortex'. *Cerebral Cortex* 10, no. 3 (January 2000): 295–307. https://doi.org/10.1093/cercor/10.3.295.

Benesh, Rudolf, and Joan Benesh. *An Introduction to Benesh Movement-Notation: Dance*, vol. 16 (Dance Horizons, 1969).

Bernstein, Bonnie. 'Empowerment-Focused Dance/Movement Therapy for Trauma Recovery'. In *Social Justice in Dance/Movement Therapy: Practice, Research and Education*, edited by Laura Downey and Susan Kierr (Cham: Springer Nature, 2022), 55–75. https://doi.org/10.1007/978-3-031-19451-1_5.

Birdwhistell, Ray L. *Kinesics and Context: Essays on Body Motion Communication* (University of Pennsylvania Press, 2010).

Bloom, Katya, Barbara Adrian, Tom Casciero, Jennifer Mizenko, and Claire Porter. *The Laban Workbook for Actors: A Practical Training Guide with Video* (Bloomsbury Publishing, 2017).

Breit, Sigrid, Aleksandra Kupferberg, Gerhard Rogler, and Gregor Hasler. 'Vagus Nerve as Modulator of the Brain – Gut Axis in Psychiatric and Inflammatory Disorders'. *Frontiers in Psychiatry* 9 (2018). www.frontiersin.org/articles/10.3389/fpsyt.2018.00044.

Bullough, Edward. '"Psychical Distance" as a Factor in Art and an Aesthetic Principle'. *British Journal of Psychology* 5, no. 2 (1912): 87–118.

Calais-Germain, Blandine. *Anatomy of Movement* (Kagaku Shinbun Sha, 1993).

Caldwell, Christine. *Bodyfulness: Somatic Practices for Presence, Empowerment, and Waking Up in This Life* (Shambhala Publications, 2018).

Caldwell, Christine, and Rae Johnson. 'Embodying Difference: Addressing Issues of Diversity and Social Justice in Dance/Movement Therapy Research'. In *Dance/Movement Therapists in Action: A Working Guide to Research Options*, 2nd ed. (Charles C Thomas Publisher, 2012), 121–140. https://play.google.com/books/reader?id=aOnmCAAAQBAJ&hl=en&pg=GBS.PR4.

Calouste Gulbenkian Foundation and Centre for Ageing Better. 'Evaluation of Transitions in Later Life Pilot Projects'. Project Evaluation (Calouste Gulbenkian Foundation and Centre for Ageing Better, 2017). https://gulbenkian.pt/uk-branch/publication/evaluation-transitions-later-life-pilot-projects/.

Çatay, Zeynep, and Marcia Plevin. 'A Way to Embodiment Through Aesthetic Relationship: Transformational Body Tracings'. In *Dance and Creativity Within Dance Movement Therapy*, edited by Hilda Wengrower and Sharon Chaiklin (Routledge, 2020), 84–95. https://doi.org/10.4324/9780429442308-9.

Clement, Evelyne. *Cognitive Flexibility: The Cornerstone of Learning* (John Wiley & Sons, 2022).

Connors, Brenda L., Carol-Lynne Moore, Richard Rende, and Timothy J. Colton. 'Movement Pattern Analysis (MPA): Decoding Individual Differences in Embodied Decision-Making'. In *The Sage Handbook of Personality and Individual Differences: The Science of Personality and Individual Differences* (Sage Reference, 2018), 257–277. https://doi.org/10.4135/9781526451163.n11.

Connors, Brenda L., and Richard Rende. 'Embodied Decision-Making Style: Below and Beyond Cognition'. *Frontiers in Psychology* 9 (2018). https://doi.org/10.3389/fpsyg.2018.01123.

Connors, Brenda L., Richard Rende, and Timothy J. Colton. 'Beyond Self-Report: Emerging Methods for Capturing Individual Differences in Decision-Making Process'. *Frontiers in Psychology* 7 (2016). https://doi.org/10.3389/fpsyg.2016.00312.

Connors, Brenda L., Richard Rende, and Timothy J. Colton. 'Decision-Making Style in Leaders: Uncovering Cognitive Motivation Using Signature Movement Patterns'. *International Journal of Psychological Studies* 7, no. 2 (2015): 105.

Connors, Brenda L., Richard Rende, and Timothy J. Colton. 'Predicting Individual Differences in Decision-Making Process from Signature Movement Styles: An Illustrative Study of Leaders'. *Frontiers in Psychology* 4 (2013). https://doi.org/10.3389/fpsyg.2013.00658.

Cruz, Robyn Flaum. 'Validity of the Movement Psychodiagnostic Inventory'. *American Journal of Dance Therapy* 31 (2009): 122–135. https://doi.org/10.1007/s10465-009-9072-4.

Cruz, Robyn Flaum, and Cynthia F. Berrol. *Dance/Movement Therapists in Action: A Working Guide to Research Options*, 2nd ed. (Charles C Thomas Publisher, 2012). https://play.google.com/books/reader?id=aOnmCAAAQBAJ&hl=en&pg=GBS.PR4.

Csordas, Thomas J. *Embodiment and Experience: The Existential Ground of Culture and Self* (Cambridge University Press, 1994).

Csordas, Thomas J. 'Somatic Modes of Attention'. *Cultural Anthropology* 8, no. 2 (1993): 135–156.

Cuevas, Kimberly, and Martha Ann Bell. 'Infant Attention and Early Childhood Executive Function'. *Child Development* 85, no. 2 (March 2014): 397–404. https://doi.org/10.1111/cdev.12126.

Daly, Ann. 'Movement Analysis: Piecing Together the Puzzle'. *TDR: The Drama Review* 32, no. 4 (1988): 40–52.

Damasio, Antonio R., and Hanna Damasio, eds. *Neurobiology of Decision-Making* (Springer Science & Business Media, 2012).

Davies, Eden. *Beyond Dance: Laban's Legacy of Movement Analysis* (New York: Routledge, 2006). https://doi.org/10.4324/9780203960066.

Davis, Martha. 'Movement Characteristics of Hospitalized Psychiatric Patients'. *American Journal of Dance Therapy* 4, no. 1 (1981): 52–71.

Davis, Martha, Dianne Dulicai, and Ildiko Viczian. 'Hitler's Movement Signature'. *TDR (1988–)* 36, no. 2 (1992): 152–172. https://doi.org/10.2307/1146204.

References

Davis, Martha, and Keith A. Markus. 'Misleading Cues, Misplaced Confidence: An Analysis of Deception Detection Patterns'. *American Journal of Dance Therapy* 28, no. 2 (October 2006): 107–126. https://doi.org/10.1007/s10465-006-9018-z.

Davis, Martha, Stan B. Walters, Neal Vorus, and Brenda Connors. 'Defensive Demeanor Profiles'. *American Journal of Dance Therapy* 22, no. 2 (June 2000): 103–121. https://doi.org/10.1023/A:1026582324633.

Dell, Cecily. *A Primer for Movement Description Using Effort-Shape and Supplementary Concepts* (New York: Dance Notation Bureau Press, 1977).

Dell, Cecily. *Space Harmony: Basic Terms*. Edited by Irmgard Bartenieff and Aileen Crow (New York: Dance Notation Bureau Press, 1977).

Denzin, Norman K., and Yvonna S. Lincoln. *The Sage Handbook of Qualitative Research* (Sage, 2011).

De Ridder, Dirk, Mark Llewellyn Smith, and Divya Adhia. 'Chapter 4 – Autonomic Nervous System and the Triple Network: An Evolutionary Perspective with Clinical Implications'. In *Introduction to Quantitative EEG and Neurofeedback*, edited by Dan R. Chartier, Mary Blair Dellinger, James R. Evans, and Helen Kogan Budzynski, 3rd ed. (Academic Press, 2023), 63–77. https://doi.org/10.1016/B978-0-323-89827-0.00016-4.

Devereaux, Christina. 'An Interview with Dr. Stephen W. Porges'. *American Journal of Dance Therapy* 39, no. 1 (June 2017): 27–35. https://doi.org/10.1007/s10465-017-9252-6.

Dieterich-Hartwell, Rebekka. 'Dance/Movement Therapy in the Treatment of Post Traumatic Stress: A Reference Model'. *The Arts in Psychotherapy* 54 (July 2017): 38–46. https://doi.org/10.1016/j.aip.2017.02.010.

Dieterich-Hartwell, Rebekka, and Anne Margrethe Melsom. *Dance/Movement Therapy for Trauma Survivors: Theoretical, Clinical, and Cultural Perspectives* (Routledge, 2022).

Dosamantes-Beaudry, Irma. 'Somatic Transference and Countertransference in Psychoanalytic Intersubjective Dance/Movement Therapy'. *American Journal of Dance Therapy* 29, no. 2 (August 2007): 73–89. https://doi.org/10.1007/s10465-007-9035-6.

Dumas, Tracy L., and Jeffrey Sanchez-Burks. 'The Professional, the Personal, and the Ideal Worker: Pressures and Objectives Shaping the Boundary Between Life Domains'. *The Academy of Management Annals* 9, no. 1 (January 2015): 803–843. https://doi.org/10.1080/19416520.2015.1028810.

Eddy, Martha. 'Body Cues and Conflict: LMA-Derived Approaches to Educational Violence Prevention' (2002). www.wellnesscke.net/downloadables/Body-Cues-Conflict.pdf.

Eddy, Martha. 'The Role of Dance in Violence Prevention Programs for Youth'. *Dance: Current Selected Research* 7 (2009): 93–143.

Eddy, Martha. 'The Role of Physical Activity in Educational Violence Prevention Programs for Youth' (PhD Thesis, Columbia University, 1998).

Ekman, Paul, Wallace V. Freisen, and Sonia Ancoli. 'Facial Signs of Emotional Experience'. *Journal of Personality and Social Psychology* 39, no. 6 (1980): 1125–1134. https://doi.org/10.1037/h0077722.

Ellingson, Laura L. 'Embodied Knowledge: Writing Researchers' Bodies into Qualitative Health Research'. *Qualitative Health Research* 16, no. 2 (February 2006): 298–310. https://doi.org/10.1177/1049732305281944.

Ellingson, Laura L. *Interview as Embodied Communication* (Sage Publications, Inc., 2012). https://doi.org/10.4135/9781452218403.n37.

Ellis, Carolyn, and Art Bochner. 'Autoethnography, Personal Narrative, Reflexivity: Researcher as Subject'. In *Handbook of Qualitative Research*, edited by Norman K. Denzin and Yvonna S. Lincoln, 2nd ed. (2000), 733–768. https://digitalcommons.usf.edu/spe_facpub/91.

Erikson, Erik. 'Theory of Identity Development'. In *Identity and the Life Cycle* (New York: International Universities Press, 1959), 42–57. www.bpi.edu/ourpages/auto/2018/11/21/57748242/theory%20of%20identity%20erikson.pdf.

Evans, Elizabeth, Martin Hyde, Jason Davies, Suzanne Moffatt, Nicola O'Brien, and Gill Windle. *Navigating Later Life Transitions: An Evaluation of Emotional and Psychological Interventions* (Calouste Gulbenkian Foundation UK; Centre for Ageing Better; Swansea University, 2019). https://europepmc.org/backend/ptpmcrender.fcgi?accid=PMC4318792&blobtype=pdf.

Fancourt, Daisy, and Tim Joss. 'Aesop: A Framework for Developing and Researching Arts in Health Programmes'. *Arts & Health* 7, no. 1 (January 2015): 1–13. https://doi.org/10.1080/17533015.2014.924974.

Fetterman, Adam K., and Michael D. Robinson. 'Do You Use Your Head or Follow Your Heart? Self-Location Predicts Personality, Emotion, Decision-Making, and Performance'. *Journal of Personality and Social Psychology* 105, no. 2 (2013): 316–334.

Finlay, Linda. '"Reflexive Embodied Empathy": A Phenomenology of Participant-Researcher Intersubjectivity'. *The Humanistic Psychologist* 33, no. 4 (October 2005): 271–292. https://doi.org/10.1207/s15473333thp3304_4.

Finucane, M. L., and C. M. Gullion. 'Developing a Tool for Measuring the Decision-Making Competence of Older Adults.' *Psychology and Aging* 25, no. 2 (June 2010): 271–288. https://doi.org/10.1037/a0019106.

Foglia, Lucia, and Robert A. Wilson. 'Embodied Cognition'. *WIREs Cognitive Science* 4, no. 3 (2013): 319–325. https://doi.org/10.1002/wcs.1226.

Fraenkel, Danielle L., and Jeffrey Mehr. *LivingDance~LivingMusic: Keeping Your Shape in Shifting Times* (New Orleans: American Dance Therapy, 2004).

Fukuzaki, Toshiki, and Shinya Takeda. 'The Relationship Between Cognitive Flexibility, Depression, and Work Performance: Employee Assessments Using Cognitive Flexibility Tests'. *Journal of Affective Disorders Reports* 10 (December 2022): 100388. https://doi.org/10.1016/j.jadr.2022.100388.

Gallagher, Shaun. *Embodied and Enactive Approaches to Cognition Elements in Philosophy of Mind* (Cambridge: Cambridge University Press, 2023). https://doi.org/10.1017/9781009209793.

Galotti, Kathleen M., Elizabeth Ciner, Hope E. Altenbaumer, Heather J. Geerts, Allison Rupp, and Julie Woulfe. 'Decision-Making Styles in a Real-Life Decision: Choosing a College Major'. *Personality and Individual Differences* 41, no. 4 (September 2006): 629–639. https://doi.org/10.1016/j.paid.2006.03.003.

References

Girshon, Alexander, and Ekaterina Karatygina. 'Psychological Re-Sources in Integral Dance and Dance/Movement Therapy'. In *The Routledge International Handbook of Embodied Perspectives in Psychotherapy* (Routledge, 2019).

Goodman, Jane, Nancy K. Schlossberg, and Mary L. Anderson. *Counseling Adults in Transition: Linking Practices with Theory* (New York: Springer Publishing Company, 2006). http://ebookcentral.proquest.com/lib/usw/detail.action?docID=291321.

Grant-Beuttler, Marybeth, Laura M. Glynn, Amy L. Salisbury, Elysia Poggi Davis, Carol Holliday, and Curt A. Sandman. 'Development of Fetal Movement Between 26 and 36-Weeks' Gestation in Response to Vibro-Acoustic Stimulation'. *Frontiers in Psychology* 2 (December 2011). https://doi.org/10.3389/fpsyg.2011.00350.

Gray, Amber Elizabeth Lynn. 'Body as Voice: Restorative Dance/Movement Psychotherapy with Survivors of Relational Trauma'. In *The Routledge International Handbook of Embodied Perspectives in Psychotherapy* (Routledge, 2019).

Gray, Amber Elizabeth Lynn. 'Polyvagal-Informed Dance/Movement Therapy for Trauma: A Global Perspective'. *American Journal of Dance Therapy* 39, no. 1 (June 2017): 43–46. https://doi.org/10.1007/s10465-017-9254-4.

Gray, Amber Elizabeth Lynn, and J. Ryan Kennedy. 'Marian Chace Foundation 2022 Lecture & Introduction from the 57th Annual American Dance Therapy Association Conference, Heartlines: Gathering Wisdom from Many Streams; Montreal, Canada'. *American Journal of Dance Therapy* 45, no. 1 (June 2023): 88–108. https://doi.org/10.1007/s10465-023-09384-7.

Hackney, Peggy. *Making Connections: Total Body Integration Through Bartenieff Fundamentals* (New York: Routledge, 2002).

Hamilton, Peter. *George Herbert Mead: Critical Assessments* (Taylor & Francis, 1992).

Hanna, Judith Lynne. *To Dance Is Human: A Theory of Nonverbal Communication* (Austin: University of Texas Press, 1979).

Hanson, Katie, Thomas L. Webb, Paschal Sheeran, and Graham Turpin. 'Attitudes and Preferences Towards Self-Help Treatments for Depression in Comparison to Psychotherapy and Antidepressant Medication'. *Behavioural and Cognitive Psychotherapy* 44, no. 2 (March 2016): 129–139. https://doi.org/10.1017/S1352465815000041.

Harris, David Alan. 'The Paradox of Expressing Speechless Terror: Ritual Liminality in the Creative Arts Therapies' Treatment of Posttraumatic Distress'. *The Arts in Psychotherapy* 36, no. 2 (2009): 94–104.

Hershler, Abby. 'Window of Tolerance'. In *Looking at Trauma: A Tool Kit for Clinicians*, edited by Abby Hershler, Lesley Hughes, Patricia Nguyen, and Shelley Wall (Penn State University Press, 2021), 25–28. https://doi.org/10.1515/9780271092287-008.

Hervey, Lenore, and Rena Kornblum. 'An Evaluation of Kornblum's Body-Based Violence Prevention Curriculum for Children'. *The Arts in Psychotherapy* 33, no. 2 (2006): 113–129. https://doi.org/10.1016/j.aip.2005.08.001.

Hervey, Lenore Wadsworth. 'Embodied Ethical Decision-Making'. *American Journal of Dance Therapy* 29, no. 2 (December 2007): 91–108. https://doi.org/10.1007/s10465-007-9036-5.

Hess, Kyra. 'Witnessing Another, Witnessing Oneself'. *Dance/Movement Therapy Theses* (May 2018). https://core.ac.uk/download/pdf/217287591.pdf.

Hofstede, Geert. 'Dimensionalizing Cultures: The Hofstede Model in Context'. *Online Readings in Psychology and Culture* 2, no. 1 (2011): 1–26.

Homann, Kalila B. 'Embodied Concepts of Neurobiology in Dance/Movement Therapy Practice'. *American Journal of Dance Therapy* 32, no. 2 (December 2010): 80–99. https://doi.org/10.1007/s10465-010-9099-6.

Hutchinson Guest, Ann. *Your Move: A New Approach to the Study of Movement and Dance | Teacher's Guide* (Taylor & Francis Ltd., 1983).

Imus, Susan D., Aisha Bell Robinson, Valerie Blanc, and Jessica Young. 'More Than One Story, More Than One Man: Laban Movement Analysis Re-Examined'. *American Journal of Dance Therapy* 44, no. 2 (December 2022): 168–185. https://doi.org/10.1007/s10465-022-09370-5.

Jackson, Naomi, and Toni Shapiro-Phim, eds. *Dance, Human Rights and Social Justice: Dignity in Motion* (Plymouth, UK: Scarecrow Press, Inc., 2008).

Joo, Baek-Kyoo, and Insuk Lee. 'Workplace Happiness: Work Engagement, Career Satisfaction, and Subjective Well-Being'. *Evidence-Based HRM: A Global Forum for Empirical Scholarship* 5, no. 2 (January 2017): 206–221. https://doi.org/10.1108/EBHRM-04-2015-0011.

Jung, C. G. *The Archetypes and the Collective Unconscious*, 2nd ed. Collected Works of C. G. Jung, vol. 9 (London: Routledge, 2014).

Kapit, Wynn, and Lawrence Elson. *The Anatomy Coloring Book*, 4th ed. (Pearson, 2013).

Karkouti, Ibrahim Mohamad. 'Examining Psychosocial Identity Development Theories: A Guideline for Professional Practice'. *Education* 135, no. 2 (December 2014): 257–264.

Katzman, Erika R. 'Embodied Reflexivity: Knowledge and the Body in Professional Practice'. In *The Body in Professional Practice, Learning and Education: Body/Practice*, edited by Bill Green and Nick Hopwood Professional and Practice-Based Learning (Cham: Springer International Publishing, 2015), 157–172. https://doi.org/10.1007/978-3-319-00140-1_10.

Kawano, Tomoyo, and Meg Chang. 'Applying Critical Consciousness to Dance/Movement Therapy Pedagogy and the Politics of the Body'. In *Social Justice in Dance/Movement Therapy: Practice, Research and Education*, edited by Laura Downey and Susan Kierr (Cham: Springer Nature Switzerland, 2022), 97–118. https://doi.org/10.1007/978-3-031-19451-1_7.

Kelly, Martina, Joy de Vries-Erich, Esther Helmich, Tim Dornan, and Nigel King. 'Embodied Reflexivity in Qualitative Analysis: A Role for Selfies'. *Forum Qualitative Sozialforschung/Forum: Qualitative Social Research* 18, no. 2 (May 2017). https://doi.org/10.17169/fqs-18.2.2701.

Kenner, Carole, and Welma Lubbe. 'Fetal Stimulation – A Preventative Therapy'. *Newborn and Infant Nursing Reviews, Fetal Therapeutics* 7, no. 4 (December 2007): 227–230. https://doi.org/10.1053/j.nainr.2007.06.013.

Kestenberg Amighi, Janet, Susan Loman, Penny Lewis, and K. Mark Sossin. *The Meaning of Movement: Developmental and Clinical Perspectives of the Kestenberg Movement Profile* (Amsterdam, The Netherlands: Gordon and Breach, 1999).

Koch, Sabine C. 'Arts and Health: Active Factors and a Theory Framework of Embodied Aesthetics'. *The Arts in Psychotherapy* 54 (July 2017): 85–91. https://doi.org/10.1016/j.aip.2017.02.002.

Koch, Sabine C. 'Movement Analysis in Dance Therapy: Semantics of Movement Qualities, Rhythm and Shape According to Laban and Kestenberg'. *Acta Universitatis Carolinae. Medica* 47, no. 2 (2011): 1–8.

Koch, Sabine C., and Diana Fischman. 'Embodied Enactive Dance/Movement Therapy'. *American Journal of Dance Therapy* 33, no. 1 (June 2011): 57–72. https://doi.org/10.1007/s10465-011-9108-4.

Kolk, Bessel A. van der. 'Beyond the Talking Cure: Somatic Experience and Subcortical Imprints in the Treatment of Trauma'. In *EMDR as an Integrative Psychotherapy Approach: Experts of Diverse Orientations Explore the Paradigm Prism* (Washington, DC: American Psychological Association, 2002), 57–83. www.essentia.fr/blog/wp-content/uploads/2011/09/vanderKolk-Beyond-the-talking-cure.pdf.

Kolk, Bessel A van der. 'The Body Keeps the Score: Memory and the Evolving Psychobiology of Posttraumatic Stress'. *Harvard Review of Psychiatry* 1, no. 5 (1994): 253–265.

Kolk, Bessel A. van der, and Alexander C. McFarlane. *Traumatic Stress: The Effects of Overwhelming Experience on Mind, Body, and Society* (Guilford Press, 2012).

Komorowski, Marlen, and Justin Lewis. *The Covid-19 Self-Employment Income Support Scheme: How Will It Help Freelancers in the Creative Industries in Wales?* (Cardiff, Wales: Creative Cardiff | Caerdydd Creadigol, April 2020). www.creativecardiff.org.uk/sites/default/files/Creative%20Cardiff%20study%20on%20COVID-19%20Support%20Scheme%202.4.20.pdf.

Konie, Robin. 'A Brief Overview of Laban Movement Analysis' (2011). http://psychomotorischetherapie.info/website/wp-content/uploads/2015/10/LMA-Workshop-Sheet-Laban.pdf.

Konie, Robin. 'Laban Movement Analysis: Worksheet 2' (2011). https://studylib.net/doc/8395068/laban-movement-analysis.

Kornblum, Rena. *Disarming the Playground: Violence Prevention Through Movement and Pro-Social Skills, Activity Book* (Oklahoma City: Wood 'N' Barnes Publishing, 2002).

Kossek, Ellen Ernst, Monique Valcour, and Pamela Lirio. 'The Sustainable Workforce: Organizational Strategies for Promoting Work – Life Balance and Wellbeing'. *Wellbeing: A Complete Reference Guide* (2014): 1–24.

Laban, Rudolf. *Choreutics*. Edited by Lisa Ullmann, 2nd ed. (London: Macdonald & Evans, 1966).

Lamb, Warren. *Posture and Gesture: An Introduction to the Study of Physical Behaviour* (G. Duckworth, 1965).

Lamb, Warren, and Elizabeth M. Watson. *Body Code: The Meaning in Movement* (London and Boston: Routledge & Kegan Paul, 1979).

Lamb, Warren. 'The Recruiter's Responsibility for Judging People: The Need to Observe Body Movement'. *Journal of Management Development* 1, no. 1 (1982): 63–74.

Lamb, Warren. 'Body-Mind Functioning in the Workplace'. *The Educational Forum* 54, no. 1 (March 1990): 71–76. https://doi.org/10.1080/00131728909335519.

Lamb, Warren, and Eden Davies. *A Framework for Understanding Movement: My Seven Creative Concepts* (London: Brechin Books Ltd., 2012).

Landy, Robert J. 'The Use of Distancing in Drama Therapy'. *The Arts in Psychotherapy* 10, no. 3 (September 1983): 175–185. https://doi.org/10.1016/0197-4556(83)90006-0.

Lauffenburger, Sandra Kay. '"Something More": The Unique Features of Dance Movement Therapy/Psychotherapy'. *American Journal of Dance Therapy* 42, no. 1 (June 2020): 16–32. https://doi.org/10.1007/s10465-020-09321-y.

Laumond, Jean-Paul, and Naoko Abe. *Dance Notations and Robot Motion* (Springer, 2016). https://doi.org/10.1007/978-3-319-25739-6.

Leder, Drew. *The Absent Body* (Chicago and London: University of Chicago Press, 1990).

Leigh, Jennifer, and Richard Bailey. 'Reflection, Reflective Practice and Embodied Reflective Practice'. *Body, Movement and Dance in Psychotherapy* 8, no. 3 (August 2013): 160–171. https://doi.org/10.1080/17432979.2013.797498.

Lerner, Jennifer S., Ye Li, Piercarlo Valdesolo, and Karim S. Kassam. 'Emotion and Decision-Making'. *Annual Review of Psychology* 66 (January 2015): 799–823. https://doi.org/10.1146/annurev-psych-010213-115043.

Levine, Peter A. *In an Unspoken Voice: How the Body Releases Trauma and Restores Goodness* (Berkeley: North Atlantic Books, 2010).

Linden, Paul. 'Aikido Roots and Branches: Body Awareness Training Methods and Their Applications in Daily Life'. In *International Aiki Extensions Conference* (Germany, 2002), 1–26. https://www.being-in-movement.com/wp-content/plugins/pdf-poster/pdfjs/web/viewer.html?file=https://www.being-in-movement.com/wp-content/uploads/2020/08/Aikido-Roots-and-Branches-Body-awareness-training-methods-and-their-applications-In-daily-life-Paul-Linden.pdf&download=true&print=vera&openfile=false.

Linden, Paul. *Embodied Peacemaking: Body Awareness, Self-Regulation and Conflict Resolution* (Columbus, OH: CCMS Publications, 2007). www.being-in-movement.com.

Loman, Susan, Hilary White, and Melanie Johnson French. 'Kestenberg Movement Profile (KMP) Approaches to Working with Young Children and Caregivers in Dance/Movement Therapy'. *Journal of Infant, Child, and Adolescent Psychotherapy* 20, no. 1 (January 2021): 36–50. https://doi.org/10.1080/15289168.2021.1875703.

Longstaff, Jeffrey Scott. 'Continuous Flux in Flow of Effort and Flow of Shape'. *Movement and Dance Magazine of the Laban Guild; Motus Humanus Supplement* 27, no. 4 (2008): 22–28.

Longstaff, Jeffrey Scott. 'Laban Analysis Reviews: Effort Elements, Factors, States, & Drive' (2004). www.laban-analyses.org/laban_analysis_reviews/laban_analysis_notation/effort_dynamics_eukinetics/element_factor_state_drive.htm.

March, James G. *Primer on Decision-Making: How Decisions Happen* (Simon and Schuster, 1994).

McCaw, Dick. *An Eye for Movement: Warren Lamb's Career in Movement Analysis* (London: Brechin Books Ltd., 2006).

McCaw, Dick. 'Understanding the Meaning of Movement'. *Theatre, Dance and Performance Training* (July 2015). www.tandfonline.com/doi/pdf/10.1080/19443927.2015.1027453?casa_token=ZzM1Gjkt9iwAAAAA:3KEIJNshuM LPa92-yKvJjUuxY0IFwEo2iZxBFf5lEWLsWeLd_gcJ3iKi3dDDWElveX6t2egk-qg.

References

McNamee, M. J., and S. J. Parry. *Ethics and Sport* (London: Routledge, 2002).

Mead, George Herbert. *George Herbert Mead; Essays on His Social Philosophy* (New York: Teachers College Press, 1968).

Meekums, Bonnie. 'Embodied Narratives in Becoming a Counselling Trainer: An Autoethnographic Study'. *British Journal of Guidance & Counselling* 36, no. 3 (August 2008): 287–301. https://doi.org/10.1080/03069880802088952.

Merlo, Gia, and Steven G. Sugden. 'Trauma Considerations'. In *Lifestyle Psychiatry* (CRC Press, 2023).

Merleau-Ponty, Maurice. *Phenomenology of Perception* (Humanities Press, 1962).

Miller, Diane L. 'The Stages of Group Development: A Retrospective Study of Dynamic Team Processes'. *Canadian Journal of Administrative Sciences/Revue Canadienne Des Sciences de l'Administration* 20, no. 2 (2003): 121–134. https://doi.org/10.1111/j.1936-4490.2003.tb00698.x.

Miyake, Akira, Naomi P. Friedman, Michael J. Emerson, Alexander H. Witzki, Amy Howerter, and Tor D. Wager. 'The Unity and Diversity of Executive Functions and Their Contributions to Complex "Frontal Lobe" Tasks: A Latent Variable Analysis'. *Cognitive Psychology* 41, no. 1 (August 2000): 49–100. https://doi.org/10.1006/cogp.1999.0734.

Moore, Carol-Lynne. 'Body Metaphors: Some Implications for Movement Education.' *Interchange* 18, no. 3 (1987): 31–37.

Moore, Carol-Lynne. 'Effort and Inner Life'. Website (MoveScape Center, 2015). https://movescapecenter.com/tag/effort-drive/.

Moore, Carol-Lynne. *Movement and Making Decisions: The Body-Mind Connection in the Workplace* (New York: Dance & Movement Press, 2005).

Moore, Carol-Lynne. 'On Flow, Lamb, and Kestenberg' (MoveScape Center, 2015). https://movescapecenter.com/on-flow-lamb-and-kestenberg/.

Moore, Carol-Lynne, and Eden Davies. 'Remembering Warren Lamb'. *American Journal of Dance Therapy* 36, no. 1 (2014): 130–134.

Moore, Carol-Lynne, and Kaoru Yamamoto. *Beyond Words: Movement Observation and Analysis* (Routledge, 2012).

Novick, Jack, and Kerry Kelly. 'Projection and Externalization'. *The Psychoanalytic Study of the Child* (January 1970). www.tandfonline.com/doi/abs/10.1080/00797308.1970.11823276.

Ogden, Pat. 'Emotion, Mindfulness, and Movement'. In *The Healing Power of Emotions, Affective Neuroscience, Development, and Clinical Practice* (New York: Norton, 2009).

Ogden, Pat, and Kekuni Minton. 'Sensorimotor Psychotherapy: One Method for Processing Traumatic Memory'. *Traumatology* 6, no. 3 (2000): 149–173.

Oliver, Wendy, Crystal U. Davis, Susan R. Koff, Selene Carter, Teresa Heiland, Beth Megill, Mahzarin R. Banaji, Anthony G. Greenwald, Ralph Buck, and Jeff Meiners. 'Dance in a World of Change: A Vision for Global Aesthetics and Universal Ethics'. *Journal of Dance Education* 20, no. 1 (2020): 51–54.

Pallaro, Patrizia. *Authentic Movement: Moving the Body, Moving the Self, Being Moved: A Collection of Essays*, vol. 2 (London and Philadelphia: Jessica Kingsley Publishers, 2007).

Parker, Andrew M., and Baruch Fischhoff. 'Decision-Making Competence: External Validation Through an Individual-Differences Approach'. *Journal of Behavioral Decision-Making; Chichester* 18, no. 1 (January 2005): 1–28.

Payne, Helen. 'The Psycho-Neurology of Embodiment with Examples from Authentic Movement and Laban Movement Analysis'. *American Journal of Dance Therapy* 39, no. 2 (December 2017): 163–178. https://doi.org/10.1007/s10465-017-9256-2.

Porges, Stephen W. *Polyvagal Safety: Attachment, Communication, Self-Regulation* (New York: WW Norton & Co., 2021).

Porges, Stephen W. *The Polyvagal Theory: Neurophysiological Foundations of Emotions, Attachment, Communication, and Self-Regulation (Norton Series on Interpersonal Neurobiology)* (WW Norton & Company, 2011).

Porges, Stephen W. 'The Polyvagal Theory: New Insights into Adaptive Reactions of the Autonomic Nervous System'. *Cleveland Clinic Journal of Medicine* 76, no. 4, supplement 2 (February 2009): S86–S90. https://doi.org/10.3949/ccjm.76.s2.17.

Preda, Rachele. 'Power Dynamics in Dance Movement Therapy'. *Body, Movement and Dance in Psychotherapy* 17, no. 1 (January 2022): 71–80. https://doi.org/10.1080/17432979.2021.1994010

Proske, Uwe, and Simon C. Gandevia. 'The Proprioceptive Senses: Their Roles in Signaling Body Shape, Body Position and Movement, and Muscle Force'. *Physiological Reviews* 92, no. 4 (October 2012): 1651–1697. https://doi.org/10.1152/physrev.00048.2011.

'Protected Characteristics' (Equality and Human Rights Commission, 2021). www.equalityhumanrights.com/equality/equality-act-2010/protected-characteristics.

Pryor, Robert G. L., and James E. H. Bright. 'The Value of Failing in Career Development: A Chaos Theory Perspective'. *International Journal for Educational and Vocational Guidance; Dordrecht* 12, no. 1 (March 2012): 67–79. http://dx.doi.org.ergo.southwales.ac.uk/10.1007/s10775-011-9194-3.

Pryor, Robert G. L., and Jim E. H. Bright. 'Applying Chaos Theory to Careers: Attraction and Attractors'. *Journal of Vocational Behavior* 71, no. 3 (December 2007): 375–400. https://doi.org/10.1016/j.jvb.2007.05.002.

Public Health Wales. 'Primary Care One – Social Prescribing' (Gofal Sylaenol | Primary Care One, 2019). www.primarycareone.wales.nhs.uk/social-prescribing.

Quenk, Naomi L. *Essentials of Myers-Briggs Type Indicator Assessment* (John Wiley & Sons, 2009).

Ramsden, Pamela J. 'The Action Profile® System of Movement Assessment for Self-Development'. *Dance Movement Therapy: Theory and Practice. London*, no. 1992 (2003): 218–241.

Ramsden, Pamela J. 'The Power of Individual Motivation in Management'. *Journal of General Management* 3, no. 2 (December 1975): 52–66. https://doi.org/10.1177/030630707500300206.

Ramsden, Pamela J. *Top Team Planning*, 1st ed. (London: Littlehampton Book Services Ltd., 1973).

Ramsden, Pamela J., and Jody Zacharias. 'The Action Profile System of Movement Assessment for Self Development'. In *Action Profiling: Generating Competitive Edge Through Realizing Management Potential* (Ashgate Pub Co., 1993).

Rivera, María, Charné Furcron, and Nancy Beardall. 'Embodied Conversations: Culturally and Trauma-Informed Healing Practices in Dance/Movement Therapy'. In *Dance/Movement Therapy for Trauma Survivors* (Routledge, 2022), 24–39.

Robinson, Aisha Bell, kyla marie Gilmore, and Charla Weatherby. 'Embodied Cultural Competence Framework: A Body-Based Method to Examine Cultural Identity Development and Bias'. *American Journal of Dance Therapy* (March 2024). https://doi.org/10.1007/s10465-024-09399-8.

References

Romanowska, Julia, Gerry Larsson, and Töres Theorell. 'Effects on Leaders of an Art-Based Leadership Intervention'. *Journal of Management Development* 32, no. 9 (January 2013): 1004–1022. https://doi.org/10.1108/JMD-02-2012-0029.

Rowe, Alan J., James D. Boulgarides, and Michael R. McGrath. *Managerial Decision-Making* (Citeseer, 1984).

Ruff, Holly Alliger, and Mary Klevjord Rothbart. *Attention in Early Development: Themes and Variations* (Oxford University Press, 2001).

Schmais, Claire. 'Healing Processes in Group Dance Therapy'. *American Journal of Dance Therapy* 8, no. 1 (December 1985): 17–36. https://doi.org/10.1007/BF02251439.

Schmais, Claire, and Elissa Q. White. 'Introduction to Dance Therapy'. *American Journal of Dance Therapy* 9, no. 1 (December 1986): 23–30. https://doi.org/10.1007/BF02274236.

Selioni, Kiki. *Laban – Aristotle – Ζώον (Zoon) in Theatre Πράξις (Praxis): Towards a Methodology for Movement Training for the Actor and in Acting* (Athens, Greece: Ellinoekdotiki, 2020). https://ellinoekdotiki.gr/gr/ekdoseis/i/laban-aristotle.

Shafir, Tal. 'Movement-Based Strategies for Emotion Regulation'. In *Handbook on Emotion Regulation: Processes, Cognitive Effects and Social Consequences* (New York: Nova Science Publishers, Inc., 2015), 231–249.

Shafir, Tal. 'Neurophysiological Aspects of Dance Movement Therapy for Psychiatric Rehabilitation'. In *Arts Therapies in Psychiatric Rehabilitation*, edited by Umberto Volpe (Cham: Springer International Publishing, 2021), 117–120. https://doi.org/10.1007/978-3-030-76208-7_14.

Shafir, Tal, Rachelle P. Tsachor, and Kathleen B. Welch. 'Emotion Regulation Through Movement: Unique Sets of Movement Characteristics Are Associated with and Enhance Basic Emotions'. *Frontiers in Psychology* 6 (2016). https://doi.org/10.3389/fpsyg.2015.02030.

Shank, Michael, and Lisa Schirch. 'Strategic Arts-Based Peacebuilding'. *Peace & Change* 33, no. 2 (2008): 217–242.

Shapiro-Phim, Toni. 'Dance, Music and the Nature of Terror in Democratic Kampuchea'. In *Annihilating Difference: The Anthropology of Genocide*, edited by Alexander Laban Hinton (University of California Press, 2002), 179–193.

Sheets-Johnstone, Maxine. *The Phenomenology of Dance*, 2nd ed. (London: Dance Books Ltd., 1979).

Sheets-Johnstone, Maxine. *The Roots of Power: Animate Form and Gendered Bodies* (Open Court Publishing, 1994).

Shweder, Richard A., and Edmund J. Bourne. 'Does the Concept of the Person Vary Cross-Culturally?' In *Cultural Conceptions of Mental Health and Therapy (Culture, Illness, and Healing)*, edited by Anthony J. Marsella and Geoffrey M. White, vol. 4 (Springer Netherlands, 1982), 97–137. http://dx.doi.org/10.1007/978-94-010-9220-3_4.

Sommer, Robert. 'Studies in Personal Space'. *Sociometry* 22, no. 3 (September 1959): 247. https://doi.org/10.2307/2785668.

Sovereign, Genevieve, and Benjamin R. Walker. 'Mind, Body and Wellbeing: Reinforcement Sensitivity Theory and Self-Cultivation Systems as Wellbeing Influencers'. *Journal of Happiness Studies* (January 2020). https://doi.org/10.1007/s10902-019-00216-5.

Studd, Karen A., and Laura L. Cox. *Everybody Is a Body* (Indianapolis, IN: Dog Ear Publishing, LLC, 2013).

Sullivan, Sherry E., and Akram Al Ariss. 'Making Sense of Different Perspectives on Career Transitions: A Review and Agenda for Future Research'. *Human Resource Management Review* 31, no. 1 (March 2021): 100727. https://doi.org/10.1016/j.hrmr.2019.100727.

Tantia, Jennifer Frank. 'Is Intuition Embodied? A Phenomenological Study of Clinical Intuition in Somatic Psychotherapy Practice'. *Body, Movement and Dance in Psychotherapy* 9, no. 4 (2014): 211–223.

Tantia, Jennifer Frank. 'Mindfulness and Dance/Movement Therapy for Treating Trauma'. In *Mindfulness in the Creative Arts Therapies*, edited by L. Rappaport (London: Jessica Kingsley Publishers, 2012), 96–107.

Tantia, Jennifer Frank. 'Viva Las Vagus! The Innervation of Embodied Clinical Intuition'. *The USA Body Psychotherapy Journal Editorial* 10, no. 1 (2011).

Thomas, Helen. *Dance, Modernity, and Culture: Explorations in the Sociology of Dance* (London: Routledge, 1995). http://site.ebrary.com/id/10099778?ppg=180.

Trif, Elliotte. 'A Dance/Movement Therapist's Experience of Vicarious Trauma and Burn-Out: An Autoethnography'. *Creative Arts Therapies Theses* (August 2010). https://digitalcommons.colum.edu/theses_dmt/11.

Trinity College Dublin. 'Why Babies Need to Move in the Womb'. *ScienceDaily* (2018). www.sciencedaily.com/releases/2018/03/180312104014.htm.

White, Elissa Queyquep. 'Laban's Movement Theories: A Dance/Movement Therapist's Perspective'. In *The Art and Science of Dance/Movement Therapy* (Routledge, 2015), 235–253.

Witte, Martina de, Hod Orkibi, Rebecca Zarate, Vicky Karkou, Nisha Sajnani, Bani Malhotra, Rainbow Tin Hung Ho, Girija Kaimal, Felicity A. Baker, and Sabine C. Koch. 'From Therapeutic Factors to Mechanisms of Change in the Creative Arts Therapies: A Scoping Review'. *Frontiers in Psychology* 12 (2021). www.frontiersin.org/articles/10.3389/fpsyg.2021.678397.

World Health Organization (WHO). *Mental Health in the Workplace* (World Health Organization, 2019). www.who.int/mental_health/in_the_workplace/en/.

World Health Organization (WHO), Daisy Fancourt, and Saoirse Finn. *Health Evidence Network Synthesis Report 67: What Is the Evidence on the Role of the Arts in Improving Health and Well-Being? A Scoping Review (2019)* (World Health Organization, November 2019). www.euro.who.int/en/publications/abstracts/what-is-the-evidence-on-the-role-of-the-arts-in-improving-health-and-well-being-a-scoping-review-2019.

Wyman-McGinty, W. 'The Body in Analysis: Authentic Movement and Witnessing in Analytic Practice'. *The Journal of Analytical Psychology* 43, no. 2 (April 1998): 239–260. https://doi.org/10.1111/1465-5922.00023.

INDEX

Note: Page numbers in *italics* indicate a figure and page numbers in **bold** indicate a table on the corresponding page.

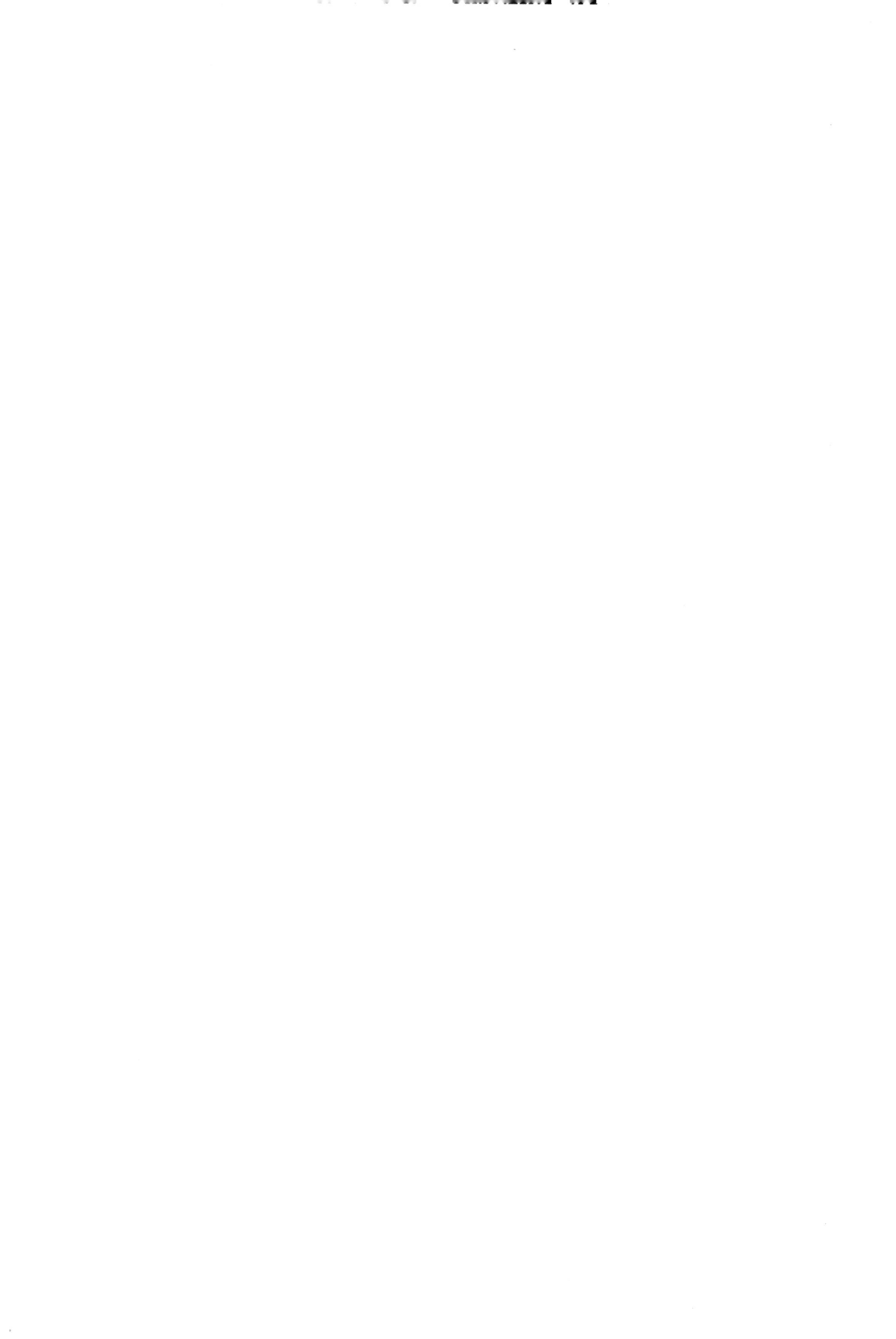

For Product Safety Concerns and Information please contact our EU
representative GPSR@taylorandfrancis.com
Taylor & Francis Verlag GmbH, Kaufingerstraße 24, 80331 München, Germany